FOOD
and the
CITY

FOOD
and the
CITY

New York's Professional Chefs,
Restaurateurs, Line Cooks, Street Vendors,
and Purveyors Talk About What They
Do and Why They Do It

INA YALOF

G. P. PUTNAM'S SONS · NEW YORK

PUTNAM

G. P. PUTNAM'S SONS
Publishers Since 1838
An imprint of Penguin Random House LLC
375 Hudson Street
New York, New York 10014

ISBN 978-0-399-16892-5

Printed in the United States of America
1   3   5   7   9   10   8   6   4   2

Illustrations by Rita Carroll
Book design by Gretchen Achilles

To my family

Contents

Author's Note

Caveat lector: I am not and never have been a restaurant critic, cookbook writer, or food blogger. Nor have I worked as a burger flipper, cheesemonger, waitress, or for that matter in a kitchen supply store. I am an investigative journalist whose interest is in exploring the depths of specific subjects. In this book, I focus my lens on the New York City food world, but first and foremost, this is a book about people. People of multiple cultures, ages, incomes, and tastes, all of whom share a common ground: They drive the story of food in this inimitable city. More than that, they *are* the story—its heart and soul and guts. They are the gastronomes; I'm just the one with the tape recorder.

But I *am* an expert in one food-related area. Eating. At that, I am world class.

Introduction

I grew up in Miami Beach, a child of parents who didn't cook—unless throwing frozen TV dinners into the oven every night is your idea of cooking. There were, however, two exceptions. The first featured my father's "famous" (more like "infamous" to my brother and me) Sunday night salmon croquettes. Into a chipped green medium-sized bowl he emptied a can of Bumble Bee salmon, two eggs, and as much Pepperidge Farm bread crumbs as the dish would hold. Next, he melted a quarter stick of butter in a cast-iron pan until it began to sizzle—or burn, depending on whether or not he had left the room to get a cigarette. Into this pan he slid the four fish patties, browned them on both sides, and voilà! Leo's Famous Croquettes. The second exception was when we went out for dinner—an infrequent event, to say the least. When we did go, our destination was either Wolfie's or Junior's coffee shop. And on very special occasions, the Hickory House, a *real* restaurant.

It was only when I married a New York boy who loved to eat—and met his mother—that I saw what I had been missing all those years. My mother-in-law lived in the Olcott Hotel on 72nd Street in what was known at that time as an "efficiency apartment." Meaning it had a kitchen—if you want to call it that. It was actually a converted closet with a tiny sink, a two-burner hot plate, and an electric oven that rested on a makeshift counter. The refrigerator stood majestically in a corner of her bedroom, covered with vine-patterned Con-Tact paper so it would "fit in" with the décor. And whereas my mother kept golf balls in our refrigerator because she believed it increased their distance, my mother-in-law jammed enough food to feed a hockey team into hers.

It was she who taught me how to cook. And it was her son who taught me how to eat like a New Yorker. By the time our kids could say "bagel," we were already dragging them around with us for catsup-smeared crinkle-cut fries at Nathan's in Coney Island, bialys and whitefish at Barney Greengrass, and frozen hot chocolate at Serendipity. For years, we traditionally broke the Yom Kippur fast at Peking Duck House in Chinatown and then walked two blocks to seal the deal with cannoli from Ferrara's. I was in heaven. Sometimes even literally. Pig Heaven was one of my favorite Chinese restaurants (which, as it turns out, was the brainchild of Ed Schoenfeld, whose story begins on page 215.)

Fast-forward a few decades and a few million food trends, and here I am, more fascinated than ever by the gastronomic landscape of New York City, where what to eat and where seems to be all anyone talks about.

What got me started on this book was a chance encounter on a balmy early March afternoon—the kind of day that summons thoughts of spring. Walking home from lunch at some new vegan restaurant, I passed a butcher shop on Amsterdam Avenue on the Upper West Side. The door was wide open, and inside I glimpsed a heavyset man in a white coat, seated behind a low counter against the back wall, talking to a customer. I kept walking, but something—who can ever say what that "something" is?—told me to circle around and look again. I did. This time the customer was gone and the man was staring straight ahead at the doorway, almost as if he were expecting me. I went in and ordered two pounds of chopped meat. While an employee was grinding it fresh in the back, the owner and I began talking about what it means to be a butcher these days. His repartee was so entertaining, his observations so intriguing, his passion for his work so infectious, that it got me thinking: How many others like him are there around this city? How many others might have stories worth sharing?

It turns out there are a lot.

After several years of intensive research in all five boroughs, I can tell you that there are more than enough to fill an encyclopedic number of volumes. Since I could do just one, an equally encyclopedic number of choices had to be made. I began with a long list of people who have influenced what and how New Yorkers eat, but ultimately chucked that list and started all over again, because the people with the most riveting tales to tell were, more often than not, people I'd never heard of or read about.

I found some of my best subjects in unexpected and often serendipitous ways. One weekday in midtown, for example, I followed the irresistible scent of grilled onions, which led me directly to the food cart of an Egyptian-American guy—Mohamed Abouelenein—who was producing plates of halal lamb at warp speed for a block-long line of hungry people working in the area. It turns out that for years, that particular food cart has been the most popular, and the most imitated, venue of its kind in the city.

This being New York, of course, there was also networking involved. Someone knew someone who knew someone else who could get me in touch with Bobby Weiss, a fourth-generation fish wholesaler at the New Fulton Fish Market in the Bronx . . . or Lauren Clark, a praline artisan in Brooklyn . . . or Miriam Tsionov, an Israeli-Uzbeki waitress with a following all her own. My own daughter introduced me to Lulu Powers, a much-in-demand caterer, who sent me to her foodie sister, who connected me to the general manager of a four-star restaurant, who arranged for me to meet Ghaya Oliveira, their new executive pastry chef, who ended up being one of the best of all possible subjects. And so it went.

This book is an oral history in which the characters speak for and about themselves. They are executive chefs and line cooks, restaurant owners and night managers, wholesale suppliers, cheese purveyors, bread bakers, street vendors, caterers, institutional meal planners, and more. Together, their narratives shine a spotlight on the competitive, unpredictable, often grueling but mostly satisfying lives they live in this epicurean culture where restaurants open and close before anyone knows their name, dreams are toppled and rebuilt, and things can and do turn on a dime.

They are a disparate group, to be sure, hailing from the ethnic enclaves of the four outer boroughs to the tony neighborhoods of Manhattan. Their backgrounds range from Egyptian to Italian, Dominican to Croatian, Mexican to American. Some names will be familiar to any casual observer of the food world; others may be unknown even to those for whom they work. I specifically avoided the so-called rock-star chefs, reasoning that they're already overexposed—at least to the eighty-eight million viewers of the Food Network.

I taped these interviews on a palm-sized recorder, which was never far, especially when I had the great good fortune to be led into my subject's inner sanctum. I explored an icy meat locker in Hunts Point in the Bronx, and observed from the perimeter more than my share of oppressively hot kitchens. I studied the New York art of slicing lox from a Zabar's pro, listened to tales of jilted grooms from a Pierre Hotel banquet director, and didn't notice I was freezing to death in the "21" Club's wine cellar, so entranced was I by reading the labels on some of the 4,897 bottles surrounding me. There were breakfasts, lunches, tea in places as highly regarded as Daniel, as edgy as the 24/7 Chelsea watering hole Cafeteria, and as newly discovered, for me at least, as the Bukharan restaurant Cheburechnaya, in Rego Park. And if all those culinary adventures weren't savory enough, at the end of each interview I carried home in my recorder gems of immeasurable value.

Certain themes recur in these stories. Almost everyone has his or her own version of Proust's madeleine, a singular taste memory that unlocks the door to the past. But not everyone has the chance to translate those memories into reality in the here and now. Were just such recollections the trigger for Betony's Eamon Rockey when he devised a drink he calls Old Dog Shandy, using flavors that evoke memories of the smoke from his grandfather's pipe and the honey from his grandmother's cherished beehives? Was it Eddie Schoenfeld's memories of eating Chinese food with his parents as a young boy that, twenty-two years later, turned into his sautéed lobster, egg, & chopped pork dish at RedFarm? Did Alexander Smalls's recollections of the stories he heard about his great-grandparents, all slaves, lead to his fascination with the African diaspora that is the basis of his restaurant, The Cecil? I'm guessing yes, yes, and yes.

The power of the media was another theme that ran through a number of interviews. This doesn't come as a surprise in this day and age of information sharing. And it seems when it comes to food, two particular Forces (capital "F" intended) can literally make or break the objects of their evaluation. The first are food blogs such as *Eater* and *Grub Street*—the overwhelming craze for Dominique Ansel's runaway best-selling Cronut can attest to that. Also, the *New York Times*, whose food critics' attendance in their dining rooms directly impacted the future of a number of restaurant people I spoke to. The other Force is Oprah, whose television show has been off the air for five years now, but whose effect still resonates with the success of those she has touched. Can anyone put a price on the value of a simple affirmative nod from this woman? Just ask Nino Esposito of Sette Mezzo or the women from Levain Bakery.

Finally, the repetition of certain words and phrases became a theme in itself. "Passion" and "love" and "American dream" were uttered more often than "sacrifice" and "no family life." Although the latter came in a close second.

If I've learned anything from my extended immersion in the rich soil of New York City's food world, it's this: What makes the great ones great—waiters to caterers, executive chefs to line cooks, newly arrived to fourth-generationals—is that when it comes to food, they know even the most minute detail can make a huge difference. It doesn't matter if you're slicing a steak or selling it, embellishing a cake or serving it, raising a flock of ducks or lowering the price of olive oil, in the end, as line cook MacKenzie Arrington told me: "You're all there with the same mindset and drive and passion for food. That's what comes first and that's all that matters. *The food, the food, the food.*"

PART I

Starting from Scratch

Each of the eight narrators in this chapter created and built a food-centered business from scratch. None went to business school. None were cushioned by trust funds or had friends in high places paving their way. Most are immigrants, hailing from Poland and Greece, Egypt, Croatia, and France. Not one is a native New Yorker. And yet, instead of seeking small ponds for a big-fish advantage, every one of these people plunged into the biggest pond of all. New York, New York . . . hear the music?

If I can make it there . . .

And make it they did. Somehow, in this food-crazed metropolis already overrun with food-centered businesses, there was room for eight more—these eight, anyway. A rugelach specialist. A wholesale butcher. A halal-cart chef. A tortilla supplier, praline artisan, pastry king, a couple of restaurateurs. But why, while so many others have come and gone, do these eight entrepreneurs continue to flourish? Diverse though their industries may be, are there certain ingredients common to all—maybe even a shared secret recipe for success?

Common sense plus a quick Google inquiry into "entrepreneurial qualities" will yield adjectives like "passion," "drive," "perseverance," "resourcefulness," "vision," and "self-confidence." Pretty much all of them describe the subjects of this chapter—just as pretty much all of them describe every other self-made man or woman in any field. But we're talking about men and women who work with, in, and around food. Not laptops or screwdrivers or cars or shoes or archaeological sites, but food. Glorious food.

Why the food world? For those involved with their native fare, there's clearly the comfort factor of working within the culture of their native home. But there are so many other possibilities as well. Such as the many prospects for entry-level jobs that require no English and little training; or maybe the ever-expanding eating establishments and markets that pepper the city's landscape are the draw. Or maybe it was a philosophical choice that even they themselves were unaware of. Food is a—and in some cases *the*—locus of family life. It triggers memory. It gives pleasure and comfort and warmth, emotional and otherwise. Food is energy; without energy, forget about passion, drive, perseverance, and the other facets of entrepreneurial spirit. Forget, for that matter, entrepreneurs—and everyone else. Food sustains life. Food *is* life. Can't live for long without it.

And then there's love. Neighborly love, romantic love, familial love, animal love, self-love—what is preparing and serving food, for oneself or others, if not an act of love as well as survival? The subjects of this chapter share this awareness, and perhaps that's the ingredient they have in common: They feed people, and in so doing they comfort and sustain themselves.

Dominique Ansel

DOMINIQUE ANSEL BAKERY

He seems a happy guy. Tall, dark, and lanky. Despite being in this country for almost ten years, he still speaks with a heavy French accent. He's been cooking professionally since he left high school at sixteen, ultimately landing a plum position at the long-established Paris épicerie Fauchon. From there, it was on to New York City and restaurant Daniel, where he toiled for six years under Daniel Boulud as executive pastry chef. During his tenure at Daniel, the restaurant won three stars from Michelin and four from the New York Times. *In 2013, he left to open his eponymous bakery in SoHo.*

Opening day of Dominique Ansel Bakery is still so clear in my mind. I was very nervous. Holding my breath. I didn't know how many people were going to show up—if any. I didn't know what their reaction would be to my pastries or my bakery. I went in very early that morning to get everything set up and ready to open. The last thing was to remove the brown paper that the builders had left covering the inside of the windows facing the street. When I pulled down the paper, I saw with great relief at least ten people standing there, some of them trying to open the doors. Well, that's New Yorkers for you. They see something new is coming and they immediately have to know all about it.

Within a few days, we got a small write-up in the *New York Times*, and that was all it took. That first weekend it seemed everyone knew we were open. We got so slammed! We weren't ready for it. We had opened the shop with a very small team of six people. Very humble, very simple. And boom! Right away we had to hire more people to up our production and increase our customer service. I was completely overwhelmed.

When something like that happens, you very quickly realize you aren't working for someone anymore. This isn't a job and it isn't a dream. This is reality. *Your* reality. When you're the boss, everything's on you. If no one shows up to clean the bathroom—you clean it. No one to take out the trash? That's your job, too. That's the difference between a chef and a business owner. Once you're a business owner, you have to be dedicated to your business night and day—day off or not. If, that is, you can even get a day off.

The DKA pastry was one of my first hits here. It's a pastry I discovered back in France when I was working at Fauchon. I called it DKA, for Dominique's Kouign Amann. *Kouign amann*—which means "buttery cake" in Celtic—traditionally uses leftover bread dough. Years ago, when bakers portioned their dough, they took whatever was left over, put a big hunk of butter and sugar inside, and baked it in the oven. The finished product came out very heavy, greasy, and sugary. My version is much different. It's individual-sized. I use less than half the butter and sugar. I repeat thin layers of dough, butter, and sugar. What you get is a caramelized croissant. It's a highly addictive pastry. Seriously. Somebody buys a DKA, starts eating it on the way out of the bakery, gets halfway down the block, makes a U-turn, and comes back to get another one. It makes me laugh to see this.

The Cronut came about almost as a fluke. No one could ever have predicted that outcome. It started with a staff meeting at the beginning of 2013. In these meetings, we always talk about new innovations and things we can do, and someone said, "Maybe we can do a special doughnut." I said, "You know, I'm French. They didn't make doughnuts in France, so I don't have a recipe for that, but maybe I can create something that will be like it." I experimented for three months, through lots of trial and error and minor adjustments of time and temperature, until I finally came up with a way to make a laminated dough with flaky layers that resembled a croissant. We formed it into a doughnut shape with the hole in the center, and filled it with a cream. Because it was a hybrid croissant and doughnut, we called it a Cronut. And because I thought it was so delicious, I put it on our list of pastries.

Not long afterward, one of the writers from *Grub Street—New York* magazine's food blog—happened to stop in the bakery for coffee. He asked if we were doing anything new. I said, "We're just now launching this." And I showed him the Cronut. He tasted it, photographed it, and wrote an article about it for the blog. The article showed up on May 9, 2013, at exactly 2:10 p.m. That same night, we got a call from the *Grub Street* people. "Hey, guys, I don't know if you realize it, but this Cronut thing is going to be big. You should make a few more for tomorrow." They told us they had an increase of 300 percent of traffic on the website, and over 140,000 hits in just that one afternoon.

Naturally, I was very happy to see the article. But did I expect it to have that kind of an effect? Never! I made our usual fifty or so Cronuts for that next morning, and when I opened the shop for business, there were maybe fifty people waiting outside. I'm wondering, "What's all this?" Every morning, I open the door of the bakery myself. It's become a tradition. I want to see my first customer and wish them welcome. By the third day after the *Grub Street* article, I opened the door to find over a hundred people waiting in line! I still had no idea what was happening.

Every day the number of Cronuts we made increased a little. But the number of customers who showed up to buy them increased a lot! To the extent that we had to set up some rules just to keep things fair. I hated doing that, but we had no choice, because we sold out early every single day. We couldn't just keep making more and more. Our bakery is small and we have many other pastries to get out as well. Rule one: Maximum two Cronuts per person. This lets us sell to as many different people as possible. Rule two: Everyone waits in line. No exceptions. If we get food writers, TV stars, anyone, we kindly ask him or her to wait in line. We have a lot of respect for all our customers, especially the ones that wake up at five or six in the morning to come here and wait. It wouldn't be fair for me to give a Cronut away to someone just because they are "important"—whatever that means.

No one could have imagined a scenario like this. Especially me. Then I started thinking: "As great as the success of this Cronut is, I want my bakery to be known for more than just one pastry. I don't want to let our creations kill our creativity." In other words, just because you've found a winner doesn't mean you should rest on your laurels. Think of an artist with a beautiful painting. Or a writer with a best seller. They don't stop there. They keep making something new; they keep innovating and trying different techniques.

After the Cronut, we launched a new creation we called a Frozen S'more, which starts with a marshmallow, inside of which is frozen vanilla custard with a chocolate wafer. The whole concoction sits on a branch that has been smoked, so it smells like fire, and we torch it so the outside shell of the marshmallow is caramelized, like a thin shell of *crème brûlée.* Beneath this shell, the marshmallow is slightly chewy, the frozen custard is creamy and cold, and you have the crunch of the chocolate wafer. The whole thing plays with texture, temperature, presentation, and taste. I didn't want people just to eat a scoop of ice cream. I wanted them to have a different experience. Then we created the Magic Soufflé—molten chocolate encased inside a rectangular tower of orange blossom brioche with a drop of Grand Marnier. We heat it for you in the oven for a few minutes and you eat it hot. We just keep trying new things.

Every aspect of care—down to the tiniest detail—is important to me here at the bakery. I learned that from working with Daniel Boulud. From the minute you step into his restaurant until the time you leave, someone is welcoming you, sitting you down, bringing butter and bread, serving water, taking your order, explaining the dishes on the menu, serving the meal, bringing dessert and coffee and the little chocolates you get at the end, and finally, wishing you a good night, and getting a taxi for you in the street. Every detail is important to him. Which is why we service our customers often before they even step inside the bakery. I still open the doors for the first time at eight a.m., but if customers show up an hour or two before, one of us will step outside every fifteen minutes or so to greet them. We'll pass freshly made little madeleines to keep them warm and thank them for coming. We don't ever take a single person for granted. To the contrary. We're both grateful and honored that our customers are there, because we know they are waiting for us.

Noe Baltazar

BUENA VISTA TORTILLAS

The Buena Vista Tortillas factory is situated in a large Brooklyn warehouse. On this particular morning, the overhead metal doors to the street are raised and forklifts roll in and out, transporting sealed boxes of tortillas and supplies. Deeper inside the factory, the aroma of warm, cooked corn curls through the air. Toward the back of the large expanse, a machine mixes and sheets the tortilla dough. Another cuts it into six-and-a-quarter-inch circles, and drops them onto a conveyor belt that carries them through a 500-degree oven and then a cooling tube. The tube spits out the now fully cooked tortillas at a rate of hundreds per minute into large, plastic bins—and then the humans step in. Five gloved workers begin a choreographed series of quick and deliberate movements, counting and stacking the soft disks, stuffing them into bags, and securing each bag with twist ties. There's no kidding around on this job. And not surprisingly, there is no talking.

He owns the company. A congenial man, solidly built, thick dark hair and mustache. He immediately apologizes for his broken English. "I love America," he tells me, gesturing large with his arms. "America gave me the opportunity. In my hometown, Puebla, you don't have anything. Nothing. Only your dreams. You want to make it, you come here. When the Twin Towers came down, I cried, because this country feels like family. In this country they give you food, they give you medical. When I got here, someone like me, with nothing, could go to the hospital and they would take care of you and then ask how much you can pay. In Mexico, you have to pay first. If you have no money you have to stay outside. They don't care if you die. If you die, then you die. That's it."

I was five years old when I started working with my mom on a farm picking tomatoes and green peppers. I had a little basket and I put the tomatoes there. When I was eight, she would go to work and leave me home to watch my brothers. We were little boys and little boys get hungry, and sometimes your mother is not there to feed you so you have to cook yourself. For my brothers and me, I made tortillas by hand. It's not so hard to do it. You put corn flour and water into a bowl and mix it until it's like a little elastic ball of dough. Then you put it between two sheets of plastic paper, and with the heel of your hand you keep pushing it down until it's flattened. Then you take it out of the plastic paper, put it into a hot pan, cook it for a little while, flip it over, and it's ready. Of course you can buy a machine in the supermarket that flattens them and trims them for you. But we never had money for that.

Life is hard in my small town where I grew up; there's no work there. You work for six months a year if you're lucky. But you eat twelve months a year, you know? So you're always looking for something better for your family. And you have to hope that it's here in America.

When I came to New York, I got a job working the line at a tortilla factory. It's what I knew. My job was to feed the machines and pack the boxes. Whatever they needed, I did it. For twenty years, I did it. Then one day, a close family member died and I had to go to Texas for the funeral. And when I came back, no more job. And I couldn't find another one. It's not easy when the only thing you know is tortillas. So I decided to go out on my own. What did I have to lose? I already had nothing.

I rented a small, run-down factory in Flushing that was once a tortilla place. I bought two old machines and repaired them and went to work. When I opened the doors, there were already a lot of people asking for tortillas. A good sign. First I called my business "Ole Mexican" but then I decided to change the name to "Buena Vista," after my hometown in Puebla. When I put that name up on the sign, my business got even better. A lot of people in this town know Buena Vista and they wanted to come.

For the first four years I worked like a dog. I didn't see any money. Hours and hours and everything I had to do I did myself. My wife and I and our children lived in the tiniest possible apartment. In those really early days we had nothing to eat. Nothing. And believe me, it was hard not to quit and look for a job when you see that your children are hungry. But we did the best we could and I kept going. Working seventeen-hour days, seven days a week. I was always tired and hated being away from my family. Some days, all I could think of was how much I wanted to go home.

When I started, I was competing with all the big companies. I knew if I wanted to stand out, I had to be different. So I went for high quality. A tortilla is only flour and water. That's the whole deal. No oil, no flavorings, nothing else. So the quality of the flour you use is the most important thing. There is first quality, second quality, and third quality. The third quality, you can eat it or give it to the animals. It's good,

I'm not saying it's not good. But it's third-grade stuff. I used the best corn flour I could find. You can use cheaper flour, you only sell it once. If they don't like it, it doesn't matter if you give it to them free. If they don't like it, that's it. If they like it, they tell their friends and that's how your reputation gets made.

In the beginning, I was the whole show. I would cook half a day and the second half I would go out with my truck and sell and deliver to grocery stores and supermarkets. Eventually, I got two people to help me. We started by making twenty to forty cases a day—36,000 single tortillas a day in my small space. My customers told me my tortillas were the best. Authentic, they said. What a tortilla should taste like. The result was, within three years I outgrew that space and moved here. Here I have around 5,000 square feet with fifteen people working full time. We now put out 450,000 tortillas a day for supermarkets, grocers, and restaurants, locally and out of state. It's good, no?

Tortillas are the bread for Mexicans. The people, if they don't have tortillas on the table, it's like you're not eating anything. It's like the Chinese. Chinese have to eat rice. If they don't eat rice, then they don't feel it's been a meal for them. Same for us with tortillas. You have some and then you feel full. Mexicans know.

The Mexican people are lucky to be here, but I think New York is also lucky to have so many Mexicans. We are what makes the food industry. You know what people say? They say if all the Mexicans went home tomorrow, there wouldn't *be* a food industry in this city.

Sam Solasz

MASTER PURVEYORS

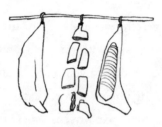

On this crisp December morning, with daylight still an hour away, I arrived outside of Unit B-14 at the Hunts Point Meat Market in the South Bronx. A trio of white-coated workers stood on the loading dock, rubbing their gloved hands together and stomping their feet to warm them. A guy with a dark wool cap pulled down over his ears explained that they were waiting for a trailer to arrive from Chicago. "It'll be hauling the carcasses of a hundred steers. Once it gets here, we're lookin' at four, five hours to unload the stuff."

A young worker in a yellow safety helmet led me inside and up a short flight of stairs into a conference room, where Sam Solasz, the owner, was waiting. He's a short, solidly built man with hands that look thick enough to wrestle a bull to the ground in less than thirty seconds. At eighty-three, he's still going strong. Dressed in a heavy sweater under a butcher's coat, he closed the door and waved me into a chair across the table from him. I turned on my tape recorder and began with one of my usual first questions: Where are you from? I was hardly prepared for what followed.

I grew up in Bialystok, Poland. At the very beginning of the war, 1939, all the Jews from my town, including my family, were rounded up and sent to live in a ghetto—an area walled off from the rest of the city. At one time, there were sixty-five thousand Jews crammed into this one space, which was designed for perhaps one-tenth that number. For the next several years, the ghetto operated as a forced labor camp. You did what the Germans needed you to do, what they told you to do. Those of us who could butcher animals—my father, who was a butcher, taught me how—we were trucked every morning by the Germans to a slaughterhouse outside the ghetto where we processed meat for the German army. In the afternoon they brought us back and left us off inside the ghetto walls. Periodically, they would come to get some of the people, rounding them up for deportation to a concentration camp. Out of so many thousands, maybe fifty, fifty-five survived.

You ask me, how did I survive? I'll tell you how. In 1942, I already was twenty-three months in the ghetto when, one morning, eight thousand of us were told to get on a train; they were transporting us to Treblinka, one of the camps built by the Nazis in occupied Poland. I was only thirteen years old, but I knew already about Treblinka, and I knew what was in store for us. Don't ask how we knew. People knew.

Just three kilometers from the entrance to Treblinka, I jumped from the train. I ran as fast as I could into the nearby forest, where I found a large group of partisans hiding out in secret encampments. They were not only Jews. They were Russians, too, and others who, like me, were trying desperately to stay out of sight of the Nazis. We stayed in hiding in the forest, foraging for food and sometimes receiving it from the kindness of strangers, until the end of June 1944, when the Russians found us. They told us, "We liberated you. Now you have to do something for us." They needed us to help them because by then we knew every inch of the forest. The Germans had hidden live mines in there, and bombs, and we knew where these mines were. And where it was safe and unsafe to trespass.

I stayed there with the Russians for four weeks and then I escaped. I made my way to Warsaw, then to Lodz, to Czechoslovakia, and finally to Munich, Germany. It was by then 1945. The war had been over for four months and I was put into a displaced persons' camp. I was sixteen years old. In Munich, they had places where survivors could get help searching for relatives. I spoke only Polish, so I got someone to write a letter for me to the *Forverts* [a Jewish newspaper] in New York, where my grandparents and my uncle had emigrated in 1922. One Saturday, right after synagogue, a relative of my father's came across my letter in the newspaper. Right away, he called up my uncle and said, "Hey, I just found somebody. It's a boy. He's looking for you."

Five months later, I was on a ship to America.

When I arrived in New York, my whole family came to the docks to greet me. At the docks also were people looking for men who wanted to work. One guy was looking for butchers. My uncle took me over to him and I got his business card, which I put in my pocket. It turned out that he was from the third-largest food company in the United States—Hygrade Food Products. The next day my uncle took me over to Hygrade. The manager gave me a white coat, an apron, a set of knives, and said, "Show me what you can do." So I sharpened the knives the way I like them and I worked for two hours straight. The following day, I had a job.

After my first day's work, they told me my salary would be three hundred dollars a week. That was a lot of money in those days. People at the time were making $1.65 per hour. A gallon of gas was thirty-five cents. Gum was a nickel a pack and a carton of cigarettes was

$1.20. I was butchering meat the way I knew from home, but he thought I was special. He wanted me to teach his workers how I did it. I showed them how to cut beef, how to break up the cattle into sides. In their slaughterhouse, I butchered hogs, pigs, cattle, and other things. Always working and teaching.

And then, 1956 rolled around, and I decided it was time to strike out on my own. With sixty-five hundred dollars I had saved, I gave my boss two weeks' notice, took the bus to 14th Street, and rented a space in the wholesale meat district. It all happened so fast, when the landlord asked the name of my business, I didn't have one. My first thought was to call it "Meister's." In Europe, a *meister* is someone who knows everything. At Hygrade, anytime they needed something in the company they said, "Call Saul. He's a real *meister*." I added the word "Purveyors," because that meant I sold provisions as well. Then a friend said, "You know, Saul, you're in America now. You should use the English word." In English, *meister* means "master." And that's how we became "Master Purveyors." We got all the legal stuff out of the way, and on August 16, 1957, Master Purveyors opened for business.

August 16 was a lucky day for me. A very sad, but also very lucky day. August 16 was the date when they killed all the people in Bialystok. But they didn't kill me.

The business kept growing, and as it did, we'd move into larger and larger quarters. Finally, in 2001, we left the meatpacking district. The area was undergoing a gentrification into a nightlife and shopping destination. Rents went up, and like so many others, we moved our operation to Hunts Point in the Bronx. Which is where we are today. Even in these new surroundings, we have continued to do business the old-fashioned way. I buy cattle straight from the slaughterhouse.

Close to five hundred thousand pounds of meat arrive here every week. Maybe around seventy thousand pounds a day. Give or take. And only the top, top of the line. All our beef comes from steer. Those are male cows that have been castrated. They do that when the cow is a calf so it develops muscles and weight. You also get quality, taste, and everything you want in a piece of meat. When I call up a slaughter-house and order fifty steers, they arrive already quartered. That means two hundred pieces. As soon as the trailer pulls up to our loading dock, each of my "luggers" grabs a quarter, which weighs between 220 and 250 pounds, and hangs it on a hook that is attached to a bar on a roller. Immediately someone slaps our Master's stamp on every quarter. We stamp it again when we break it down, so I can recognize whether it's my product or not. If one of my customers complains the meat is bad and he's looking here for credit, I'll say, "Yeah? Show me the stamp."

Once the meat is hung and stamped, it gets rolled through the door. While it's still on the hooks, one guy is there with an electric power saw and he cuts it right away into two pieces. Then the next guy, and the next guy and the next guy. Each one has his own part to do. Two hours later, the hindquarter has been broken into ten pieces, and those get cut again by my butchers into large portions of sirloins, ribs, bris-ket, and so on. I taught every one of my guys how to cut the way I want it. On a smaller scale, we have benchers. In response to the orders that come in, the benchers take the meat from the cooler, put it on the bench, and cut it into filet steaks, sirloin steaks. Whatever you want, we do for you. We try to accommodate everyone. Amy Rubenstein, one of the owners of Peter Luger's, comes in every Thursday morning to personally select her restaurant's weekly supply. She's been doing that for years. She chooses what she wants, stamps her selections with the Peter Luger insignia, and that way we both know it's hers.

I work eighteen hours a day, five days a week. Always have. I start my day at eight thirty. That's p.m., not a.m. I come in at night because I want to see what product is coming in and what's going out. I leave here at two in the afternoon. Usually, I meet my wife at a restaurant. This is our time together. She has lunch, I have dinner. I eat five times a week steak. And I don't eat a little hamburger. I eat a steak. One and a half pounds, sometimes two pounds. I don't let my wife cook. She deserves to be treated well. It hasn't always been easy for her since I'm never home at the normal times. But we've been married fifty-six years, so I'm guessing she's used to me by now.

By four o'clock in the afternoon, I'm ready for bed. I sleep maybe four hours, until eight, eight fifteen p.m., when I get up and go to work. My kids work with me here so they're up crazy hours, too. We're all night owls. Scott, my younger son, comes in at ten p.m. Mark, my oldest boy, comes in at midnight. My son-in-law, who used to be a doctor but recently hung up his stethoscope to join our team, comes in a half hour later. And then my workers start drifting in at different times after that. I've been doing it like this from day one that I came to this country. Sixty-three years and I've always worked nights. Always. I can do it blindfolded.

Jelena Pasic

HARLEM SHAKE

She was born in Rijeka, Croatia, a town of about 150,000 people. While studying at the university, she also worked for Procter & Gamble, which paid her in American dollars, providing her with a "fantastic" standard of living. But after graduating in 2000, she decided to start the new millennium in grand style. She would go to America.

She arrived here on a J-1 exchange visa—meaning she could work for five months and travel for one—with two hundred dollars in her pocket and a promised job in Myrtle Beach, South Carolina. "On day one, I learned that the job entailed picking up cigarette butts and garbage. I never even finished the day." After several more employment debacles, including a job selling temporary tattoos, she headed for New York City and became a waitress. She's thirty-eight.

I met my future husband while I was waitressing. He had always wanted to open a restaurant. Our parents gave us some financial help and we became partners in a series of small, successful cafés in Washington Heights. Seven years later, after our marriage fell apart, I learned that I had never really been a partner in the cafés at all. Which left me, after our divorce, without a job, almost broke, and with two kids to raise. I had a choice: Work for someone else for the rest of my life, or think of something really cool that would turn my life around. I had a business degree, and I knew how to run a café, so I'm thinking, "Why not keep going with that? Why not open my own restaurant?"

My goals were, first, to survive and feed my children, and second, to create a place that's beautiful, practical, and has some culture. In short, a nice place where a mom and two kids can go to eat together, that's affordable for them. I knew it would be a huge gamble, but I figured that if I took things conservatively so as not to lose whatever money I had left, I could do it.

In May 2012, I decided to give it a go. First up was the location. I knew Harlem was up and coming. Marcus Samuelsson's Red Rooster restaurant was thriving, as were Corner Social and other upscale eateries. But at the same time, there were few really cool, casual places to eat. And I figured, if I could fill that void, my place would be a hit. To me, the architecture along Lenox Avenue looked like a Parisian boulevard, and after Red Rooster opened and people started going up there, it became clear to me that perhaps the area might develop into something special.

I learned of a vacant corner spot on Lenox and 124th and went to check it out. The space itself was horrible. Eight layers of dropped ceiling, no windows, and a disgusting wood floor. But when I looked at it—all I saw was a corner. Just what I wanted. The landlord was a seventy-five-year-old man who was no longer even thinking of renting the space because there had been so many unsuccessful restaurants there. For three months I negotiated that lease like I was negotiating a country's destiny. I ended up taking it for fifteen years, which was a pretty big commitment—and I think he was just happy to lock some-one in for a long time. And the rent itself was a blessing.

The day I signed the lease, I remember standing on the corner, thinking, "Okay, Jelena. What exactly are you going to do here?" I knew I wanted a casual restaurant, but what kind? And then, it just came to me. A burger and shake restaurant! For a mom with two kids, it's a much better way to make a living than working late at night with liquor involved. Shake Shack was my inspiration. The food is delicious and of good quality and the restaurant is now a New York tourist attraction. From what I could see, there was no burger place with this type of concept up here in Harlem. I wanted to do something like that. In Harlem. For Harlem.

It can be tough for a white person to come in and try to do business within a black culture. I knew that even though my intentions might be the best and I'm trying to provide an amazing product, I needed someone who could bridge the gap. I called Dennis Decker, a brilliant and creative designer who has been living in Harlem for thirteen years. We decided together to highlight Harlem culture and make the restaurant a place that Harlem could be proud of. And the name had to be something Harlem-specific; that I was sure of. I was thinking Har-lem this, Harlem that, Harlem burgers. And then a friend of mine very casually tossed off, "How about Harlem Shake?" "That's it!" I said. "I'm going to be selling shakes. That's perfect!" The next day, I called my lawyer and we trademarked the name.

And that's when the fun began.

In February 2013, we were still renovating when my friend Kenji Alt e-mailed me. He said, "Jelena, there's something strange going on. There's a video on YouTube you need to watch." Kenji is very big on trends. He's a much-revered blogger, food writer, and food critic, and he's very tuned in to everything that's hip. He said, "There's a clip of different people doing these dance moves. It's called the 'Harlem Shake.' This is totally ridiculous, but it seems it's going viral!"

Up to that point, the restaurant had 384 "likes" on Facebook. I could never figure out why there were so many—or even any—because we weren't open yet. But suddenly, after the YouTube clip, we started getting seven to eight thousand "likes" a day. People were going crazy. There were hundreds of videos all over YouTube of different groups— old people, young people, black and white—all doing the same dance moves. It's like a flash mob. The "Harlem Shake" starts with one dancer, dancing on his own somewhere; it could be in the middle of Grand Central Station. He appears oblivious to the people surrounding him, and they are seemingly oblivious to him. Then, suddenly, they all join him, repeating the same dance moves as a crowd. The video has been replicated by all kinds of groups. I heard that the University of Georgia men's swim and dive team did it underwater, and members of the Norwegian army did it, too. All these people danced with their own group, and posted the tapes on YouTube. It was wild! I got e-mails from trademark brokers offering all kinds of money for the name. My Harlem Shake ended up having 27,000 "likes" on Facebook before we even opened.

Suddenly I began to worry that people might resent me and my restaurant, thinking that this white lady is trying to cash in on the name "Harlem Shake" and maybe demeaning their culture. I feared it was going to be a disaster for my business. I needed to do something fast. Because we were under construction, we had put up a fifty-foot plywood safety wall surrounding the restaurant while it was being built out. So we hired a graffiti artist named Kindo Harper to design something special. In huge, six-foot-tall letters, he painted the words:

"Do the real Harlem Shake." And that was all it took! Within one week, that graffiti-painted plywood became a tourist attraction. Tour busses started coming up here, tourists and neighborhood people alike stopped to take pictures in front of it. It was so funny, my kids and I stood there laughing because fifty tourists are taking pictures with no idea how this came about.

I felt so lucky. The people from the neighborhood could not have been happier or prouder; they showed up in front of the plywood and danced the Harlem Shake themselves. All the New York newspapers wrote us up, which was pretty amazing. When it came time to open the restaurant, I was thinking, "How do we take this plywood down? It's a piece of art. We can't just destroy it." So we found a home for it at Wadleigh high school, a neighborhood public school of performing arts, and we donated it to them. They use it as a theatrical prop to represent the Harlem background when they put on shows.

We opened on May 13 to lines out the door and down the block. We got so slammed, it wasn't funny. I sat in my office in the basement, totally overwhelmed, saying, "Never again!" Did we have a few mishaps? More than a few those first weeks—food not ready, orders confused . . . what you'd expect from a place that newly opened to find a line a mile long waiting on the street. We were babies, and still are. We're still working out our kinks, but I'm feeling like we have a good future ahead of us.

People talk about the American dream. I'm living it. Seriously. I had sold everything when I moved to this country. I started with close to nothing. I was frightened to take the step I took, but I still took it. I'm a scuba diver and a parachutist, and I can only liken this to jumping out of a plane without knowing if your parachute is going to open.

But sometimes that's the only way. You want to do something—you have to take a chance and jump.

We've been in business a few months now. I still live in a one-bedroom apartment on 126th Street. My kids are with me two weeks out of the month. It took all my life savings to open this place, and for the time being, I can't afford anything better than that. And there still are many days that my children sit in the office with me when I know they would rather be somewhere else. But they understand that for now at least, this is what we have to do. I feel safe, right now. Like I'm where I belong. And sure, I know that I might fail, but at least for today I'm master of my own destiny.

Sammy Anastasiou

CITY DINER

In 1981, after seven years as a cop in Athens, he came to America in search of a better future. He was twenty-five years old and newly married.

Coming to the Bronx from a place like Greece was, well, like shell shock. You must understand why I was depressed. I didn't like the dark buildings. My apartment was like a jail. A gate in front and bars on the windows. In Greece, we would go out at night. Here, there was nothing to do and nowhere to go.

I started working right away, of course. What else do you do? A dishwasher in a small coffee shop was all I could get. When you don't speak English, you can either go into construction or work in a restaurant kitchen where you don't need language so much. I learned English by copying the customers. In the kitchen, I'd ask, "What's this? What's this?" All these questions. Like a kid. And then I'd go home at night and get a book and try to read it. That's how I learned English. I never went to school for it. Not one day.

Of course I didn't expect when I got here I'd be doing a dishwasher job. Everyone I knew who came here left a little richer three, four, five years later. And naturally I thought that was what I would do as well. You know, go home to Athens one day. But as I got into the system and learned my way around, met some people, got better at the language, I started to like it here. I changed my attitude about this country. And why not? In Greece, after seven years as a cop, I made $206 dollars a month. Here, as a dishwasher, it was $225 a week! I saved my money. I invested some. I bought my house. It wasn't easy in the beginning. We never went out. Couldn't afford to. My wife knew that that was how it would be. But the fact is, you change your lifestyle or you go back. And I was not going back.

There are a lot of Greek-owned diners in this city. Why? Because when people start out as immigrants, they tend to go where others like them have gone before. Greeks specifically look for the diners because they either know somebody or they just feel more comfortable there. They become dishwashers, salad men, griddle men, short-order cooks. Jobs where you only need to communicate minimally. If you get an American to do this type of work, he's here for a day and he's leaving. You have to make too many people happy. You have to make the boss happy, the manager happy, all the customers happy. It's a lot of pressure. Americans are educated and they don't like the pressure, so they don't stay. If you're an immigrant, you stay. What're you gonna do? And if you're any good, you move up. People I know who started as dishwashers became cooks and pretty soon they had their own little luncheonette. Then from the luncheonette, to a coffee shop, to a diner. Like that.

Like me.

Things in the diner business are changing, though. You won't see as many young Greeks in it anymore. At one time in the late fifties, late sixties, Greeks owned a large percentage of the coffee shops and luncheonettes in Manhattan. Not anymore. Kids don't want to continue their father's hard work in the restaurant. They don't want to work seven days a week, fourteen hours a day—holidays and weekends. So they go off and become something else. And who can blame them?

The first place I opened for myself was in the Bronx. Three of us were partners. I'd get up at two in the morning and go home at seven at night. It was a small place. I cooked, cleaned, served. Did it all. After some years there, we sold it and opened the Manhattan Diner on the corner of 77th Street and Broadway. That was like hitting the big time! I loved that place, I can't even say how much. I loved the neighborhood and I loved the customers. We knew them all—the nannies, the doormen, the supers, the families. And they knew us. We all got along. I poured my heart and soul into that place for eleven years.

Then one day, early in 2011, just like that, the wrecking ball comes and it's over.

Typical New York style—the building's owners pulled the lease and closed our diner, along with the other small shops on the block, to make way for a twenty-story luxury apartment building. Now you see us, now you don't. Our whole block. Gone. Curl Up & Dye Hair Salon, gone. Vai Restaurant, gone. The World of Nuts & Ice Cream candy store, New Pizza Town. Demolished. Like we were never there at all. All those times we gave lollipops to the little kids and let them close the cash register drawer. Gone.

We never even got to say good-bye to them. The customers whose preferences we knew from memory. Before you even sat down, we had for you your half-caf, half-decaf coffee with half a spoon of sugar and a bagel well toasted, no butter. My waiters knew without asking who liked their scrambled eggs well done and who very loose. Gone like they never happened. Block destruction is going on all over the city, but that doesn't make me feel any better. I still go into mourning when I pass that corner.

When we closed, I was so depressed. Truly depressed. I needed to get away. Not think about things for a while. I decided to take a year off by myself and go home to Greece. I'm thinking, I'll play cards with my old buddies from school. Go out at night with the guys. Regroup. I did it, too. I went home to Greece. But the going-out-with-my-friends part didn't happen, because everybody goes to work. After seven months, I felt so bored, I couldn't wait to come home. And what's going on back in New York? Same thing. Everyone's working, including my wife. I had nothing to do. All those years I had no time for myself and I wished for it. Now I had all the time in the world and I didn't like it. What I realized was: The diner is my life. It's the only thing that fills me up.

So I started again.

With partners, I bought the diner on the Upper West Side, where I am now. Back to working seven days a week, fourteen hours a day. Same as before. You have no holidays, no weekends, and my kids never see me. All along I've felt like I've missed my kids growing up. But I saw no other way to change my life. What're you gonna do?

Missing your family is only one of the downsides of owning a diner. Finding good people to work for you is another. It's not easy to find good kitchen help—and if you do, to keep them. I have ten people working the kitchen now. The grill and sandwich guys are upstairs. But most of the others are cooking in the basement kitchen. Some do the gravy, dressings, some do the baking. The dishwashers are down there, too. It's tough to be downstairs all day. I get that. There's no windows. But that's the job.

Today, the only ones who want to work hard are the Mexicans. It's the truth. You try to give other people jobs, they work one, two days and that's it. I hire a dishwasher and after five minutes, he complains, "This is not for me." I mean, come on! You come to answer an ad for dishwasher. What do you expect to do? Wait on tables? When the Mexicans stop working, that's it. We're all cooked.

We're facing a new challenge, I'm noticing. Our clientele is getting older. And sometimes that presents a predicament. Young people don't want to come in here and see an old man walking with a cane. They want to have fun. Today, dining is not only about the food. It's also about the atmosphere. I have a man in his nineties who's been coming every day. Twenty-five years he's coming here. So now he's got a few problems and every so often he might upset a customer a little bit because he walks slowly or doesn't look so good. What am I going to tell him? Don't come anymore? He will never hear that from me. Never! Same thing goes for the famous people. We're on the Upper West Side. Lots of theater people live around here and they come in all the time. Famous authors. Celebrities from Page Six. You name it. By me, everyone gets the same treatment. I mean, if someone comes every morning for coffee and eggs, who'm I going to treat better? A famous person or the man who comes every day? Right.

At any diner, if you're an owner, you work all the shifts and you meet so many different people. I could write a book just about all the characters I meet over here. You see the same faces over and over, which makes them like friends. The best part is the families. Watching the kids grow up. First I give them high chairs, then booster chairs, and then they become big boys and I love to watch that. They come for ice cream after soccer and then for lunch after graduation from school. And then they come in with their own credit cards. And I'm laughing inside me. I say, "Look at you kids! You go to other places, other restaurants, they don't know you. You come to my diner, we will always know you."

Lauren Clark

SUCRE MORT PRALINES

She's been a New Yorker for almost a decade, but she still sports a soft, unmistakable Louisiana accent. She's in her early thirties. Tall, with dark hair and eyes. She currently works as an editor and website manager for a war photography project called Nuba Reports, which covers the civil war in the Sudan. "Working from home makes life easy, although it can be somewhat of a vampire existence. Still, it's helpful because it frees me up to make my pralines." At first she appears shy, but in a short time her face and hands come alive as she reflects on her hometown.

In August 2005, Hurricane Katrina struck the town where I grew up—Mandeville, Louisiana, just outside of New Orleans. It's a small town, full of gravel roads and bayous and good cooks. It's situated right on Lake Pontchartrain, the lake that literally filled up and flowed over the sides during the hurricane. In many ways, it was a memorably beautiful sight to see something so dramatic, but at the same time, it was terribly painful for me. I was living in Brooklyn, watching it play out on television from the comfort of my living room and feeling so guilty and helpless that I wasn't there, experiencing it like every-one else.

In an effort to make myself feel better, I started making pralines in my Brooklyn flat, using my grandmother's original recipe. Pralines—that's pronounced PRAH-leen, not PRAY-leen—are a flat, round, fudge-like candy that consists mostly of sugar and pecans. They're native to New Orleans, so cooking them just somehow made me feel connected to home.

For generations, Southern cooking has been a tradition in my fam-ily. When Hurricane Katrina hit us, it hit hard in many different ways. Suddenly everyone was struck with the fear that along with so many of our homes, our traditions would also be washed away. And in many cases, unfortunately, they were correct. But what didn't wash away was our ability to cook New Orleans–style food. I remember there was one story of a woman who thought that she had lost all of her cook-books and the favorite recipes that she herself had written. One morn-ing, as she was going through what was left of her home, she found them in tattered, water-stained form. She was so relieved. She was, like, "I lost my home, but at least I didn't lose my recipes." Carrying on traditions is part of the way a city revives itself. When they returned to New Orleans, people started reviving the things that were so special. One of those quintessential New Orleans traditions is pralines.

I can't pinpoint the exact time I came up with the idea of turning my praline avocation into a vocation. I think it was probably in the back of my mind for a while. Do I realize we're pretty far north of the Mason-Dixon line? Of course. But it's easy to get skewed when you grew up with this candy being such a natural part of your life. In my hometown, nobody gets married or buried without someone bringing a plate of pralines. You bring them to church, to a christening; you share them with your next-door neighbor. Thanksgiving dinner wouldn't feel right if you didn't finish it off with a good ol' praline. And I'm thinking, "Why wouldn't people want to walk up Broadway, munching on something this delicious?"

I guess a large part of what drove my dream was meeting Dosia Sanford a few years ago. Dosia and I worked together in a retail store, and at lunchtime, we'd sit around talking about our visions for the future and about all the things we wished for. We learned that we both had a passion for food. Hers was more about cooking—she's very imaginative and quirky in the way that she cooks. My fantasy was to start a business. I've always been drawn to doing something where you can work for yourself and make good money and really like what you're doing. Brooklyn was beginning to burst at the seams with new food artisans popping up every day and I wanted to hop on that train. So I put forth the idea to her that we use her crazy cooking skills and my grandmother's recipe for pralines and we start a little business of our own. Dosia jumped on board immediately, and although we kept our day jobs, we became partners in a two-employee company, which we named Sucre Mort.

Sucre Mort literally translates to "dead sugar," or "sugar death." And that's what the process is of cooking a praline; you're literally killing the sugar when you burn it. But the term also refers to the bliss of eating sugar—well, bliss, that is, until you overdo it and start bouncing off the walls.

Making a praline isn't all that hard. Basically you just caramelize sugar in buttermilk until it turns a really dark color. The only hard part is the amount of time it takes. You have at least twenty-five minutes of cooking, during which time you're standing and stirring and stirring and stirring. You can't walk away for even a minute or they can burn. And they will! Trust me. When the mixture hits a certain texture—after you've been doing this a while you just know when—it turns the right color and it smells the right way and it's done. That's it. At that point, you take the pot off the fire, drop spoonfuls of the mixture in small circles onto waxed paper and let them cool. That's the whole deal. But you have to be 100 percent present. No leaving, ever, or they'll burn just like that.

Dosia and I always cook together. You can imagine how well you get to know somebody when you're sharing a stovetop and there's about twelve inches distance between the two of you. We tell each other long stories from our past, and try to mend each other's broken hearts. Because we already know everything there is to know about each other, the thing we've been doing a lot lately, especially during the winter, is we make up ghost stories. When we're standing and stirring and starting to fall asleep, our goal is to scare each other awake.

Our first order came from a Carroll Gardens store called By Brooklyn. The owner started us with an order for fourteen bags. When those sold out, she ordered more and so did a few other vendors. Now that we had some real orders, we needed a place to cook. In New York City, if you have a business, you're supposed to be cooking in a licensed kitchen. And we do, but not everyone does. A lot of cooks in the city are finding clandestine ways to work. They're renting spaces from one another, they're sharing time in certain kitchens, but in truth, that's because they have no choice—at least in the beginning. It's ridiculously expensive to rent a kitchen on a regular basis. I've seen them go for a thousand dollars a month for four two-hour time slots. A thousand dollars for eight hours a month? That's a lot of pralines!

When you start a small business, at first it's all about the quality of the product. Somewhere along the line, a real transition takes place.

That is, you have to start thinking about your product in terms of money. We're interested in growing, so we have to confront the reality that we need a business plan, and a loan. So far we've been getting by by the skin of our teeth and it's been working. We're not making money, but we're not in debt, either. We price a bag of six pralines at $10 retail. It costs us $5.50 in ingredients and packaging materials. That's not including our time and labor. Then we have to wrap and transport them, which also takes hours. And we can't stock them because they are so perishable. They taste best when they're just made, and after about three weeks, they lose the flavor that makes them so wonderful. It's not like jewelry, which can stay around forever. With pralines, you're constantly thinking about the timing.

We laugh constantly about how small we are, and how the demands are so much larger than we can actually provide. It's thrilling to us, of course, but it's sometimes a comedy of errors. It will be four thirty in the morning and we've gotten giddy. You can't daydream too much because you need to pay attention to what you're doing. I have lots of little burn blisters all over my wrists that attest to the wisdom of that. And so we try to figure out which of us is the more tired and the other will say, "One of us has to sleep tonight. You do it."

Alvin Lee Smalls

LEE LEE'S BAKED GOODS

On the north side of 118th Street in South Harlem stands a small bakery with a red-and-white-striped awning. In the window, a sign proclaims: "Rugelach by a Brother." It's three o'clock. Inside the shop, a glass counter displays what's left of the day's offerings—a few carrot muffins, sweet potato pie, red velvet cake, some assorted pastries, and a few dozen rugelach. Two rectangular, fabric-covered tables sit nestled against corner banquettes on either side of the door. Fading red-and-white-print wallpaper covers the walls.

Mr. Lee, as he likes to be addressed, is a large man, graying, in his midseventies. He's wearing a white baker's apron. Flour dusts his muscular arms. He's the first to tell you he moves a little slower these days, but according to those who stop by the table where we sit talking, his pastries have lost none of their punch over the years. It seems everyone who comes in buys something. Except the kids, who walk in empty-handed and walk out with a free cookie. He's been at this a lifetime.

I have no family life. Never did have none. I have my son and a daughter. Don't see them much, though. My son works for me on occasion, but he's not into this kind of work. He's not into it 100 percent, anyway. You got to be 100 percent to do this.

I was born in 1942, in Georgetown, South Carolina. I came to New York at nineteen. I got a job right away at New York Hospital in the kitchen. First try. Right off they put me in the vegetable room, peeling onions. And boy, I peeled them onions like nobody's business! Never shed a tear. No sir. But you know how it is. After a year of peeling onions, doesn't matter how good you are, you want to do something else. Well, every so often I'd pass by the guys who worked in the bakery and they looked pretty happy, so I'm thinking, "Maybe that's for me."

I asked the chef to move me over there and he did. No more peeling onions. Now I was greasing pans. Two years. All I did was grease those pans. There were seven different bakers in there and each had a different specialty. One guy made rolls, one made cookies, one pies. And you know, in those days we made everything from scratch. It's not like it is now, where it's all formulated out for you. I wanted to know more about the baking, so on my days off, I took a class to learn to bake. Just your basic stuff. But that was for me. And eventually, those guys saw what I could do and they let me bake right along with them.

One day, I saw a recipe for rugelach in the newspaper and decided to try it out. Rugelach is a small, rolled pastry—two bites' worth at most. I used to eat it back when I was younger, when the old Jewish and German bakeries were in business. Those guys are long gone now. It's all factory-made today. Anyway, I tried out the recipe in the paper and they came out hard as bricks. So, that became a challenge for me. I kept playing around with the recipe, adding more flour, less sugar, more butter. I cooked the raisins in honey, which I learned kept the insides moist, and this and that. You know how it is. And when I got them the way I wanted them, I put them out for the staff in the hospital kitchen at holiday time. They loved it! Ate 'em like crazy. Asked me for more. Couldn't believe a black man could make a Jewish pastry so good.

That was back in '87. Right around that time, the hospital bakery was starting to bring in goods from these big commercial bakeries, so I figured it was just a matter of time for us to be out of a job. Time to start my own bakery. I opened my first place on Amsterdam Avenue. Made everything from scratch. Danish, pies, rolls. And of course my apricot and chocolate rugelach. I put everything into that shop. Heart and soul. And all the money I had. And we were doing just fine. In the eighties, people still came for their sweets to a bakery. Used to line up on the streets, especially around holiday time. Not like now, when you can get baked goods at just about any store.

As luck would have it, in 1994, my spine gave out. Too much time on my feet, the doctor said. Who knows? I had an operation and after that I had to close my bakery. I put everything in storage and for almost ten years, I only worked part time. But I missed my baking. I missed my customers. And I was bored. You can't even imagine. Then one day I found this little place. I pulled my cooking stuff out of storage and with the highest hopes; I opened Lee Lee's Baked Goods. That was in 2001. September 10, to be exact.

Well sir, if you remember, that was the day before 9/11.

My family told me the towers coming down was a bad omen. That business would be bad after that. But the truth is, there wasn't much business to *go* bad. It was pretty desolate around here. Most of my customers were the staff and the outpatients from the methadone clinic across the street. For the better part of a year, I spent my own money keeping this place afloat. And then slowly but surely, the neighbor-hood started changing. Little by little, business improved. And I hung on for seven or eight years. Then the recession came. Then the metha-done clinic closed and business slowed to a crawl. It was up. Then down. Up. Down. Story of my life. I was back to using all my savings to stay afloat. And eventually, my money ran out. So on May 31, 2010, I closed my doors.

But that's not the end of the story. Seems like shutting the place down didn't sit all that well with some of the neighborhood people. They liked Lee Lee's. Their kids did, too. The kids knew if they came here after school, they got a free cookie. So a group of neighbors started a campaign on the computer to help me out. They put out the word on the Internet, asked people to buy from me as much as they could—to keep me in the community.

New York people. Ain't they somethin'?

So I reopened. And my business went crazy after that. Some of the neighbors helped me set up a website selling my rugelach, and other goods as well. On the Web, people are ordering from every state. Two months ago, I shipped goods to Morocco. That lady paid forty-eight dollars just in shipping, but she wanted my pastries that bad.

Today, I sell at least two hundred rugelach a day. More, if I can make more. I've done up to a thousand on a weekend. I make other goods, too. You know, lemon pie, cookies, cupcakes, and red velvet cake. I don't know why everyone's so partial to my rugelach. People ask for my recipe all the time. I never tell them, except to say I use real butter instead of shortening, and the best cream cheese and flour money can buy. And I never use preservatives, which is not neces-sary anyway because we sell out of everything just about every day. My biggest problem is, I can only make so much at one time. This is a little place and I have only a half-sized oven to work from and one person sometimes to help me. So a sheet tray goes in and when it comes out, another tray goes in right away. That's how we have to do it.

Recently I had an offer from a factory in New Jersey that wanted to package my rugelach, carrot cake, and bread pudding. They wanted to sell it as frozen product with my picture on the back and my story. You know, a black man making rugelach. I turned 'em down. I'm not good at business and I didn't want to do it. No, sir. I'm fine with what I've got right now. Maybe when I retire and look back on this, I'll think I should have done things different. You know, got more people to work with me. Maybe, maybe not. Am I going to die a poor man? Probably. But I can tell you this: I'm going to die a happy man. Because when I'm baking, I've never had a bad day in my life.

Mohamed Abouelenein

THE HALAL GUYS

The Halal Guys food cart has been a New York staple for years. Residing at the corner of 53rd Street and Sixth Avenue in Manhattan, it has become perhaps the city's most well-known alfresco dining destination. The lines to purchase an aluminum plate of food from this cart ($6) often stretch from Sixth to Seventh Avenue. Once the food is in hand, with no headwaiter to guide you, it's then up to you to decide where to sit and eat it.

His office is in a bland building in an industrial neighborhood in Astoria, Queens—the kind of building you might drive by and never notice if you weren't seeking it out. It's one flight up from street level. When I arrive, he's seated at his desk, on the telephone. With his free hand, he motions me to sit down on a well-worn sofa. Within a few minutes, he returns the phone receiver to its cradle and swings his chair around to face me. As we talk, every so often the blaring music from a car radio reverberates so loudly through the open window, I have to ask him to repeat himself. He doesn't seem to notice the noise.

In Egypt, it's the aim of any family for their children to get a higher education—to be a doctor or an engineer or something like that. I ended up with a doctorate in veterinary medicine, but only because that was the desire of my family. Me? I wanted to be a soccer player. I was very good at it, too.

After I received my doctorate, I worked as a vet, but after six months, I quit to come to America in search of a better future. I joined a friend here in New York and started to study for my vet's license, but studying and trying to make enough money to live on at the same time was almost impossible. So I went to work. First as a dishwasher. Then as a waiter. Then I met a guy who said, "Come work with me selling hot dogs on the street. You can make more money." I told him, "I don't know anything about working on the street." "I'll teach you," he said, this friend. I was thirty years old at the time.

I started with a small pushcart, selling hot dogs, pretzels, and soda, on 61st Street and Fifth Avenue. It was okay for me. When you're looking for money, you forget your profession. You want to buy a car, and you want to get married. That's what was in my mind at the time. I didn't need anymore to be a veterinarian. I was just looking for money. With my hot dogs, I made about fifty or sixty dollars a day, and as I got better at it, I reached a hundred dollars a day. But the hours were tough. I started at nine a.m. and finished at nine p.m. And then, every night, after twelve hours working, I had to push my cart down the street and into a garage that was blocks and blocks away. Then I can go home.

A guy named Abdul owned the garage I parked my cart in. Abdul was a smart guy. He had his food cart in a spot on 53rd Street and Sixth Avenue. He started by selling hot dogs and pretzels from a small cart like mine. But all night long, when the cabdrivers—mostly guys from the Middle East—stopped by to eat, they asked him to change the food he was selling. They told him, "We want a big dinner, a decent meal. Not hot dogs and sausages every night. Make us something better." So Abdul changed from a small pushcart to a bigger one, and from his new cart, he started selling falafel, chicken, *kofta*, and salad—stuff the cabdrivers would like. Right away, lots of people started coming—and not just cab- and limo drivers. Other people, too. And they came by the carload, especially at nighttime. He used to end his day at midnight, but when he saw that the drivers stayed working until four a.m., he increased his hours to accommodate them. So he started staying until five a.m. when, by arrangement, a coffee-and-rolls guy would move into Abdul's spot for a few hours and then Abdul would come back around noon.

One day, as I parked my cart in his garage, Abdul said he was moving back to Egypt and asked me if I wanted to buy his spot. I didn't have the money, I told him. My aim was to bring my family here and I needed my money for that. And besides, I said, I was happy with the hundred dollars a day I was making selling hot dogs. Still every night, as I pushed my cart into his garage, he would ask me again. Always I said no. Finally, he said, "Okay, Mohamed. You are always honest. Other people want my spot, but you're the only one I trust. If you can't buy it yourself, I'll get my brother in Egypt to share it with you. And you only pay half." To that, I could agree.

By law, you do not have to pay for any spot in the city that is zoned for food carts. Any pushcart can be in any of the areas of the city that are not restricted. What you have to pay for is a vendor's license to operate a food cart, and those are not so easy to acquire. But as far as where you park your cart, that's legally open to anyone as long as there is a parking space available. The thing is, if you want to have a business, you have to keep returning to the same spot so customers know where to find you. After you build up a business, that spot becomes more and more valuable. And at the same time, others with carts know it's "your spot." It's like an unwritten agreement.

His spot was a winner! Fifty-third Street and Sixth Avenue is in the heart of midtown, directly across from the New York Hilton—one of the city's busiest commercial and tourist hotels. The Hilton restaurant is very expensive, so a lot of the guests come outside and buy food from us. If you buy a can of soda inside, it's four dollars. If you buy from me, it's a dollar. A plate of my food is only six dollars. Where are you going to find anything like that in the city? And by day—a huge number of businesspeople and workmen take our food for lunch. It's also the area where the limousine drivers congregate at night, because most of the nighttime drivers are Muslims and they are looking for halal.

Halal is very important to the Muslims. It's like kosher to the Jewish people. In our religion, when you cut the neck of an animal, like a cow, steer, buffalo, or camel—you have to say aloud the name of Allah—which means "God" in Arabic. And you must immediately drain all the blood from the carcass, which is considered healthier, because bacteria grow in an animal's blood. We are certified halal.

Because we sold authentic halal, I felt I should put the name "Halal Food" on my truck where people could see it. It turned out I was the first in the city to do that, so now people knew where to get it. If you're Muslim, you go to any city in the world and you want to eat good food but don't know where to go—who do you ask? A cabdriver! And all the cabdrivers told people about us. They made a good reputation for us. And not just with the Muslim tourists. The American ones, too! And then the construction people started coming. And soon we were so busy, we started to have lines waiting for the food.

A lot of people don't mind waiting in line. They're talking. They're hanging out with their friends. They're making new friends. It's an adventure. Sometimes there can be up to fifty people on line. But it moves fast. The most you'll wait is between twenty and thirty minutes, depending on the time of day and if it's a weekend or not. We never let anyone cut the line. No one! We watch it very closely. The only people we give preference to are the cabdrivers because they have been so good to us. When a cabdriver comes for food, they need to be served fast because they have a break for fifteen, thirty minutes maximum. So they stand on the other side of the cart and we feed them right away. The customers in line understand, and they don't mind.

For us, the lines waiting to buy our food are our best advertisement. You come to us, you see the line halfway down the block. Day and night. You know something is happening. And you're going to want in. I heard a joke about that once. A guy bends over to tie his shoelace and another guy stops short right behind him so as not to bump into him. Seeing the two guys, one behind the other, a third guy gets behind the second guy, and then a few more line up behind them. When the first guy comes up from tying his shoe, he wonders what everyone is waiting for. But he thinks, "Hey, I'm first in this line, I'm not leaving now!" The line got so long that finally the second guy in line asked the first, "What's everyone waiting for?" And the first guy says, "I don't know but I'm sure it's something really good . . ."

We have four guys working on the weekdays and five on the weekend. Three are cooks and one takes the money. We move fast. It takes about five seconds from the time you order until the time we hand you your food. Almost before you can spit out the word "chicken," the plate is in a bag and in your hands.

People always ask me, "Mohamed, what are you doing that you're so busy when the guys across the street or on the next block who sell the same food have nobody waiting?" I tell them there are no tricks to this business. Just good common sense. When you build something with a good foundation, the building will be strong. What's the foundation for my business? Customer service. That's the first thing. Make the customer happy. When I train an employee, I explain that a happy customer will talk to somebody else. You get a lot of new people this way. But if one customer gets mad, they will tell others the same way and I will lose business. Rule two: The food must be fresh. Most vendors, if they have something left over, they serve it the next day. For me, it doesn't matter how much is left over, at the end of the day, I throw it away.

Next thing: Keep the area around the truck clean at all times. I hire someone just to keep it clean. It can get very dirty very fast if you don't keep up all the time. People come at lunchtime or on the way home, if they see garbage on the ground, they keep walking. And who would blame them? Next thing: Price the food right. We sell a plate of food in a foil container for six dollars. You hear? Six dollars is *nothing!* If you try to get this quality and amount of food at any New York restaurant, you're paying at least fifteen.

People think I am a millionaire. I'm not. People think all this money comes in and I don't spend it. I do spend it. We have expenses. Huge expenses. The building that houses the kitchen where we clean and prepare the food before it goes to the truck costs a lot of money. The truck itself is not cheap. My employees, the products we buy to prepare the food. We have too many expenses. If I don't sell all the volume, I can't make ends meet.

We don't cheat the people. I know some people that sell food *say* it's halal but it's not. Halal is more expensive because in the slaughterhouse they have to hire more people to kill the animals right and to mention the name of Allah. We get a certified paper weekly that says this is halal. That's why the customer trusts us.

Okay, final rule: You have to show up every single day, so the people can count on you. I remember one day there was a big snowstorm and Mayor Giuliani gave the order that no cars should come into the city from New Jersey. That day we were working. It was quiet all around us. Everything white. Only two or three cabs on the street. So a cop comes up to us and he goes, "You know you guys are famous?" "Why?" I asked. "You didn't hear? CBS is talking about you!" The city had come to a standstill. We were the only pushcart open in the city. Our yellow-and-red cart sticking out from all the white snow. Believe it or not, on that day I made very good money. That day, Jason Kidd, the Knicks player, came by in a stretch limo with about eleven guys with him. They stayed with us for about forty-five minutes, talking and eating sandwich by sandwich. It was freezing cold out, but they were very happy. I was happy, too. I was making money!

Only one day I have ever missed and that was during Hurricane Sandy. And even on that day, we went to work for a few hours until they forced us to leave. I remember the police officer came and said, "Guys, there are only two departments working in the city right now, the police department and the Halal Guys department. But you guys gotta leave."

Some people look at us and what they see is a vendor in the street and nothing more. They think we just want the easy way to work to make money. Some people look at us as foreigners, uneducated Muslims. But they don't know anything about us. My right-hand man, Omar, is an engineer. And I have my doctorate. Most of our workers are citizens of the U.S.A. They pay taxes like everyone else. You think I care what they think? No. I don't. Because today, we are the most famous food vendor in the city and how many of them can say that?

PART II

Duck and Other Dynasties

As you've just read, to take an idea for a food-centric business and turn it into the real thing is one kind of challenge. To inherit that business and preserve its integrity for the next generation is quite another. And though this dynamic may play out more quietly in the food world, under the radar of public awareness—unlike, say, in politics or sports or media—the issues are no less complicated, and possibly more so. A recent study by the Small Business Administration revealed that in contrast to other industries, the vast majority of food companies are family owned or controlled while also facing a tougher generational transition. When control of a business shifts from the first to the second generation, there's a 25 to 30 percent success rate. That rate falls to 10 to 15 percent when the business moves to the third generation. Less than 3 percent make it to the fourth generation and beyond.

Why food families should have a dicier time at the inheritance game is only minimally explained. One thought is that the food industry in particular is subject to more intensive rules, regulation, and inspection by federal and state agencies concerning food safety and labeling requirements. Another consideration takes into account Mother Nature's unpredictable behavior and its possibly damning effects on crops, production, shipping, and the like.

But none of these cites the far more compelling human factor. Sharing a family's bloodline doesn't guarantee the ability to successfully run the family-owned business—just look at the history of kingship. And even if you *do* happen to have the head for the job, maybe you don't have the heart. Maybe you're set on a career as a vet, or an artist, or a cop—or simply dead set against a career in business altogether. What then? Do you succumb to family expectations regardless of the consequences? On the other hand, stepping into the shoes already broken in by your father and his father before him, preserving their legacy while keeping the business vital for your own children, could be what you've wanted all along.

The following stories reveal that the ways of bringing it all back home can be as varied as the individual personalities involved. But what appears to be a mishmash of straightaways and hairpin turns, unexpected cul-de-sacs and prolonged detours, all ultimately converges at a common end-point. Douglas Corwin, born on the family duck farm, and Bobby Weiss, heir to a thriving fish business, rode the straightaway into those businesses—both the fourth generation to lead them. Palma Denino married the second-generation owner of a renowned Staten Island pizzeria knowing nothing about her husband's responsibilities; she learned what they entailed the hard way, when he died unexpectedly and she was forced to take over. Alexander Poulos, David Fox, Amy Rubenstein, and Wilson Tang took early detours but were ultimately either lured away from other lives, or willingly found their way back home. Today they, too, are currently carrying the mantle for the next generation.

And speaking of that next generation, so far, seven of our eight inheritors already have members waiting in the wings. Maybe they'll beat the SBA statistics after all? Time will tell.

Wilson Tang

Nom Wah Tea Parlor is the oldest Chinese restaurant in New York. It could also be the only Chinese restaurant in the world to use red-checkered table-cloths, Italian-cliché style. In 1920, the Choy family opened the place; in 1950, the owners hired sixteen-year-old Wally Tang to help out; in the 1970s, Wally bought the restaurant from his former employers and ran it for the next thirty-odd years before passing it along to his nephew, Wilson. Those red-checkered tablecloths are still there, part of a décor mashup—mirrored pillars and a ceramic-tiled floor are other features—but Wilson, a whirlwind of energy at twenty-nine, is hardly marching in place. Restaurant number two is already on the drawing board.

Nom Wah was always a hub for our family. Wherever we went, we always seemed to end our day or evening there. I grew up in Chinatown and lived there until grade school, when my father moved us to the suburbs because he thought it would be safer for me. Also, he didn't want me hanging around the restaurant all the time and not knowing that there was another world out there. He said I should aspire to do more with my life. "Be a doctor," he said. "Be a lawyer. Just don't look at this place too much." And yet, on weekends, all through my school years and all during the summers, our family would constantly drift back to Nom Wah. When I graduated from college, I went to work for Morgan Stanley. Personally? I did it to please my father. It was not what I wanted for myself. My office was in Two World Trade Center. On the seventy-fourth floor.

And that's where I was on 9/11.

That morning was like any other for me. It required two elevators to get up to my office—the express to forty-four, and then the local to seventy-four. I got into the elevator at eight fifteen, rode up to forty-four, stopped in at the cafeteria on that floor for my usual two eggs, sausage patties, and hash browns to go. I got back on the local and arrived at my office on seventy-four, turned on my computer, and started in on my breakfast. That's when my office mate stopped by my desk and said, "Hey, the fire alarm went off, I think there's a drill or something." My first thought was, "Cool. I can go downstairs now and goof off for a bit." So we took the elevator back down to forty-four. When the doors opened, we're told there's a real fire and we have to take the stairs the rest of the way. The funny thing was that when I was still in my office, I saw all this paper flying outside, and I remember thinking, "Is this like a ticker-tape parade? The Yankees? World Series? Is there a parade today?" I was young. And I was oblivious.

As we were descending the stairs from forty-four, somewhere around the sixteenth floor, there was an announcement that everything is fine. You can go back to your floor. And people did turn around. My thinking was, walking down sixteen flights is so much easier than walking up twenty, I'll walk to the first floor and take an express elevator back up. People were just heading down, no one was panicked at all. The firefighters kept passing us heading up, and I'm still oblivious.

There was so much commotion in the lobby that I walked outside to see what was going on. And that was when I understood—but I did not yet absorb the magnitude of what had happened. When you looked up, the area where the plane went in looked so small that I figured it was some guy flying one of those private planes and I was thinking, "How terrible for him." Next thing you know, the second plane hit and everyone starts yelling and we're being pushed further and further away from the building. It was pandemonium. Chaos. Crazy. Nobody you asked knew much of anything except to get away. Fast. I could only think to go to Nom Wah. Where else would I go? Along with a load of stunned people, I started walking north toward Chinatown, heading for the restaurant. Suddenly, the crowd around me started turning around, looking backward and yelling. I turned to see what they were looking at and that's when I watched the first tower on its way down. And then I saw the second one go, too.

I still try not to think about it.

Morgan Stanley relocated in Harborside, New Jersey. I hated the commute from New York and I decided if I was ever going to strike out on my own, now was the time. I found a small bakery for sale, bought it, and hired a master baker to teach me to make bread. It ran fairly successfully for around four years, but the hours were killer. Every day—five a.m. to eight p.m.—I never saw daylight. I rarely saw my family or my friends, and I'm thinking, "I'm a young guy. My buddies are all out having fun, going to clubs, doing crazy things and I'm here, running a bakery." And . . . I wasn't meeting any chicks.

All that changed in 2010 when my Uncle Wally made a proposition to me to take over Nom Wah. It was a very simple proposition.

"Wilson," he said, "I'm eighty-five. I need to get the fuck out." For me, those were words from heaven. I was so sure this was my calling, my chance to do what I had always wanted to do. I knew my father would be disappointed, but I told him, "I'm never going to be happy putting on a tie every day and being told what to do, what time to go home, what time to come in, what days to work, when I can go on vacation. This is my opportunity."

My "inheritance" wasn't much to look at in the beginning. Over the forty years Uncle Wally had been at the helm, the restaurant had been falling apart bit by bit. Paint was chipping; there was a stray cat slinking around. Uncle Wally owns the building but he wasn't really serving food anymore. The place had become his social club. He had his gang of hooligans in the back, smoking and playing cards. When a customer came in, if they wanted to stay, he would make them some-thing to eat. He never thought of the place as closed. In his eyes, "I'm open" meant "I've got cookies. You can have a cup of tea, use the bath-room. Whatever." I said yes, under the condition that I do things my way, and that I have help in the kitchen. He agreed to both. The kitchen help he got me is still with me to this day.

Nom Wah is and has always been a dim sum parlor. Dim sum is a style of Cantonese food that's prepared as small bite-sized or individ-ual portions. In most restaurants, ready-to-serve dim sum dishes are rolled from the kitchen on a cart around the restaurant, with the server stopping at each table for customers to choose their orders. Tra-ditionally, dim sum is a breakfast, brunch, or lunch type of cuisine. The story goes back five thousand years, when people were traveling along the Silk Road and they would stop off at little shops for a snack and a cup of tea. Chefs have to train for years to get everything right in every dumpling; the skins, the portions, the marinades, the folds, and the pleats all matter. And of course the filling is of equal importance.

For me, the problem with doing the traditional dim sum for breakfast and brunch meant I had to get up too early—I might as well have stayed with the bakery. I wanted to break that mold. I wanted to do dim sum for dinner, which meant starting later and staying open later. To serve it with beer and wine. My dad said, "You're crazy. Dim sum for dinner? Who does that?" I said, "I do." It made perfect sense to me. After all, it's just like Spanish tapas. You go to a tapas restaurant and have little Spanish dishes, a glass of wine, and you sit and eat. Why not do that with Chinese food? When I announced my intention to Uncle Wally, he said, "I don't care what you do, Wilson. Just don't fuck it up. Keep the store open and let the legacy live on." Wally has been in Chinatown for fifty years and he's well known in the community. Even though he passed his place on to me, it's still his identity. And for a while after I moved in, I did let his cronies play cards in the back room.

Eventually, I started opening later and closing at ten p.m. My next step was to educate the public. We're in the age of social media and I'm young enough to understand that. I made a Facebook page for the restaurant and the next thing you know, the editor of the *Daily News* messages me, "I've been going to Nom Wah since I was eight. I have to write a story about your reopening." So we got in touch. In January 2011, we had a two-page spread in the Sunday *Daily News* and that was the beginning of Nom Wah's comeback.

The last three years have been a whirlwind experience for me. We were in the *New York Times* twice, including on the front page of the Wednesday dining section. Even more exciting: I held a party here for Jeremy Lin's first game as a New York Knick. I'm a big basketball fan. I am six foot five. Taller than anyone in my family. When Jeremy Lin came to the Knicks, I thought, "Wow, that's amazing. He's like me—a tall Chinese boy, born and bred in America." Then, out of the blue, I was approached by a PR firm about hosting a viewing party here for his first game in New York. I thought, "How cool! Knicks lovers will be here, and they will give out free stuff." Other restaurant owners were like, "What do you mean, a viewing party?" "How much does it pay?" "What, you're going to take up the whole dining room and put TVs in here?"

It was fantastic. ESPN had a live feed in here, and because it was a big game, it was broadcast nationally. The Knicks City Dancers were here. John Wallace, a former Knicks forward, signed autographs for whoever asked him. All the big guns from Madison Square Garden came. We were the talk of the town for weeks and business was great.

So much has happened in the course of my life and more things just keep coming my way. I feel so grateful and also so lucky. I think a lot these days about what's next for me and my business. But mostly I think about my son. In my whole life, I never took a vacation with my dad because he was always working. I want to make sure I don't miss these moments with my son. It seems like just yesterday he was born and he's already walking and talking and I've been busy. I want to be able to experience things with him. I want to go to Little League, I want to go to soccer practice, I want to take him on hiking trips, run a marathon with him. I didn't get that with my father. I hope I can have it with my son.

Douglas Corwin

CRESCENT DUCK FARM

In 1873, one male and three female Pekin ducks arrived in the United States from China. No one knows exactly how it happened, but all four ducks ended up on Long Island. What we do know is that the members of this quartet became the progenitors of Crescent Duck Farm's current flock, and that these descendants now populate the menus of some of New York's best restaurants. Corwin, a fourth-generation duck farmer, was born and raised on Long Island, on the land once tended by his great-grandfather, grandfather, and father, and on which he's raising his own children—along with, per year, more than a million ducks.

The duck industry started on Long Island in the 1860s. By the 1960s, six million ducks were produced in America, five million of which were grown on Long Island. But ten years later, things started to change. Just about the whole industry migrated to other parts of the country. I never did get exactly why; maybe energy production was cheaper elsewhere, maybe labor was cheaper. I don't know. But by the time I got out of college, there were only thirty-five duck farms left on the Island. Today, there's our farm and one other small farm. That's it. There was no way my family would ever have considered leaving this place. First, because we have one hundred and forty-five acres here and half of us live on this land. But also, some of it has been in the family since the 1600s. How are you going to leave that?

At Crescent Duck Farm, we breed ducks. We hatch them, we grow them, and then we harvest them—or as some call it—"process" them. Yes, we process them, too. It's a real family business. What makes it work so well is that each of our generations has contributed something different. My great-grandfather was the first to start farming ducks here in 1908. His son was a master carpenter. We have barns all around to attest to how good a builder he was. My father was the first college-educated Corwin. He came into the business right after graduating from Cornell. Dad had a very strong business sense and focused his attention on our bottom line, making sure we'd have something to carry us into the future. I came in straight from college too, but my contribution is in developing the genetics of the Crescent Farm bird. I want it to be meatier and more succulent than our competitors'. Which, by the way, it is.

We breed our birds for all the best characteristics. They're still white Pekin ducks, but we've managed them such that a chef will know instantly that he's cooking our ducks versus someone else's. I've probably got well over 50 percent of the white-tablecloth trade up here in the metropolitan area for one reason alone: We simply have a better bird. I've been told the Four Seasons Restaurant has had our ducks on their menu for twenty-five years now.

A lot of my time is spent doing advance breeding. That means selecting the best of our best birds for reproduction. What you mainly look for in a breeder bird is overall health. How do the eyes look? What does the feathering look like? Then you want to know that it excels physically as well. Is the bird's frame straight? Are the legs good and sturdy? Is it going to be strong enough to carry what you want to put on that frame? How long, how wide is the breast? How thick is the muscle tissue? How thick is the skin? If it looks like a breeder, you put a wing band on it so you can go back and check it as it grows. That way, you start refining your product. But it takes an awful lot of time.

And money. You want to produce a great bird? It's going to cost you. You have to house them. If they're going to be happy and grow properly, they need enough room to move around. We've got thirty different barns here. Inside each one, we allot a certain amount of square footage per bird, depending on the season. You want them to be comfortable. On any given day we have 150,000 ducks at varying stages of growth. In six weeks, they go from wet ducklings to big enough to eat. Egg to harvest. They grow fast, these guys. Every day in front of your eyes. Bigger and bigger and bigger.

If you took a little walk into my biggest barn right now, what you'd see is an ocean of white feathers. Twelve thousand busy ducks waddling around, quacking their heads off. My smaller barns might have up to four thousand ducks in each. We hatch flocks twice a week. And there are thousands in every flock. And every one of those thousands wants to eat. So of course you have to feed them well. We've always given our ducks the best possible diet—natural grains and no hormones. It takes twenty pounds or so of various different kinds of feed to produce a single six-pound duck.

Then you have to factor in the fact that we're always building something new here. We recently put up a $3 million waste treatment plant. We compost all of the solid waste we screen off. It's a nice process because it ties up the nitrogen, makes it so it doesn't go in the groundwater, and the by-product is an excellent fertilizer that we turn around and use. We have a digester where we cook the wastewater from the farm, and get gas from it. We take that gas and burn it through our motors. The motors help us make other parts of our waste stream, where the bacteria that are fostered by the oxygen eat up the rest of the waste. What's left gets filtered through an artificial wetlands, so by the time we're done, we have a very clean waste stream. It's all good for the environment.

I work eighty to ninety hours a week. You ask me what I'm doing for those hours, I can't really explain it—even to myself sometimes. I look at ducks. Lots and lots of ducks. Hours and hours of looking at ducks and more ducks. I don't know how much of a social life I have, but I go out if I can. Once a year I take the family out to a city restaurant. And yes, I order the duck.

The beauty of a family business is that each generation, if it's going to be a success, comes in with a certain energy, a certain amount of ideas. My grandfather built barns. My dad organized and developed the operation into a thriving business. I developed the bird that I was given. And the next generation is coming up fast. I've got two sons who are pretty much full time now. The oldest is a builder like his grandfather. He's a hard worker and he likes doing everything from a physical aspect. And while the ducks are pretty much my domain, my younger boy works directly with all the other farm animals.

For me, being able to work for yourself means being able to control your own destiny. And there's a family closeness, which is a very wonderful thing if it can happen. It doesn't always happen, of course. There are different personalities, and different goals. Some people might want to work harder than others, some people might not want to go in the same direction you want to go in, some people step on each other's toes too much. But if the business is big enough and you can each find your own niche, a family business, no matter what it is, can be pretty amazing.

Palma Denino

DENINO'S PIZZERIA AND TAVERN

Denino's Pizzeria, which was once just a small tavern, sits at the north end of what is still partially a residential block on Staten Island. After the latest addition to the restaurant, it now looks like two awkwardly joined brick buildings that could easily house anything from a bridal shop to a dental clinic. Walk through the front door, however, and there is no mistaking where you are. What hits you first is the smell of burnt bread, melting mozzarella cheese, garlic, and sweet, ripe tomato sauce: a smell so rich, it can come only from baking several hundred pizza pies a day, every day. Which is what has been happening here for the last sixty-three years.

Up front in the barroom, two muted TV sets broadcasting sports compete for wall space with shelves crowded with liquor bottles. As the bar fills up with the lunch crowd, people's voices slowly drown out the sounds of Frankie Valli crooning "My Eyes Adored You" from a corner jukebox. The well-lit, windowless dining room is farther back. Dark vinyl-cushioned booths line the walls. She and I occupy one of them. As she talks, I grow hungrier by the minute.

My father-in-law, John Denino, whom I never had the pleasure of meeting, left Italy with his family and arrived in Manhattan when he was a boy. Here, he met Mary; they got married and moved to Staten Island, which is where my husband Carlie—short for Carlo— was born and raised. In 1937, John opened Denino's as a tavern. When he died in 1951, he left it to his only son. Carlie didn't really want to take over this place. He was a welder, making good money working over at the shipyard, whereas the tavern was just about breaking even. But what was his choice? The tavern sold liquor but very little food, and it wasn't long before Carlie realized he needed to put something in here that was going to turn a profit. Pizza seemed as good an idea as any. To no one's surprise, it was a big hit.

I first met Carlie in this very dining room. I was in my early twenties and had come in with someone else. "Hello, how are you?" "Hello. Nice to meet you." That was the sum total of our first conversation. The next time I met him, I was married and nine months pregnant. "Hello, Palma." "Hello, Carlie. Nice to see you again." When I ran into him for the *third* time three years later, I was divorced with a son, Michael, and he was divorced with a son, Michael. I know what you're thinking and, yes, it got confusing. When we started dating, we took to calling them big Michael and little Michael. Old Michael and young Michael. He also had a daughter, Carla. So there were Carlie and Carla, and the two Michaels. Don't ask.

I was twenty-seven and he was fifty-four when we got married. We had a long and happy marriage until, at age seventy-seven, he died suddenly on the golf course. I'm sure he died happy. But I'm equally sure leaving me clueless about this place wasn't part of his plan. Suddenly, I'm fifty years old, and I'm the owner of a restaurant. Sure, we worked here together, but he was the one who made all the decisions.

The only one. I never pushed for anything, even if I thought it would help the business. Denino's was Carlie's place and that was all there was to it.

The first few months after he died, I had no idea what I was doing. Nothing was really in the right order; things were all over the place. It was tough. But I pulled it together following what I thought was the way he would have wanted things to be done. And surprisingly, we did just fine. As Staten Island started building up, the restaurant got increasingly busy. Lines of people waiting for tables started to be out the door. We bought the two-story house next door, knocked it down, and expanded our space. And still more people kept coming, which was crazy, because we never advertised. We still don't. What's even crazier is that we keep winning awards as Best Restaurant this and Best Restaurant that and we're not really a restaurant. We're a pizzeria. We don't even serve pasta here. Just pizza, twenty different ways. And a few appetizers like Buffalo wings, scungilli, and calamari. We have salads and hero sandwiches and Italian wedding soup sometimes, but we don't do real dinner. Still, in 2014, TripAdvisor ranked us number one of 698 restaurants on Staten Island. Zagat's named us sixty-fifth in the top one hundred New York City restaurants, which is really something to be proud of, considering there are around twenty thousand restaurants in the five boroughs.

Carlie's son Michael has branched out into his own restaurant, and our other two kids, my Michael and his Carla, have pretty much taken over the place today. My son Michael was with the fire department, but he has always had an interest here, too. And Carla, though she's had other jobs, she keeps coming back to work at Denino's. So where does that leave me? Right now I'm in charge of the books and paperwork. I had heart surgery twice. It took a lot out of me. If everything is not just the way it should be, I get upset, which I'm not supposed to do. Everyone knows that working with your kids can get frustrating at times. You want to yell at them. I still look at Carla and go, "Uh-huh," and she goes, "You're shaking your head, Ma. What's-a-matter?" So I say, "Carla. You're here so many years. How do you not know how to do this? Don't you look? Don't you see what I see?" Stuff like that. I'm better off I work from home, so that's what I do now mostly.

Yesterday I spent twelve hours in the office at home. We have closed-circuit cameras in the kitchen and the front of the restaurant that I can access from home. We got them when an employee fell and accused us of being negligent. I said, "There's nothing there to fall on!" And nobody saw that person fall but we got sued anyway. So that's how it started. I also tell them all the time, "If you need me, call me. I'll run down." Do they call me? No.

Doesn't matter. I can see on my closed-circuit monitor if they need help. If it's really busy, I'll call them sometimes. Or if I see some of the employees sitting down, I'll call in and say, "What are you doing sitting down?" And then they look up at the camera and wave at me and they crack up, laughing.

This year marks the tenth anniversary since Carlie died. I don't think he ever could have imagined how incredibly successful Denino's would become. But I do know one thing. I know he would have looked at his family and how we're running his place and he would have been proud as hell.

Michael Burke (Palma's son)

DENINO'S PIZZERIA AND TAVERN

At forty, he's next in line to take over the place.

I was five when my mother married Carlie Denino, so I kind of grew up in this place. And as I grew up, Carlie used to tell me, "Mike, always keep your options open in case something happens to the restaurant." I always wanted to reply, "We've been here since 1937, Carlie. What's going to happen?" But I listened to him. You always listened to Carlie. So for the twenty-eight years I've been working here, I always had a second job. My latest was with the Staten Island fire department. I started there on November 14, 1999, and left, reluctantly, after 9/11, when they forced me to retire because of health issues. I was on-site when Building Seven came down, and spent every day, all day, for three months afterward, doing search and rescue and cleanup at Ground Zero. As a result, I lost 38 percent of my lung capacity, so I couldn't pass the firefighter's requisite breathing test anymore. Since then I've been here at the restaurant full time.

Everything I know about pizza I learned in this kitchen before I was twelve. Which tells you something, doesn't it? It's so basic. People constantly say, "Your pizza's so great. What's your secret?" Secret? What secret? We keep it simple. That's our secret. Sometimes, the simpler something is, the better it is. A lot of people throw different ingredients into the dough. We don't. We use a basic recipe. Flour, water, yeast, salt. We let it sit for two days, stretch it out, and done. Ready to go. The way we prepare our pies is a little different. A lot of places put the sauce on first. We put the cheese on and then the sauce. If there's a secret, that's it. Oh, and the other thing we do is we use bread crumbs on the bottom instead of flour or cornmeal. Which is where the crunchiness and taste come from. Is that a secret?

There must be hundreds of pizzerias on Staten Island. You read articles about who has the best pizza and how we are in competition with each other. That's utter nonsense. There's room on Staten Island for all of us—Lee's, and Joe and Pat's. We're all friends. If we need something, we go to each other. If we run out of an ingredient, we lend it to each other. As long as everybody can make a living, it's like any other job.

The last two weeks have been insane. Bill de Blasio was in the restaurant during his campaign for mayor of New York City. He came in right before a fundraiser. He ordered the calamari and the pizza and he loved them. So afterward, he goes to this fancy dinner at the Excelsior Grand with six hundred people in attendance and from the podium, he's talking for ten minutes about the great food he just had at Denino's. All during his speech, I'm getting text messages and phone calls from friends who are in the audience listening to him. He started his speech by saying, "If I had known the calamari and pizza like I just had at Denino's was this good, I would have been here years ago . . ."*

The minute people heard about de Blasio's comments, they started lining up at the door. And that was just one incident. We have a wall of plaques out in the entry that show that we've been in the top three pizzerias in the city for the last fifteen years. I can't tell you what makes us so special. If I knew, I'd bottle it and sell it. Maybe it's the family atmosphere. We serve everyone here from dockworkers in construction boots, who stop by for lunch or a couple of beers after work, to lawyers in business suits. You have billionaires and guys making minimum wage hanging out together. We get high school kids coming in after their athletic games. And of course we get families. People bring their children, especially on weekends. I've watched those children grow up and bring their children. It's amazing how many generations still come here. As the families of Staten Island grow, so do we.

We used to be 80 percent family working here. My aunt Rose, Carlie's sister, started at fourteen and worked up until two weeks before she died at eighty-nine. She was the hostess and, before that, a waitress. All our waitresses were aunts and cousins, and their kids bussed. As they grew up, we had to fill a gap, and so friends came in. A lot of friends' wives work here now, or my sister's friends. Many of the guys in the

---

*Bill de Blasio, as newly elected mayor of New York City, visited Staten Island, where he ate a slice of pizza using a knife and fork. This horrific food faux pas caused such a furor as to have the press label the incident "Pizzagate." And worse, it elicited the following admonition from comedian Jon Stewart: "De Blasio! . . . You're supposed to be championing the middle class. Two weeks into your term, and we catch you eating pizza à la Trump? Look, I understand there is a learning curve to being mayor, but here is lesson No. 1: Learn how to eat your city's signature dish. If you were mayor of Philadelphia, would you eat a Philly cheese steak with a knife and fork? If you were mayor of Buffalo, would you eat Buffalo wings with a knife and fork? . . . Admittedly, your predecessor Bloomberg did not eat it with his hands . . . But you are not that. You're a man of the people! EAT LIKE ONE!"

kitchen have been here for over twenty years. They came here young, as dishwashers. We got them all citizenships, and today, they're like family. So I guess you could call us a family restaurant in more ways than one.

My wife and I debate whether or not our kids should become the next generation at Denino's. I say yes. She says no. And not just no. Emphatically, *"No!"* Look, I know it's a rough business. Yes, it's seven days a week, and yes, it's a lot of hours. But my kids seem to love it here. They come in, they go right to work. My son is ten. He goes to the computer. He answers the phones, he puts the orders in. He has my personality in that he loves talking to people but he hates getting dirty. He's a front-of-the-house kid. He takes money or your credit card, swipes it, "Can you sign this, please? And thank you very much." So it's in him already. My daughter, who's nine, is the opposite. She likes to make the pizza and is happy in the kitchen covered in flour. It's amazing how they fall right into it and have picked things up already. Children adapt well, and if nothing else, this will be a fallback for them. Honestly? I think at least one of them will definitely stay in it. The fourth generation. Kind of has a nice ring to it, doesn't it?

Bobby Weiss

BLUE RIBBON FISH COMPANY

The Fulton Fish Market is located in Hunts Point, the Bronx, inside a building that resembles a large airplane hangar. The structure is more than a quarter of a mile long, about the size of the Empire State Building laid on its side. Golf-cart-sized delivery vehicles run up and down a narrow, four-lane passage at the market's center, moving hundreds of tons of seafood in and out daily. The space is climate-controlled at forty degrees all year round—a bit chilly for the workers, perhaps, but great for the fish and the tons of ice that further ensure their freshness.

Weiss, the fourth generation of his family to work at Blue Ribbon, hopes that his seventeen-year-old son will be the fifth. "Today is his first day of work," Weiss says. "He came in with me at midnight and right now he's over there in the corner, sleeping."

My great-grandfather started this business. Even when I went to college, I knew I was headed here. I had worked here eight summers, paid my dues, and was thoroughly prepared for the challenge.

I have a bunch of guys working for me. My regular guys and my purveyors. The regular guys help with the inventory, deliver to the restaurants, and sell the fish on the floor. The purveyors process the fish. Some of our product goes out whole but a lot of it is butchered by these guys. One cuts it, someone else skins it, someone else pulls the pin bones. That guy is like a machine, *rat-a-tat-tat-tat*. He can pull twenty bones in five seconds, which is about as fast as you can get.

We process from fifty to a hundred thousand pounds of seafood a day, between shellfish and frozen product. None of it goes to waste. There's even a market for the bones that are left over after butchering. People use them to make soup, or stock. Or they take the whole rack from the tuna, and they spoon out several ounces between each bone. They take that and grind it up for tuna burgers or use it for spicy tuna roll. We used to throw the bones out with the rest of the garbage. That is, until a year ago, when some guy with a truck pulled up to our back door, walked into the processing room, and offered my men a few dollars every day for the fish bones we were throwing away. This went on for some time until I found out about it. Then I, personally, took the bones outside. The next thing I knew, I was coming away with thousands of dollars a week from him. That guy was getting away with murder.

Our seafood comes from across the world. And of course this country. But in America we're dealing now with conservation laws. In my grandfather's day, there were a zillion pounds of fish in the ocean. Today, the environmentalists and other powers that be worry about preservation of the species. Our edible fish are in danger of being fished out. So now there are quotas on what American fishermen can catch. I have a guy who works here whose full-time job is to keep track of anything that I get directly from a boat. I have to report the catch to the Department of Conservation of the federal government. I'm not complaining, because conservation works. I've seen fish stock replenish to record levels within one, two, and three years. Still, it's tough on the fishermen. You don't want to let them overfish, but you also don't want to cut the allotments back so far where you let them catch so little it doesn't pay for them to go out at all. Eventually, they'll all go out of business.

It's happening already. This year they cut codfish back by 81 percent, a big cut for a fish that has been a staple item for decades. The ban is for three years. As a result, I'm sourcing cod from Iceland and Norway. It's outstanding product, every bit as good as ours if not better. It costs me more, but I charge my customers more, so it's fine with me. But it's not fine with our fishermen. What are they supposed to do? Wait around? In three years, those guys are of necessity going to have a different job, and they're not going to come back.

This is night work. To deliver fresh seafood in the morning, you have to be here to receive it and sell it in the wee small hours. My day starts at midnight and ends around ten thirty in the morning. The hours actually work perfectly for me. I'm divorced and my two older children are with me half the time. I probably spend a lot more time with my kids than some of my friends who work full time in the city and go out and entertain afterward. I eat dinner with my nine-year-old daughter every night around five p.m. And then I go to bed. I get up for work at eleven. I've been doing it for the last ten years.

When I first started in the 1980s, we all came in to work at four a.m. It's gotten progressively earlier over the years because one company decided to start earlier to get the edge on the competition, and then of course we all had to follow suit. We adjusted, our customers adjusted, and it's been like that ever since. Now you'll see customers wandering up and down the "street" at two or three in the morning and thinking nothing of it.

At one a.m., I'm in my Carhartt jumpsuit and down in the trenches with my guys. We distribute the ice and set up displays of the new fish that have just arrived. We all walk around with these big giant grappling hooks slung over our shoulders that we use for grabbing fish or boxes, dragging, pulling, and yanking thousands of pounds of seafood. For the next few hours, that hook will be an extension of my arm. By two a.m., maybe 50 to 75 percent of the product is already in. That's when the buyers from the restaurants and the markets start showing up and we start selling and putting up their orders. By eight a.m., all the orders have been processed. I go back upstairs, change into my street clothes, and do other administrative tasks until ten, which is when I leave for the day. Usually for the golf course. *Mostly* for the golf course. It's not a bad way to end the day.

Amy Rubenstein

PETER LUGER STEAK HOUSE

Peter Luger Steak House, which stands in the shadow of the Williamsburg Bridge in Brooklyn, has been the institution most beloved by New York's discerning carnivores since her father bought it over sixty-five years ago. Through recessions and boom times, hurricanes and blackouts, reservations have been (and still are) all but impossible to secure. Something must be working. It's certainly not the décor. The bar has been in the restaurant since Carl Luger, Peter's father, opened the place in 1887. Plain wood panels cover the walls and floor, nondescript chandeliers hang from the ceiling, and vinyl-covered bentwood chairs flank clothless tables. And that's it. The star of this setting is clearly the steak.

She's one of three women who currently sit at the restaurant's helm. The others are her sister, Marilyn Spiera, and her niece, Jody Storch. Considering the fact that steak houses are such a bastion of male dominance, as is the entire meat industry, you'd think that three women at the top would give rise to some comments here and there. But she says that never happens. "The one thing my father always insisted on was that all bills be paid weekly and that there be no debt. We pay every bill immediately and women or not, everyone loves us."

I was eleven years old when my father, Sol Forman, bought Peter Luger. My dad came from very poor circumstances. His older siblings had moved out on their own, leaving him, at fourteen, with his parents to support. He dropped out of school and eventually joined his brothers in Forman Family, a company that manufactured metalware. The factory was located at 185 Broadway, and whenever he could, my father took prospective clients to lunch at his favorite restaurant across the street—Peter Luger. In fact, he ate there every day himself, even when he didn't have clients.

In June 1950, the Luger family got into some financial difficulty and they were forced to put their restaurant up for auction. At the time, my father was looking for other things to do in addition to the metal business, so he went to the auction, prepared to bid on the restaurant and the surrounding properties the Lugers owned. As it turned out, he was the only person who showed up. Sol Forman was now in the restaurant business.

Did it occur to him that he knew nothing about running a restaurant? Not *my* father. He figured he could put his buying and manufacturing expertise into the restaurant business, and that's just what he did. First up were the purveyors. Instead of counting on a single supplier, he got prices from several people and selected from there. And he insisted that every piece of beef he sold had to be all prime and USDA stamped.

To ensure the quality, he put my mother in charge of selecting every piece of meat that came into the restaurant. But she knew as much about picking meat as he did about running a restaurant. She was a pianist. With a master's degree in music from Columbia. Sadly, my brother had died not all that long before, so at that point in her life, my mother was looking to immerse herself in something completely different, something to get herself out of the house. And this seemed to be the perfect opportunity.

She spent two years learning. She was tutored by Joe Dowd, a retired USDA meat grader. I still remember how she'd put on her fur coat and hat and go with him twice a week to the meatpacking district, which at that time was near the West Side Highway. There, she would change into a white butcher's coat and galoshes, and she and Joe would go inside the processing areas to choose the meat. In time, my mother learned everything she needed to know about selecting good meat. After that, she didn't let any of the purveyors send anything into the restaurant that didn't first have her approval. She went to the market with her Peter Luger stamp and stamped every side of meat she had chosen, so that when it arrived, she knew she got just what she ordered. She did this every week until she was eighty years old.

My sister, Marilyn, joined the business around 1960. She had just graduated from Barnard when my father enlisted her help. He was still working in the metal business and he was involved in real estate as well. So even though Peter Luger was his passion, he didn't have time to spend there. So he made her the president. As for me, in the early sixties, all I was thinking about was getting married and having children. Which is what I did. Until one day in 1975, when my father called me to come to his office. He said, "Amy, your mother and I are going away on a cruise for three months. How can you leave your sister to run the restaurant all alone?"

Believe me, Marilyn was fully able to handle it without me. She had been doing just fine. But the way he said it, well, he literally guilted me into coming to work here. Before that, if I ever even mentioned the subject of working, my husband, Howard, would say, "Women should not work!" My father was adamant, though. And he offered me a deal. If I joined the company, I could work three days a week, leave for work after my children left for school and be home before they got home. So I acquiesced.

At that point, we set up a division of labor. Marilyn was the president and responsible for all the day-to-day operations. I oversaw construction as we added new rooms and a new kitchen to the restaurant. My mother, at the time, was still buying the meat. She would go once a week to the meat market and after she returned, she'd meet my dad here for lunch and they'd sit at the table and criticize the food: "This steak is a little tough." "The onions are a little sharp today." "The corned beef is a little hard." It was inevitable, and it was funny.

I'm pretty sure there are not a lot of steak houses left where every cut of meat is hand-selected by the owners. But that's essential to us. We get our meat from a number of purveyors. The ones who send it to us, where we don't make a personal selection, give us the right of refusal, which means we can return what we don't like. And once a week I'll go to the bigger places like Master Purveyor in Hunts Point. That's a real experience. For starters, you still have to dress for the show, which means you first cover your hair and your hands and then you put on a white coat and only then can you go into the meat area. George, the head of the shop, walks me in. He lifts the sides of beef to show me their short loins, which is where the porterhouse steak is cut from. The only meat that I'll even consider is USDA Prime, which represents less than 2 percent of graded beef cattle. If there's any callusing or bruising or blood dots in the meat—I don't want it. Now I hold the branding stamp, so when a piece meets my approval, I ink it and slap our name on the loin. More often than not, after a few minutes, George takes the stamp from me and whacks the loin himself because I don't go fast enough for him.

Some people think Peter Luger is stuck in the past. We don't think of it as being "stuck." We're a conscious throwback from the fifties, and that's the way we like it. We still take our reservations over the phone and enter them by hand with a pencil in a reservation book. We're always booked six weeks in advance, so apparently no one cares how we write down their name. We may, in fact, be the only restaurant in New York City that's not computerized. Our waiters take your order and write it down on a pad. They then take that ticket to the kitchen, not to some computer terminal that's in the middle of the floor. At the end of your meal, you get a handwritten check, which you pay with cash only, or one of our own credit cards. We've just started taking debit cards as well.

Our menu has remained pretty close to the original, too. Steaks and chops for the main course. Bacon slices, tomato and onion slices, and lettuce wedge appetizers. Our sides haven't changed either. Everyone still loves the German hashed brown potatoes and the creamed spinach. Top it off with one of our ten desserts and a dollop of *schlag*, and you've got your dinner right there. Nineteen fifty or 2015, it's all the same. People keep coming back and back, so why would we want to change anything?

Right now, our biggest challenge is whether or not the supply of top-quality meat will continue and whether or not the trend for lean beef will affect the quality. These days, people are looking for lean everything, but it's the fat and marbling in beef that give it the flavor. If people want fat-free beef, it's going to look like a piece of liver, and I'm not sure it will taste very good. But that's what's happening. There's a push for leaner beef, and that means grass-fed beef. The more people request it, the more the restaurants buy it, the more the restaurants buy it, the more the purveyors import it and the more the cattlemen produce it. That's how trends get started. And this one has us a little bit concerned.

Another challenge we face here is an occasional shortage of acceptable meat. Two years ago there was a shortage of lamb. No one really knew why. Maybe they didn't wean them early enough. Whatever the reason, there just wasn't enough to go around. The same thing has happened with beef. Particularly in the summer when people want meat for their barbecues. I always think it preludes a price rise. It's going on right now. They say there isn't enough prime beef. I don't know about the rest of the beef because I don't look at choice or select. But if things get really tight, rather than compromise on the quality of what we serve, we simply cut our reservations. We've done that several times.

The Peter Luger philosophy is to keep the restaurant as it was. I know that's not the *American* philosophy. We may, in fact, be the only business in this age of globalization that has not gone crazy with expansion. We have our Brooklyn and our Great Neck operations, and that's it. Somehow, I think that's in keeping with what my father would have wanted. He died fourteen years ago. My father, Sol Forman, the guy who for seventy-five years consumed a steak a day, was ninety-eight.

David Fox

FOX'S U-BET

We're in the Brooklyn office he shares with his son, Kelly, who is next in line to take over the business. Books about New York City's history and food culture are scattered about, as are leather scrapbooks, small statues, and other memorabilia depicting the good old days. As David Fox and I talk, Kelly sits eight feet away at his own desk, deeply focused on his work and oblivious to our conversation. Or at least that's how it appears.

I wish I had a dollar for every time someone asked me how we got the name Fox's U-bet. You don't have to give me a dollar. I'll explain anyway: Around the turn of the twentieth century, my grandfather Herman founded H. Fox and Company in Brooklyn as a chocolate syrup business. Grandpa Herman loved to gamble. He often went to the racetrack, sometimes raiding petty cash to support his habit. So no one was exactly surprised when this Brooklyn-born Jewish man, son of a Hungarian immigrant, went to Texas to invest in land with not a clue about what he was buying. And of course, while he was there he lost all the money he had. But he did come back with something. He came back with an expression that everyone used in the Southwest—"You bet!" "Feelin' okay today?" "You bet!" "Hot enough for ya?" "You bet!" And that, in a nutshell, is how our chocolate syrup got the name Fox's U-bet.

Some of the stories that have grown around us are legend. Especially with the Borscht Belt comedians. Don Rickles often talked about us in his act. Mel Brooks wrote an article about us in *Playboy* magazine in which he said as a young man he was never a sports star. Why? Because he was afraid of getting hurt. So instead, he was always the team's medic. That way, he could watch from the sidelines. And when an athlete was injured, he treated the guy's injury by getting him an egg cream made with Fox's U-bet. When I read that, I dropped him a line saying how much we appreciate his "Old Hebraic medical use" for our product. Harry Crane, who was a TV writer, sent us this note: "I live out in Los Angeles. Like so many other guys, I invite girls to my house all the time. I offer them Dom Pérignon. They say, 'What's the big deal?' I give them the best of caviar. That seems to bore them, too. But when I make them an egg cream with Fox's U-bet, I get lucky every time! So, thank you very much." Those anecdotes are repeated and repeated, and that creates the myth around our product. And of course the syrup itself makes a statement. You can't imagine how many people tell me they have a bottle of Fox's U-bet in their refrigerator that must have been there for ten years. It's vintage! A good, vintage chocolate syrup! Waddya think of that?

This company was formed in 1900, which puts us at a hundred and fifteen years and counting. New York was such an immigrant area back then. You had Brooklyn, Queens, Lower Manhattan, and the Bronx. And each of the boroughs had its share of candy stores. In those days, your life revolved around your neighborhood candy store with its soda fountain and swinging metal stools. You'd go there for a cup of coffee, or your newspaper, or your comic books. You'd go to the movies and come out afterward and have an ice cream sundae, and that was a great date. That was the landscape against which my grandfather started the business. His timing was perfect. People hanging out at the soda fountain bought a "two cents plain," which was essentially carbonated water, or seltzer. In an effort to up the price to a nickel, they had to add something. That something was generally cherry, orange, grape, or chocolate syrup. Which Grandpa sold to them.

At the same time, just like the milk trucks that delivered to your doorstep, a profusion of seltzer trucks went around from house to house dropping off bottles of seltzer and collecting the empties. So he created family-sized bottles of syrup just for the seltzer trucks. Now you could add a little syrup to your two cents plain and you could make in your kitchen the same thing you got in the candy store.

When my father came into the business right before the Second World War, there were maybe twenty syrup companies in New York. But over the course of time, competition became too great for some of them and they folded. Coke and Pepsi became the monster players in the marketplace, so my dad had to come up with yet another new idea, and that was to sell our product to the supermarket.

I came into the business fifty years ago. I was twenty-one and had just returned from Vietnam. My dad was ill. There were a lot of family problems by then and Fox's was in Chapter 11. When my father turned it over to me, everybody told me to sell. But I chose not to. All I could think about was survival: How will I get paid every week? How will I pay everyone else? Funny thing, though. I never thought about failure. I probably wasn't smart enough to know that you can fail. So I kept it alive. Because I felt then and I feel now like I'm just one in a line of those who came before me and those who will follow. The business started with my grandfather. Then my father and his siblings took it over. Then it was passed down to my sibling and me. Then it was just me. And now it's me and my son, Kelly.

There are a lot of theories about where the first egg cream came from, but to be honest, no one really knows. My theory is that it was a drink consisting of eggs and heavy cream. When immigrants pushed their carts along the streets or when they spent hours sewing in the sweatshops and they needed a boost or a working meal, they took an egg, put it into a glass of cream, beat it all up, and presto! No more hunger. Funny thing is, ultimately, they took out the egg and then the cream so that today, when you make an egg cream, it's with chocolate syrup, milk, and seltzer. No egg. No cream. Go figure.

There are definite camps on how to make the perfect egg cream. Some say the only way is to put in the syrup first, then the milk, and then the seltzer, which makes it foamy on top. If you go to Brooklyn, though, they tell you to put the syrup in last because the head gets different and it becomes a different color. To me, how you put the ingredients in is not what's important, it's what the ingredients are. If you use our syrup, you'll get a perfect egg cream. If you don't use our syrup, you won't. End of story.

It's funny how nostalgic people are about egg creams. On our website we ask, "What are your memories of having an egg cream?" Readers respond: "I had my first experience when I was a little girl and I'd dress up to go shopping with my mother. We always stopped for a special treat before we went home, and that day we went to a drugstore counter, ordered one egg cream and two straws, please." "I remember the first time I went to Coney Island with my family and we went to a candy store where my brother ordered an egg cream and I wanted to be just like him." The great thing is, they all speak of happy memories. It's like when you had a charlotte russe and you went, "Wow! A *charlotte russe!*" And really, what was it? A piece of cake in a tube with whipped cream and a cherry on top. But in those days, it was the greatest thing in the world. You would die for a charlotte russe. Penny candy? You would get a piece of paper with these colored dots on it and the dots tasted like flavored chalk, but you ate them anyway because everybody else did.

We're thrilled that Fox's U-bet egg creams are a part of that history, part of people's lives where they remember having good times. It's family, it's friends, it's laughing, it's having fun. Today, we carry that legacy on our shoulders. It's a hell of a history to bring forward.

Alexander Poulos

PAPAYA KING

"What is it with papaya drinks and hot dogs?" I ask Poulos, a slightly balding man with a narrow mustache. The combination is as traditional in New York as bagels and lox—but it seems to be successful only here in the city. I'm wondering why this duo can't seem to hack it anywhere else in the world. "I don't know the answer," he tells me. "We've tried expanding outside of New York many times, but haven't succeeded. I'm talking about in large cities like Boston or Philadelphia. I'm not talking Bismarck or Duluth. Maybe it's the water. They say that's why you can't get a good bagel outside of the city. Other than that, I'm as stumped as everyone else is."

After the Turks invaded Izmir in 1922 and threw the Greeks out, everyone in my family moved to Athens. Everyone, that is, except my Uncle Gus, who, at sixteen years old, came alone to New York with very little money and a lot of ambition. Ten years later, now the owner of a deli in Yorkville, he went with his buddies to Cuba, where he tasted tropical fruit drinks for the first time in his life. He fell in love. With the drinks, that is. Being the entrepreneur he was, Uncle

Gus figured if he loved these drinks so much, so would everyone else. And so in 1932, he opened a stand on the corner of 86th Street and Third Avenue, called it Hawaiian Tropical Drinks, and waited for the lines to form.

It never happened. Unfortunately, his timing was off. It was shortly after the Depression and the clouds of war were drifting in from Europe. People certainly weren't thinking about drinks made of exotic pineapples and papayas. Nor did they have the money to buy them. For months, Uncle Gus tried everything to drum up business, including playing Hawaiian music and putting women in grass skirts on the corner outside the fruit stand. This helped, but not enough. There had to be something else. Something that everyone was familiar with. And that's when he came up with the idea to sell frankfurters! They were cheap and easy to prepare. And Nathan's was already selling them on Coney Island. The location was perfect. Eighty-sixth Street and Third Avenue was Yorkville, the German area of the city. It was also home to a large Eastern European population. If there ever was a built-in demographic, this was it!

So there was Uncle Gus, selling frankfurters to the city's German population, topping them with sauerkraut, which was a favorite of the Eastern Europeans, and asking everyone to wash it all down with exotic tropical drinks—which appealed to no one. Slowly, though, the customers came around and they started to consume, and then actually enjoy, these tropical drinks. And in time, I suppose, the combination of these two different foods became so customary, no one thought about it anymore. They just ordered them together. A dog and a drink.

The name change to Papaya King came about in the fifties. How it came to be changed, no one really remembers. It was already that when my family immigrated here when I was nine. I went to school, then college, got a degree in engineering, and then a job as an engineer. I really liked engineering, and I would have stayed at it, but in 1974, my uncle's partner became ill and he needed someone to replace him. That someone, Uncle Gus decided, was me.

So why did I leave a cool job, where I went to work every day in a tie and jacket, to put on an apron and stand behind a counter flipping hot dogs for ten hours a day? I'll tell you why. After much soul searching, I admitted to myself that if I stayed at the company I was with, at best I might one day become a head engineer. Whereas if I went to Papaya King, we would expand and open up stores worldwide. I would get to travel to Paris! And London! The franchising boom for fast-food stores was just beginning—McDonald's hadn't yet come to the city—and I figured we could ride that wave. Those were my dreams—and my plans. So when Uncle Gus offered me shares of the company and promised me the title of general manager, I agreed.

I was twenty-seven years old when I reported for work that first day. I didn't even know what papaya was. I had to learn everything about the drinks, including the secret formulas. I learned that you couldn't juice a papaya, because, like a banana, it's a pulp. I learned that in order to make the drink, you had to dilute the pulp of papaya by adding lemon juice, water, or milk; what makes the drink so creamy is the way it's whipped and agitated. And I learned about "mouth feel," which is how we judge the consistency of our milk shake.

I also learned how to handle the grill. Cooking franks on a grill is no walk in the park, let me tell you. Sure, you think, "How hard can it be? You take a frank and put it on a grill." Not exactly rocket science. But there actually is an art and, yes, a science to it. You don't want the frank to be overly cooked, where it becomes burnt and tough, or undercooked, which would be worse. When you have dozens going at the same time, it's all a matter of how you move them around and how you control the temperature below them. It takes a lot of training to get somebody to do things the Papaya King way. Anyone can just serve a customer. You order a frank, I give it to you, and I take your money: "Next!" That's easy. To prepare and sell the food the right way—our way—is not so easy. Our store is only 475 square feet. That's a little more than twenty by twenty. Of that, 80 percent is customer space. In the remaining 20 percent we fit a small kitchen area and prep area, refrigerators to store our products, sinks, and a cutting area. Oh, and let's not forget the four people who work the counter. One takes the order and collects the money. Two others serve the customers and one person stands at the grill.

Three years after I started working here, we got involved in what became known as "The Hot Dog Wars of 1977." The newspapers, of course, had a field day. What happened was, Nathan's opened up a stand two doors away from us on Third Avenue. Right next to us was a Baskin-Robbins and next to that was a five-story apartment house. Two brothers rented the ground floor and turned it into a Nathan's. They were young guys who told us they would bury us, since Nathan's had a better name than we did.

Because we were essentially selling the same thing, the whole mess turned into a price war. At the time, our franks were going for fifty cents apiece. The brothers knocked the price down to forty-five cents. We went to thirty-five. They went to thirty. And finally we went down to twenty-five cents. The street was a madhouse, a zoo. Nobody was happy, most of all the neighborhood residents. We couldn't serve our regular customers properly. The crowds were insane, and people were coming in asking for ten franks at a time. They'd eat two and take the remaining eight home for dinner.

We couldn't keep up with serving the franks the way we wanted to—properly cooked, with a toasted roll—because there were just too many customers. The customers were yelling and screaming: "I was here first!" "I've been waiting!" In those days, just as today, the grill faced the customer with a Plexiglas partition between the customer and us. I was working the grill, and as soon as a customer got in front of me, I'd take care of him. But of course I didn't know who was first. How could I know who was first? And they wanted so many, we would run out of what was on the grill and have to overload it. It was awful. We were working to break even, basically. The place was filthy. Napkins all over the place.

It was pandemonium. This went on for about six months. And then Nathan's capitulated. They just shut down the store and went home. I never want to go through that again—it was sheer hell.

Papaya King is a real New York institution. And we've worked really hard to keep it that way. Including trying to keep people from attempting to pass themselves off as us. Businesses have started up with the names Papaya Kingdom, Papaya Dog, Papaya Prince, Papaya on First. I don't know how many places. Papaya is the name of a fruit, so it can't be registered. But the name "Papaya King" is registered. Over the years we've sued six or seven establishments for name infringement, and we've won, but it cost us ten or twelve thousand dollars in legal fees every time. And what does it get us? The other side takes down the "Papaya Kingdom" sign and puts up one that says "Joe's Papaya," or "Mike's Papaya." There's nothing you can do about that. We spent all that money, but what have we won? Nothing.

Do I regret leaving engineering to sell hot dogs? Not really. I mean, sure, some days are not as good as others, but that's going to happen in any business. For the most part it's been a good ride. I love the customers, particularly the ones who come in almost every day. And I'm always in awe of the celebrities who stop by, including the "foodies," like Martha Stewart and Anthony Bourdain. But you know, mixed in with the good guys, you're always gonna get the customers who make you scratch your head in wonder. For example, this drives me crazy: At one in the afternoon, when the place is loaded with people waiting and I'm putting out the hot dogs as fast as I can, I'll get a guy who starts rapping on the glass to get my attention. When I look up, he yells into the glass, "Gimme two with onions and three without." And then he points to exactly which hot dogs he wants. It's noisy, people are yelling, the radio is playing, and I can barely hear him. I have a fork in my hand, so I'll point at one: "This one?" "No. The one behind it." "*This* one?" "No! The other way. The one in *front*." Now I'm really yelling: "When you say 'front,' do you mean *your* front or *my* front?" Do I want to give that guy what for? Yes. But I won't. Because I respect that time-honored adage and still subscribe to it: The customer is always right. That, and I'll be darned if I'm going to be the one who comes between a man and his hot dog.

PART III

Taking the Heat

When we eat at a restaurant, most of us neither think nor care about what's happening back in the kitchen—unless, of course, there's a problem with the food that's coming out of it. Normally, the mechanics of it all are largely invisible, which is what both management and customers want. And as a diner, that's what I wanted, too. Did I care how my fajitas and refried beans landed on the plate as long as they were hot when they arrived in front of me? Not really. The same went for my exquisite and exquisitely expensive morel soufflé with shaved white truffles. I was happy as long as the soufflé was still high when the waiter placed it before me.

But that was then. And this is now. Now I want to know every detail, from the callout of a waiter's scribbled order to the final hand-off of the plated masterwork for its trip to the dining room. So I spent time in a number of kitchens, a wide-eyed fly on an unsalted-butter-spattered wall, taking in the action.

I must admit, I found myself transfixed by this world of hellish heat and clockwork discipline, but even more so by the clog-shod, head-wrapped, burnt-wristed, sweat-soaked, adrenaline-spiked, mostly young men and women who inhabited it. These are the line cooks, the heart and soul of the kitchen. The ones who work tirelessly every night to bring quality food to people they will probably never know as anything more than an impersonal order ticket.

Working under the chef's direction, the line cooks are charged with preparing, cooking, and plating each course—appetizers, entrées (called "protein" by the pros), salads, and sauces—and getting them out on time. Because they work in such tight quarters, I wondered why they don't accidentally poke one another with a double-pronged fork, or step on each other's Bastads more often. What sixth sense prevents the guy with the fava-bean-and-*scamorza* salad from slamming into the one bearing a vat of vinaigrette, seeing as they had their backs to each other and then wheeled around at exactly the same moment? In short, how is order imposed on what looks, to an outsider like me, like a complete free-for-all?

The answer dates back to the nineteenth century, when the French chef and culinary philosopher Auguste Escoffier codified a system known as "the kitchen brigade." It's a military-style chain of command, where each person has his or her specific station and rank, and each rank reports to the one above it. This arrangement still pertains in the hautest of haute twenty-first-century kitchens (and is elucidated in greater detail in the appendix (page 347).

It really is quite something to watch the dance of the restaurant kitchen in action. I spent one evening, from start to finish, observing the entire ballet. An hour before the first customer arrived, there was an almost meditative silence (broken only by the whir of the intake hoods) as the line cooks set out their *mise en place*—the food supplies they'd need as a dish was ordered. As service neared, grills and ovens were lit, and you could almost feel the heat and the tension rising.

A bell rang, and then came the first call from the expediting chef: "Ordering!"

And . . . action!

A steak is slammed onto the grill; a red snapper salted and slid into a pan; monkfish shut into the oven; loin of lamb seared over coals; scallops sluiced in a copper pan; ravioli dropped into steaming water; French-cut potatoes lowered into boiling oil. Chops pulled from the grill. Chicken fired, plated, and handed down the pass; brussels sprouts and roast potatoes added, chicken sauced; down the pass again now to the chef, who quickly embellishes the plate with a dusting of parsley, swipes its edges with a kitchen towel, and on it goes, onto the outstretched tray of the waiter standing by. At eight thirty, the tables start turning over; as late diners replace the earlier ones, the pace in the kitchen increases. Orders fly in now at the rate of every fifteen to thirty seconds. The kitchen gets hotter. Humidity rises. Line cooks grab bottles of water, pour them down their throats, down their necks. Rings of sweat appear on head covers, a cloth is hurriedly taped across a burned wrist. "Ordering!" "Ordering!" Tossing, grating, sliding, flipping, bending, balancing, passing.

And then . . . as abruptly as it started, the evening service is over.

More water goes down. Aprons are untied. Head covers peeled off. Towels pulled from necks. Clogs removed. Clothes changed. Lockers locked—until tomorrow, when they are opened again. Same time, same station.

I heard somewhere that the two most-used words in a restaurant kitchen are "fire" and "fuck." Having now done time in several of them, I can say that it's totally true. What kind of life can this be? And why do they do it? For the serious would-be chef, this crazy, hectic-to-the-point-of-exhaustion life is the requisite journey. The only way to get there. But not everyone who works in the kitchen wants to be a chef. Some prefer to do their jobs in anonymity. Two of the line cooks you'll meet in this chapter have worked in the Four Seasons kitchen for more than fourteen years each. They are career restaurant employees who are perfectly content with where they are. For them— as for the baker, the fish butcher, and the oyster shucker—this is a job, not a calling; they don't want the added responsibility or stress or sac- rifice required to reach the big time. I get it. From the comfort of my writing desk, I can tell you that I am completely in awe of those with chef aspirations, but to go through what they must to reach that goal? I'm pretty sure I wouldn't last a day.

MacKenzie Arrington

MOMOFUKU MÁ PÊCHE

He's twenty-six. Six foot four. A wrestler, when he's not in the kitchen. His mother had a restaurant in Maine, so cooking was all he knew growing up. And, like a lot of cooks, he landed at "the mother ship"—the Culinary Institute of America in Hyde Park. When he graduated, he ran into a friend at a bar. "My friend asked me what I was doing and I said I was helping my mom at her restaurant. He said, 'That's it? You're gonna spend the rest of your life making crab cakes?' And I'm like, 'No . . .' 'Then why the hell aren't you in New York?' When I told him I couldn't afford it, he said, 'Dude. You won't be able to afford it ever, as a cook, but you'll also never find a better cooking experience!'"

When I arrived in the city a month later, a friend of a friend set me up with a *stage*, which is essentially a working interview at a restaurant. It's also called a "shadow" or a "trail." Any New York City kitchen will make you do it before they hire you. You come in and you work for them. For free. The point is not only to see how good you are at things, but to see if you like the kitchen, see if they like you, see how clean you work, and see your attitude. And they want to know they don't have to teach you too many things. Maybe three cooks will throw certain things at you at the same time. One says, "I need this now!" The next one says, "I need this before that!" And they watch your decision-making process. At the end they'll ask the cooks, "Did you like that guy?" And they'll say you were good or you sucked. That's really how you get hired. Your résumé means shit.

The first *stage* that really interested me was at Momofuku Má Pêche under Executive Chef Tien Ho. I'd heard I'd be cutting a lot of scallions, so I figured it would be easy. I went in at two in the afternoon. Two hours later, the *chef de cuisine* came over to me and said, "All right, MacKenzie. You have one hour." I said, "What do you mean?" He said, "One hour to cook a dish." Me: "From your menu?" Him: "No, man. You have free rein. I want you to cook me dinner! One dish. Your time starts now!"

So there I am, in a strange kitchen, I don't know where anything is, and I was scared, man. I admit it. I spent the first thirty minutes wandering around just looking for stuff. Grabbing a bunch of random things wherever I could find them. And then I went to work. I started with sweet potato fries. You blanch sweet potatoes and then cut them really thin and then deep-fry. I did a really clean steak dish with a corn succotash made with sweet peppers, hominy, and scallions. I seared the steak, did a quick prime jus with some beef they had there, cooked the meat medium rare, sliced it like tenderloin, rolled it like a sushi roll, and laid it over the shoestring potatoes. The *sous chefs* were staring at me the whole time and they would say stuff to each other I couldn't hear. Then Chef Tien came by and said, "Okay, nice meeting you, MacKenzie. Have a good trail." And he left. That was it. I don't think he ever tasted what I cooked.

I was still helping on the line when service was starting to wind down later that evening, so they told me I could go to any station I wanted, to cook anything. Craig, the *sous chef*, gave me a beer and he said, "Chef will get hold of you and we'll let you know how it went." A week later, Chef Tien called and told me everyone really liked what I did. "Our busy season starts end of September," he said, "and I have a spot for you if you want it."

I rented a tiny room in my friend's Brooklyn apartment, where I shared one of the three bedrooms with another guy. We had a bunk bed, bottom shelves for my clothes, top shelves for his, and a TV. It was three hundred dollars a month per person. Including cable and Internet. I still live there but I have my own room for five hundred dollars now, which is absurd for the amount of money a cook makes—three hundred dollars a week.

Cooks in the city get paid nothing. Or next to nothing. My theory on that is this: The best restaurants in the world are in New York City and everyone knows that, so they want to work here. Half the cooks in New York work for free. They get a shot at a restaurant like Eleven Madison Park, which is considered one of the best in the city, so they're happy to work for free. But what about the guy who, without a salary, would be living on the street? What about him?

When they do pay you, it's not exactly high finance. Starting out, most cooks get nine dollars an hour. The top cooks get twelve-fifty an hour, capped at an eight-hour shift. If you're on the dinner shift, you're not supposed to come in until three thirty, but you always get in earlier. And often as early as nine in the morning. They'll say something like,

"We're not telling you to come to work that early but it would be really good for you to learn something new." So we come in at nine to butcher our own fish, even though there's a fish butcher. And of course you don't get paid for those extra hours. It's for the experience, remember? If by chance you *can* do your job by coming in right on time, if they see you're doing well at your station, they'll add more items to it. Therefore it's physically impossible to get there at three thirty and be set up and ready for the dinner service. And if you're not set up and ready, someone will be yelling and screaming at you. If the chef yells at you, it's for one of two reasons. One, because you have potential and they want to make you better, or two, they want you out of their kitchen. They either try to make you quit or make you better. And then you have to worry about losing your job and how that will look on your résumé.

So you work until twelve or one in the morning, go for dinner, go home, go to sleep, wake up, and you're back there by nine. I started on the line at Má Pêche as p.m. fish *entremet'*, which is the guy who does all the sides, all the sauces and plating after the fish cook finishes cooking the fish. You have to be totally organized to do that job, because the fish comes at you from the grill cook and you'd better have the sauces and veggies ready to go. And we're not talking just one fish! There's a constant stream of them coming at you down the line. The first three months I thought I was going to die. Half the time from exhaustion and the other half from them yelling at me. But I finally got the hang of it and got organized.

As fish *entremet'*, the quantity of stuff that's required of you is insane. Take, for example, a codfish dish. Part one: The broth. Part one, step one: You start with bushels of live whole blue crabs and put them in a food processor and turn it on until they turn into a paste. It's such a mess that you literally have to put a trash bag around the processor.

Part one, step two: You're still with the broth. You also need your mirepoix, which is essentially what I use for soups and sauces. That's made from one part carrot, one part celery, and two parts onion. You need a bunch of that cut up and that alone can take twenty minutes to do. Then you sauté it slowly and then you add it to the crab paste. You turn the heat really high, and you have to be watching it every second to make sure it doesn't burn. Step three: Then you add the water, herbs, and spices, and you take the tops of fennel and make a bed across the top to steam it like tea and set it to boil for two hours. Step four: Then you have to strain it all out. This is just part one of one dish. That's just the broth.

Part two, step one: The cod dish is garnished with ultrafine julienned leeks and that's your job, too. So every day you have seventy or eighty leeks that you have to clean, peel, and cut into tiny, narrow strips. And you'd better cut them exactly even because if you don't, someone will yell, "Who cut these, Helen Keller?"

There are probably three or four other things going on in that dish that are just as labor intensive. So you think about time frame on that, that's close to two hours of work for one person for one dish. And then you have six or seven other dishes you're also responsible for at the same time. Plus, you might also be on tap that week for family meal.

Every restaurant has family meal. It's a meal they do every day where the whole staff sits down together for lunch or dinner. Whoever is in charge that day will say, "Okay, *entremet'* is responsible for the vegetable. Fish cook is responsible for the protein. Meat cook is responsible for the starch. *Garde-mange'* is responsible for salad." That's the idea behind it. But the *entremet'* can say, "Oh my God, I can't! I have all this prepping to do still. I'm so in the shit, can someone else do the veg?" So fish cook says, "Yeah, I'll do the veg." Then he gets in the shit and then he can go to the meat cook and say, "Hey, can you do the protein and the veg?" He's like, "Yeah, sure" and then goes to the meat *entremet'* and says, "Hey . . . I'm in the shit." And it will always be on one guy, whoever's at the bottom of the barrel or whoever gets fed up enough about hearing about it will say, "Fine. I'll do it." So they cook for the staff of the whole restaurant, that's on top of all their normal prep, and it's a snowball effect.

In the kitchen, space is so tight you have to be like a ballet dancer doing pirouettes in clogs. We have to communicate amongst ourselves keeping it quiet, too. Depending on who the chef you're working for is, there might be other rules like: no smiling in the kitchen, no laughing, no talking. No banging pans. You drop something, everyone is all over you because of the noise. And logistically, if I turn while you're going behind me, without me ever saying anything, you know exactly where I am and I know exactly what you're doing.

I hate screwing up. First, because you get yelled at. But also because you have nothing else in this world. If you're a cook, you don't have money, you don't have a social life, you don't have any outside life. All you are is a station cook, so you take pride in your work to a fault. And if you can't take criticism well, you're going to start to crumble. And you'd better pretty much understand that no matter what the circumstances, you cannot talk back to chef. Ever! You always have to answer, "Yes, Chef" or "No, Chef" and that is it. At NoMad, where I was a line cook for six months, when chef calls out an order, everyone in the kitchen has to yell in unison, "*Oui!*"—meaning they understood. The chef goes, "Fire this, this, this, this!" Once he's done talking, everyone goes "*OUI!*" at the top of their lungs. And if you're out of sync with your "*ouis*," he'll make you do it again. He'll go, "You guys are a piece of shit!

You're not working together! Let's have some enthusiasm! Call it again."
"OUI!" "That's better."

And don't even *ask* about all the injuries and how they are treated in all these kitchens. "Oh," says the chef, "you cut your fingertip off? Clean it, put some glue on it, and keep working." More than once I've had to stop the bleeding of a fingertip by sealing it against the flat top of the metal pass. And you always have a burn or two trying to heal on your arm. It's part of the game. No sick days, no being late. No nothing. No relationships either, because there's never time. Here's the reality: Faced with this insane environment, only a fraction of people who walk into this world stay there.

To be a good cook requires a weird mix of personality traits. You have to be arrogant, but at the same time you have to be flexible and open to someone else's dissatisfaction. Most of all, though, you have to be really passionate. One of the most inspiring displays I think I've ever seen, even though it wasn't at a good time for me, came from one of the executive *sous chefs* when I was working at NoMad. We were in the middle of service, it was busy, and the runners—the guys who take the food from the kitchen to the table—were all hanging out, standing against the wall, waiting for the food to come up. They were laughing at a joke and the *sous chef* turned around to them and said, "Would you guys shut the fuck up? You want to talk, get the fuck out of here. This place is all I fucking have! Don't fuck it up for me!" That's a man who loves what he's doing and lets everyone know it. That's passion.

There was this kid once who worked the morning and afternoon shift. He was really awful in the kitchen and everyone hated him because he was counterproductive. One day, his service had been over for four hours and he had long since left the building when the roast cook, for the first time that night, opened the oven to put in some meat. What he found inside was something that looked like a piece of charcoal. "What the . . . ?" he yelled. "It's a fucking pork chop!" The kid forgot it in there, with the oven on, and so it just burned to a crisp. When the chef heard about it, he got so fucking heated he's, like, "This pork chop is from one of the best pork purveyors in the country! This kid is an idiot!" The next day, before he let him work, the chef made the kid handwrite a personal letter to the farmer to apologize for disrespecting his product. Normally if you mess something up, it just goes to the trash. But because the farmer comes into the restaurant a lot, the chef knew firsthand all the work that goes into that product. "The years this guy spent raising his pig, the getting up in the morning to feed him, the making sure he's healthy, and this idiot treats it like that." In a different way, that's passion, too.

My friend was right. You make no money and you marry yourself to the restaurant. So you'd damn well better love what you do. When you hear someone whine, "I work forty hours a week. I hate it. I'm so tired." Well boo-fucking-hoo. I work eighty hours a week for a quarter of your paycheck and you don't hear me complaining. Holidays off? What's that? Expect to work on Christmas, New Year's Eve, Valentine's Day, Easter Sunday, Mother's Day, and your birthday—that is, if you aren't too exhausted to remember which day is your birthday. All the days run into each other when you're in a windowless space that's a constant ninety degrees and you never get out until the sun's gone to sleep.

So why do I love it? I love food. I love creating something. It's like temporary art. But it's not just the visual, it's the experience I'll be creating for someone to hopefully remember. That's a big thing for me. They're not going to have this food again; they're not going to have the same plate from this exact moment. Who knows, maybe someone out there is getting engaged to his girlfriend tonight. They will remember this meal. They don't know I cooked it, but that's not what it's about. They had a good time and they enjoyed. For that moment, I wowed them.

A cook never sees the people he's cooking for, and that's fine with us. If a customer is a regular or someone important, they get what they call a "PS ticket." And usually the cook is, like, "I don't care if it's Michael Bloomberg, I don't care if it's Arnold Schwarzenegger, I don't care who it is! I cook the food just the same as I would for anyone else." Of course, all that not-caring goes out the window if a chef or a cook from another restaurant comes in. Then, they care. That's when everything has to be perfect because you're showing off your talent. It's a dick-swinging contest and you're essentially saying, "I'm better than you."

I left Má Pêche after eighteen months. It was an incredible learning experience in a first-class restaurant, but I had worked all the stations and it was time to move on to the next thing. I decided to trail at a bunch of the city's top restaurants just to see what they're doing. I ended up going to a few of the top ones and was horribly unimpressed. None of them could hold a candle to Má Pêche. I'll never forget one of them because I was shit on the whole time by the line cooks. And I knew I was better than all of them. So I'm working *garde-mange'* or something and this kid came up and said, "I need you to cut this much butternut squash for me exactly like this." He slaps a small container full of squash on the counter and he repeats himself, "It needs to be exactly like this. Once you've done a pint, bring it over and show me so I can make sure you're doing it right." So I start doing that and I'm, like, "Fuck this kid, I'm going to see what he's up to." So I took the squash that he cut up to demonstrate for me and I put it in the empty container. I brought it over to him and I'm, like, "Hey, how are these?" And I laid them out and he's, like, "These are fucking garbage! This is not what I showed you!" And I'm, like, "Actually, man, those are the exact ones *you fucking did for me.*" And I just walked away. He didn't bother me the rest of the *stage*.

As soon as five o'clock comes, you have to be done prepping. Stop whatever you're doing, deep-clean the kitchen, and then we have a meeting. After the meeting, you come back to your station ready to work. And if your station isn't set up yet, you hear it from the chef. They're like sharks. Once they smell blood, once you mess up even once, your day's ruined because they're going to be all over you all day. Once, I was in the middle of service on a particularly busy evening and the chef was on my case for something and he was arguing with me. I had my fingers between the counter and the drawer and I'm trying to get my work done and he's arguing with me, and I'm saying, "Yes, Chef" because you can't talk back. When I turned away from him to go back to my cooking, he yelled, "No! You fucking listen!" And with that, his knee pushes the drawer closed with my fingers in it. And he holds it there! "You need to fucking listen to me!" What I'm thinking is this: "I'm a big guy, I'm not allowed to hit you right now but I'll fucking do it if you don't let my fingers go." But I can't say that to him, I just say, "Yes, Chef." They have you trained to that point where they are the ultimate rule. You want to cook? You suck it up.

Here's the life of a cook. You eat, you drink, and you cook. And somewhere in there you sleep, but not for long. Social life? Your only friends are the guys cooking next to you or on either side of you. I remember at Momofuku, we had a keg in the walk-in refrigerator. We had just spent fourteen hours cooking. Service would be done and after cleanup, we would tap the keg, put a few pitchers on the pass, and just sit back and hang out for an hour drinking beer in the kitchen in our street clothes. Then chef says, "All right, I'm done putting in orders for tomorrow. Finish up your beer, lock up, let's go to the bar." And we would all go to a bar or restaurant together. That's the thing. You're with each other all day but you can't seem to say good night. Do you get sick of some of these people sometimes? Sure. And there are times when you take shit from them at work. But you can't hold grudges because you're there with them so much. And you have to keep them close to you because they are all you really have.

Luis
"The Mexican Menace"
Iglesias

GRAND CENTRAL OYSTER BAR

Every year, in mid-September, oyster shuckers from all over the world con-
verge at the Grand Central Oyster Bar to compete for a $3,000 Grand Prize in
the Oyster Frenzy's Professional Shucking Championships. This year, Igle-
sias will represent the restaurant in the competition again. If he wins, it will
be for the eighth time. Does he have the home advantage? Absolutely not,
according to the statewide panel of judges that changes annually. Given the
rules, it wouldn't matter. In any case, it's still quite a coup for a twenty-eight-
year-old Mexican immigrant who has yet to taste his first oyster.

I started here as a dishwasher. Then I moved up to be a helper in the
bar. I wanted to improve myself even from that, so in my break
time I watched what everyone else was doing. I liked best the oyster
shuckers, and little by little, I saw how to do it. One day, I got up my
nerve and went to see my supervisor. "I know how to shuck an oyster,"

I told him. "Can you try me out?" He tried me and he liked how I did it and now I have ten years doing this.

I work Monday to Friday. In the morning I receive the delivery—about six thousand oysters we need for that day—and bring them upstairs in crates. The restaurant opens at eleven thirty, so I shuck from then until two, when I go to the kitchen to cover the soup cook making oyster stew and pan roast.

We sell at least five thousand oysters on the half shell a day. That doesn't count what goes into the stews and pan roast. There are so many kinds—French Kiss, Naked Cowboy, East Beach Blonde. They all taste different, depending on the region where they come from. Kumamotos come from the West Coast. Wellfleet and Martha's Vineyard from Massachusetts. Malpeques from Canada. Some are briny, some are buttery. Each kind has a different flavor. But don't ask me to tell you from experience what the flavor is because I don't taste them.

I have never eaten a raw oyster. Never put one in my mouth. I've tried to, but I just can't do it. That's a problem, too, because a customer will ask a waiter which is best and then the waiter comes to me and says, "Luis! What's the best oyster we got today?" And I can't answer that one. I can tell you if an oyster is fresh, though. That's for sure. When oysters are delivered to us, they're closed tight. If it's open, you know it's dead. Sometimes, an oyster can be closed and still be dead and when you shuck it . . . Whew! You don't want to smell that!

Here at the Oyster Bar, we have four or five shuckers going all the time. We stand behind the bar where people can watch us. They love that. When the orders start flying, we get crazy. Shuck this one, shuck the next one. Shuck, shuck, shuck. You can't imagine. Sometimes, no time to even look up. I'm fast. Really fast. My record is fifteen oysters a minute.

Every year there's a contest here where shuckers come from all over to compete. The person who goes fastest, opens the most, and makes the best presentation wins the money. They put us into different groups. The first group stands at a long table; each person has his container of oysters in front of him. First you take your oysters out and line them up for shucking. Then you hold up your knife to be ready. When they give the signal to start, you put the oyster in your palm, slice open the shell, free the oyster, place it on its half shell, and place it on the tray. And then you do it for the next one and the next and next. When the timer shouts, "Stop!" you put down your knife.

The judges count how many you have shucked. Then they look at the shells you present the oyster on to see that they are not broken and the oyster itself is not cut. That's how they judge you. There are three rounds. The top four guys from Round 1 go on to Round 2, and the top two from Round 2 will advance to Round 3. And you get your winner. I keep winning. It makes me so proud and Chef Ingber so proud and my restaurant so proud. For days after, people congratulate me and they go around calling me "The Mexican Menace." I like that name.

Jesus Albino "Albi" Chauca

THE FOUR SEASONS

It's two thirty p.m. in the Grill Room, considered since the day it opened in 1959 to be one of the most beautiful rooms in the city. The masters and mistresses of the universe have stepped back into their office-bound town cars, leaving behind the power-lunch remnants of rare steak and grilled asparagus on their plates for the busboys to deal with. I'm all alone at a table on the balcony, waiting for Chauca to be done with his duties, and wondering if maybe, with enough pleading, they might hire me here in some capacity, anything that would let me ogle, for five minutes a day, every day, this gorgeous room with its twenty-foot-high ceilings, French walnut paneling, copper chain swag curtains, and perfect grid of twenty-one precisely set tables.

He is from Ecuador. He's been in this kitchen for sixteen years.

My day here starts around nine a.m. The first thing I do is check what's on for lunch. I'm responsible for nine dishes on the menu. It could be steak tartare, or smoked salmon, or melon with prosciutto, chicken salad, Caesar salad, butternut salad, and root vegetable salad. I see what I need and what I already have in my refrigerator to make up those plates, and then I go across the kitchen to the meat and fish butchers and put in my order for the things I'm missing. In our kitchen, you tell the butchers what you need and they clean it, portion it, and bring it to you.

Once I have everything I need, I start prepping. I have to get everything for the day's service ready to go at a moment's notice. It's called *mise en place*, which means that every one of the ingredients you need for every dish on the menu that day is within reach, so when an order comes in, you're on it right away. You don't have to start looking for things. I know, for instance, that a smoked salmon order gets a finely chopped hard-boiled egg yolk and finely chopped onions to go along with it. That means I have to boil tons of eggs and chop onions and have them ready before the order for salmon comes in. You can't do that stuff at the last minute. I'll also start preparing and chopping the fish for the salmon tartare, and the beef for the steak tartare.

As soon as a customer orders, the waiter comes into the kitchen and barks the order to us as he walks by. One waiter will say, "Albi, I need this!" Then another waiter says, "Albi, I need that!" Someone else comes through: "Make this and this and this!" In this kitchen, everyone on the line keeps every order in his head—no one writes anything down. There's no time. Especially during lunch in the Grill Room, where people want to be out and done in an hour, or an hour and fifteen tops. What happens if you forget something? You don't. This is your job.

This kitchen serves both of the Four Seasons dining rooms, the Grill Room and the Pool Room. Most of the regulars come for lunch to the Grill Room. Some come so often they have their own table. That's where most of the famous businesspeople and a lot of famous writers and magazine publishers and that kind of thing like to sit. We don't go out there, of course, and I don't always recognize the names, but some of the people in the kitchen do and they'll say, "So and so is outside today." Like Henry Kissinger, or Mr. Newhouse, or Mrs. Anna Wintour.

People start arriving for lunch at noon. From that moment on, we can count on a good ninety minutes of craziness. As the food orders come in, I start assembling the plates right and left. But people ask for changes all the time. Especially during lunch in the Grill Room. It's never a problem. And the waiters are used to it.

If someone requests something that's not on the menu, we do our best to make it for them. The Four Seasons never says no to a customer. If someone wants a cheeseburger with peanut butter on top of it, we'll make it. At my station, especially, a lot of people want to redesign their appetizers. "I'll have a salad, but can you take this off and put this on instead?" "No dressing, please; yes, dressing; different dressing." If they request something not on the menu and we're missing an ingredient, let's say, like, avocado—although that would never happen—we borrow one from the Brasserie. The Brasserie is around the corner but there is a loading dock that connects us so we can go right into their kitchen through the loading dock. And they can come to us, too. That way, the guest wants avocado? The guest gets avocado!

Even though I never get to actually see the people I'm cooking for, I'm very aware that our diners are first class. People with money come here. I give 100 percent every day so that things come out well and the restaurant keeps attracting those kinds of people. It feels good to be cooking for them. It makes me feel I'm a part of that life—if even just a little part.

Carmen Melendez

TOM CAT BAKERY

It's hard to spend much time on the streets of New York and not see one of Tom Cat Bakery's ubiquitous silver trucks with the cat logo emblazoned on its side. There are, after all, twenty-five of these vehicles out and about 24/7 navigating the streets day and night, delivering bread and rolls to countless restaurants, hotels, and retail markets. Three people started the business in 1987, baking together in a Long Island City garage, only one of whom—James Rath—remains. Today, the shop occupies a full city block under the 59th Street Bridge.

It's eleven a.m. and Carmen Melendez has just come off her eight-hour shift. Still in her baker's whites, she walks me through the cavernous space where similarly dressed workers mix batters in oversized vats, load baking molds, remove finished product from proofers, and propel metal carts of still-steaming baguettes to their next destination. We talk as we walk.

I was born in Managua, Nicaragua. When I was eighteen years old—and pregnant—I left to find a better life. There were more chances to get a job in America, everybody knew that. I came by myself. With no one. I took a bus from Nicaragua to Guatemala. And another bus from Guatemala to Mexico. From Mexico, I walked across the border into Texas. I walked with people who I met along the way. For three days we walked. Along the way you see dead people who didn't make it. It's bad. But you have to keep on walking. In Texas, I got on a bus to New Jersey. And then another bus to New York. The whole journey was fifteen days. My baby was born here. She's twenty-four now.

At Tom Cat, I started cold. I applied for the job because it was near where I live, but I don't know nothing about anything. They train me to do everything. Today, there's nothing I can't do. If you tell me to make the dough, I can make the dough. If you tell me to go help with the oven, I help with the oven. Stack the bread? I stack the bread. Pretty soon, I know every corner of the place. From one end of the assembly line to the other. I talk about this and my skin gets bumps—that's from the feeling I have inside about what I'm doing here. I have such happiness in what I do.

My job starts at three a.m. People are already here when I get in. There are always people here doing something. I come in and I start to seed the dough. We make it in big vats. Once the dough is made, we let it relax two hours and I'm the one who says, "Okay, this dough is now ready to be cut." Maybe we'll start with seven hundred pieces of baguette dough. First we shape the dough. Then we cut it into starter pieces. Then we stretch each one to twenty-two inches. Two hours later, we stretch again to twenty-seven inches. Now the sun is starting to come up and it's time to make the cuts in the baguettes. Some get four cuts across the top, some get five, depending on how big the bread is. Then the guy comes to put the baguettes into the proofer or the oven. Another guy comes to take them out when they're done. In this bakery, there is always something rising or baking or cooling, and sometimes all three are happening at the same time.

We have a department of research and design here. When the customer says, "I want this and this bread," our design people work on how to make it. When it's done and becomes our new product, the people from R and D come in and show me how to make it. Then I teach the others how to do it. That's the way it goes here. At the end of the day comes the best part. At the end of the day, you can see what you've done. In the morning you didn't have anything. At the end of the day, you have rolls, baguettes, loaves. Stacked all over the bakery. It's a great feeling to see this.

My daughter is a dentist and my son is a lawyer and the little one is in high school. This country gave me so much. Look at my husband and my children. Look at my house I have. Look at me in a job I love. I say thanks for this country. All the time. Thank you, country.

Guyo Pinyo Ketavanan

THE FOUR SEASONS

His mother brought him here from Thailand to go to high school. He went to Hunter College for a year but then, needing money, dropped out to work as a waiter. One evening, a customer left a fifty-cent tip for a party of two. "I thought he made a mistake. As he got up to go, I said, 'Sir, you forgot your money on the table.' The man said, 'That money is for you. Keep it.' I said, 'Fifty cents? No, thank you,' and I gave it back to him in what was probably not a very nice way. He cursed at me and went to the manager, who fired me on the spot. But then, two weeks later, I guess that same manager realized I was a good worker, because he called me to come back to work. I said, 'Only if you give me a job in the kitchen. I don't want to be a waiter ever again.'"

He gave me a job as a cook. And I was good at it, too. So good that soon I became a chef. I worked in two separate Thai restaurants until one day it occurred to me: I'm in America. I should learn to cook American food. I had heard that the Four Seasons was looking for a line cook and that sounded great to me. I came here and asked for an interview with the chef. When he read my résumé, he started calling me "Thai Food Chef." Like that was my name. I cooked some Thai food for him and he loved it. He asked me, "What did you put in there?" He wrote down all the spices that I told him and the next day, March 27, 1987, I started my job at the Four Seasons.

Even with all my chef's experience, and even though the job I interviewed for was line cook, they started me in the back cleaning vegetables. You have to understand that that's what they do in every fine restaurant. No matter who you are, no matter what you've done, no matter which restaurant you came from, they start you from the bottom. Everyone who works in a kitchen knows this. You learn their kitchen that way and they watch you operate in a low position that can't get anyone in too much trouble. So, I became the guy who cleaned and cut up the vegetables. For almost two years. That was me. It took lots of patience. Believe me what I tell you.

Finally one day, chef said, "Okay, Guyo, time to go to the line." He put me at the sauté vegetable station for a while and then I moved up to what they call "pantry." That's the guy who sears the meats in the pan. I did that for a year and then, for the next seven years, I was "butcher." The guy who cleans the fish and chicken. From there, I became "broiler" or "grill man." You roast meat in the oven and you grill the steaks, chops, fish, and everything else on the flat grill or over charcoal. That was thirteen years ago. I'm still there.

I stand midway between the grill and the broiler. Front and back. Sometimes when people walk by, they say, "It's so hot, Guyo! How can you stay here day and night?" But I'm used to it. Other people ask me if I'm not bored after all these years of the same thing. To that, my answer is strongly, "No!" In this position there's not time to get bored. You have to always be thinking. To be aware and on top of things. You're cooking all different types of meats and fish, and they all cook for different amounts of time and in different ways. And the orders keep coming at you nonstop—many at the same time. Like on a conveyor belt. So you can't stop. If you're going to get it right, you don't have time to think about anything but what you're doing. Fish. Say I get an order for cod. I'll put it in the oven to roast. Or maybe that particular fish does best on the grill. Maybe it goes in a pan and then the oven. Some of them only go in the oven. Some of them are served plain, no salt, no pepper. Some with spices. Believe me, it's a lot of remembering.

Then there's the timing. A customer orders a steak well done. Someone else at that same table wants theirs rare. Someone else at that table orders steak for two. You have to work a table together. Have to. So now, if the steak is for two people, I ask the butcher, "How many pounds?" because the weight affects the cooking time. If the meat is 24 ounces, then it has to cook a certain number of minutes until it is medium rare. If the butcher tells me 26 ounces, then I leave it two more minutes in the oven. I put on the well-done order first. When that's almost done, I start the rare or the medium rare. But remember, there's more than just that table's meat or fish in the oven or on the grill, and that can get very tricky. So I need to clue myself what's what and whose is whose. I turn the pans a certain way—horizontal for table 3, vertical for table 11. That kind of thing. Who gets what and exactly how was very hard to remember in the beginning, but when you've been doing it as long as I have, you have your own tricks and it gets easier.

This place is like a family to me. Everyone in the kitchen eats together during the dinner break. When we finish work, we talk in the locker room like old friends, which is what we are. Some nights, when we finish, we go out together. If someone has a family problem, we help when we can. If chef tells us someone got sick, we tell him, "Don't worry, Chef. With joy we'll cover him." And if you have any free time in the kitchen, you jump right in to help the guy standing next to you. We're line cooks. It's what we do.

Justo Thomas

LE BERNARDIN

At two p.m. on a weekday afternoon, it's business as usual at Le Bernardin, a four-star seafood restaurant that has topped Zagat's list of favorite New York City restaurants a record thirteen times since it opened in 1986. On this day, every table in the exquisitely modern, tranquil space is filled with impeccably dressed diners enjoying lunch. The room is softly lit, the voices almost hushed as the waiters glide from table to table.

One floor beneath the dining room, though, quite another scene is playing out. In a windowless area bright as daylight, an unending procession of white-clad workers pass each other quickly—and silently—in the hallway. I follow a fast-paced young woman in a dark tailored suit into a conference room, its shelves lined with cookbooks. This is where Justo Thomas, Le Bernardin's fish butcher, dressed in kitchen whites and a black baseball cap, will recount his story. At the end, he invites me to see his "office," which is actually a five-by-ten-foot alcove at the end of the corridor. I'm surprised at how small it is, given the amount of fish he butchers there every day. The walls are of gleaming white tile; along one is a work space that holds his cutting boards and at the far end of the room, a two-basin sink. And that's all there is. There is no chair in sight.

When I was a kid in Dominican, we were never asked what we wanted to be when we grew up because when you have no position and no money, what does it matter? You don't come from a rich family? You don't have dreams. My dad was a gardener who worked with cacao and coffee. I went to school until fourth grade and that was it. I had to quit to go to work with my family.

As I got older, I saw that in our country, you work hard but you never get anywhere. Here, we heard, you work hard and you can get somewhere. My sister was living in New York and I told her I want to go there. She helped me find this person who travels a lot, back and forth from Dominican to New York. His son has a visa and a passport, and he said I look like his son, so I could use them for the trip. They gave me a haircut so that I would look even more like his son. We traveled as father and son. It was 1984. Everybody was coming in illegally. When we landed at JFK, the guy says to me, "Justo, any questions they ask you, don't answer. I'll answer for you." So when the immigration asked me, "What do you do?" I let my "father" answer. And that's how we did it. In those days, it was not that hard to get in. Today, it's a lot harder. But of course I'm legal now.

Here at Le Bernardin, I'm the fish butcher. I cut up from seven hundred to one thousand pounds of fish a day. From the time I get here, this is what I do. Clean, cut, clean, cut. That's my day. I come in, I go to the kitchen to see what the cooks need for that day, then I go to my station. I set it up. I always arrive at least a half hour before the fish comes in from the market so that when it does, I have already started. We only get the top of the top of the line. When we order from, say, Blue Ribbon, they deliver to us direct. They know us and they know it better be good, what they send. Sometimes, if we ask for a certain kind of fish and they don't have our quality, they won't send it, because they know we'll send it right back. The fish we accept has to look nice. But more important, it has to smell like nothing or smell like the ocean. If it smells like fish, it goes right back. You'll see if you go any-time into my station, even after a day of work, it never smells like fish. That's the quality of the fish we get.

When our guys bring in the fish from the market, they know how I want it organized. Always the same order of stacking every day. Top to bottom: salmon, monk, skate, cod, halibut, snapper, bass. Like that. I always butcher the fish with scales last. Like black bass. It's served with the skin on, so I have to scale it. And when I do, my whole station gets loaded with scales. But I have a trick. The first thing I do when I get to my station in the morning is cover the walls with Saran Wrap. That way, when I'm done at the end of the day, I don't have to start scrubbing down the tiles. It's so easy to just pull off the Saran, take some bleach, wipe the walls, and my station is clean.

I get all the fish whole—the way they are taken from the ocean. That's why we order so many pounds. They don't serve seven hun-dred pounds a day, I clean seven hundred a day. Like the black bass. I get only 80 percent from it in the end. From a hundred pounds, I get eighty portions. Snapper we get 75 percent. I toss the head and the tail and the skin and the bones. I only have left the meat.

I always work in the same order. The first fish I do is salmon. I wash and dry it and then put it on the table and fillet it. If there are pin bones, I pull them out with pliers. One by one. Sometimes they break in half so you have to touch the flesh with your finger to make sure there is nothing left in there. Each piece has to be the exact same size so the chef knows exactly how long to cook it to get what he wants. And if two people order the same fish, they get the same size. Every detail is important to the chef.

Today we have halibut on special. Halibut is a thirty-five-pound fish. That makes thirty-five portions. I can cut thirty-five portions from a halibut in ten minutes because it's only one fish. I skin it. I take the fillet. And then I portion it. Three portions a minute including skinning and boning is about right for me. A lot of people who come and make a delivery, they don't want to go. They watch me and they say, "Wow, Justo. You are amazing." The chef calls me "the machine." When I'm on vacation, it takes two or three people to replace me. They take double the time to do what I do. I don't know how I got so fast. Like today. Friday is a very busy day and the delivery came late. I had to rush, because we had one hundred and fifty pounds of black bass to portion out. With the bass, I usually do eighty pounds an hour. Today, I did one hundred and fifty pounds in one half hour. It was good, but tiring.

In my station, I work alone and in peace. Nobody bothers me. I work and I concentrate. They ask me why I don't bring a radio. I don't want that. I want to concentrate on what I'm doing. I have a knife in my hand. You look away for a second, you get cut. So far, all this time, I've never cut myself.

The fresh fish that we have left over at the end of the evening, we donate to the City Harvest charity. And we eat it, too. We got special cooks for the staff. One for lunch and one for dinner. They set up a long table in the hall and we all eat together. The chef, everybody. We all eat the same food. Today we had wild salmon prepared in a special way. But it's not always fish. Sometimes we have meat. Whatever we eat, it's always very good.

It's nice to eat at the same table with your chef. Some places you work, the chef talks only to the big people. The bottom people? They don't even look at them. But here, it's not that way. Chef Ripert comes by my station all the time. He says, "Hello, Justo," to me the same way he says hello to the manager and to everybody else who works here. He asks for my wife and children. He wants you to feel a part of the whole place. Everyone else is like him, too. You come in and they all say good morning to you and to each other. From the front people to the back people. It's nice. Before they ask you to do something, they say, "How are you? How's your family?" Monday morning, it's more conversation because we're off on Sunday and everybody comes in and asks, "How was your weekend?" Or like today is Friday, they ask you, "What do you have in mind for the weekend?" It's a real family here. I know people work for money, but when you can do for money what you love, you have to feel very lucky.

PART IV

Romans à Chef

The other day, while pounding on the treadmill at the gym, I glanced at the TV monitors on my right and left to see what my fellow runners were watching. As is often the case, both were tuned to a cooking show. The young woman to my left was doing a 3.4 mile as Ina Garten whacked apart a chicken, doused the pieces with finger-fuls of salt and pepper, and then gently slid them into a cast-iron pan sizzling with butter. At a steadier but slower pace on my right, the man on a four-point incline was held rapt by a bunch of star-struck, aproned contestants scurrying around a TV-studio kitchen gathering ingredients as a nameless chef called the play-by-play. Which got me to thinking, "When and how did all of this start? When did this society proffer knighthood on those who make our food?"

These days, the Bourdains, Batalis, and Bouluds of the restaurant world hardly need the title "chef" anymore—we know exactly who they are. They have their own publicity agents, literary agents, enter-tainment agents, Twitter and Instagram feeds. They Facebook and publish books; star in TV travelogues and license their names to the producers of Scotch salmon, mixing bowls, pasta sauce, aprons, pick-les, you name it. They are what *Us* magazine calls "celebs," on a global stage.

All well and good, but what does this have to do with, you know, cooking?

The chefs you're about to meet are exactly that: chefs. Not (or not yet, at least) brands. Their names aren't likely to appear on Page Six or in the *New York Observer*, nor will you find their eponymous salad dressings on the shelves of your local supermarket. Okay, one of them did win a cooking contest on the Food Network, but that's an anomaly. Sound stages aren't their natural milieu; kitchens are. For these chefs, it's still the food that matters.

When selecting whom to include here, I wanted to show the full spectrum of what a chef can do, so you'll notice that they're all at different stages of their career and operate in quite different venues. And a word about those venues—their kitchens. I didn't expect their workplaces to have such distinctive personalities, but they do. Sure, I thought, they'd differ in size and even quality of equipment, but after that, I figured a kitchen is a kitchen is a kitchen: Ovens, grills, lowboys, refrigerators, dishwashers, good knives, cutting boards, hanging pots and pans. The chef comes in, ties on her apron, and gets things rolling. Not so. Not at all.

It's often said that long-married couples, like dogs and their owners, come to resemble each other. The same seems to be true of chefs and their work spaces. Take John Greeley's kitchen at "21." It's all "lights-camera-action!" Greeley himself is a high-energy guy, so it's not surprising that on the day of his first interview at that restaurant, the semi-chaotic state of the kitchen immediately attracted him. Luísa Fernandes's work space at Robert, on the other hand, is far calmer because she is. Toni Robertson, an exceedingly well-organized and precise woman, runs the entire food service of the Mandarin Oriental hotel, including the hotel's highly acclaimed signature restaurant, Asiate. Her kitchen seemed the most ordered. Jeb Burke has flourished for years in the almost meditative atmosphere of the executive dining room at News Corporation—perhaps not so much reflecting his own personality as that of meeting expectations of the executives he serves.

Although these chefs may differ in personality, in many respects they have much in common, too. They all started on the line. And most of them describe grueling conditions and getting screamed at by abusive, perfection-seeking chefs who believed humiliating a young cook was the right way to turn him or her into a winner. Ghaya Oliveira, the new young executive pastry chef at Daniel, started her training, she says, "with chefs who made me want to leave every day. But I said, whatever it takes, I'll do it. I don't care." None of the chefs whose stories are here seem to have been turned off by their rigorous training. To a person, they appear to have developed the thick skin and physical stamina it takes to work the unrelenting hours, all for the opportunity to do what they love. That, it seems, is the true definition of the word "passion."

Patrick Collins

THE DUTCH

As sous chef, he's executor of the chef's wishes, second in command, chef-in-waiting. He's twenty-seven, with dark hair and a handlebar mustache that for some reason looks perfectly contemporary on his face. It's with a certain panache that he describes his passion for cooking, from the dining table of his childhood to his current position in one of New York City's "hottest" kitchens.

"I walk around with a clipboard all day. I'm always losing it. I'm like the old man who can't find his glasses. The most repeated question I ask all day long is, 'Anybody seen my clipboard?' Which is followed by, 'Hopefully?' Which is followed by, 'Oh, yeah, and my phone is with it!' And that is followed by, 'Hopefully.' Without my phone and my clipboard, I fucking die . . ."

The way my parents raised us, there was no micromanaging. You know, none of this "You have to be back by this time; you have to call me at this time and tell me where you are and what you're doing. Blah, blah, blah." Even as a six-year-old kid, I had a lot of freedom. My parents made me and my brother pretty independent. Dinnertime was the only time we all had to be home. So the dinner table was where we focused ourselves. You showed up, you looked however you looked, and my parents immediately started asking questions: "What have you been doing?" "Who have you been with?" "Why are your hands dirty?" As we all got older, dinner sort of turned into this time where we laughed and had a good time as a family, although my brother and I, who are probably the loudest people on the planet, were always creating a lot of commotion. Before my dad's parents would come to visit, we had training on how to speak at the table.

When my father got a job in Nigeria, I was sent to boarding school for high school in Switzerland. In Lugano, about a half hour north of the Italian border. Now that I look back on it, it was that boarding school experience that ultimately led me to where I am today. I got in trouble a lot at boarding school, and I was always getting grounded, which meant you couldn't leave the area on weekends. And to make sure you didn't, you had to check in every two hours. I didn't have anything to do those weekends, but there were a couple of kitchens we could use, so I would go off to a couple of the shops close by and buy ingredients to cook stuff. It kept me busy and I liked it.

In my senior year, when everyone was making plans for college, I didn't want any of it. But that's not how my dad and my advisor saw it. When they both started hassling me, I made this agreement with them that they'll fucking leave me alone if I start doing some practical research into this whole concept of cooking and what it's like to be a chef. My research consisted of hanging out with these big, fat, maybe sixty-year-old Italian cooks at school who would sit downstairs and drink wine while they whipped up all this food for the students. The bonus was, if I didn't like what the kids were eating upstairs in the school dining room, I'd go downstairs and eat with these guys. We feasted on things like spaghetti carbonara and all these kinds of dishes that I didn't realize until later were really quite fancy. The kinds of dishes restaurants today sell for fifty dollars.

I ended up going to the CIA [Culinary Institute of America] in Hyde Park. Of course, anyone who even begins to look into the culinary industry realizes that New York City is the first stopping point and that's where I set my sights. For young cooks, it's like walking down an "up" escalator. Here in New York, each step is like three anywhere else. A hundred miles an hour, exhausting, and it kills you. But no one tells you that.

My first taste of things to come occurred when I moved here in 2006. I was still at the CIA and this was to be my internship before graduation. I was sent to work at Aquavit, one of the finer, Michelin-starred restaurants in the city. Talk about baptism by fire! Even though it was technically an internship, there was no holding your hand or teaching you. I got a paycheck and I was expected to operate just like anyone else working there.

Aquavit is essentially two restaurants under one roof: A café and the more formal dining room. On the café side, even though we did between sixty to a hundred covers a day, there were only two of us cooking—a hot-food chef and a cold-food chef. The other fifteen people in the kitchen were all for the dining room, which made zero sense to me. But I was just an intern. What did I know? They give you a little bit of training and put you to work under the *sous chef,* who is watching you the whole time. He might be generous enough to help you out when things get pretty bad, but it's not like, "I'm going to do this for you." It's more like, "The fuck? You're doing that all wrong!" It was super intense. My first week, I went down like a sack of shit. The guy who was supposed to set me up—that is, prepare my station so I could cook—didn't do it. So I had to grab things from different people and I had no idea what was where. Everyone knows if you throw someone into a pool and you don't give them enough guidance or at least put floaties on them, they are most likely going down. And man, I was on my way to the bottom.

At the end of my second week, I was thinking, "I don't know if I can do this. Maybe I should just reestablish my internship somewhere else." I went into the office of the *chef de cuisine* to talk about leaving and he's, like, "Yeah, go ahead and walk—you quitter!" Marcus Samuelsson, who was executive chef at the time—he currently owns the Red Rooster in Harlem—happened to be sitting in the corner, and he starts talking to me about his first job and how stressful it was, and he said, "Look, Patrick. You can always come in here and talk to me about what's going on, but I don't think you should give it up. I think you should give it more time."

At that point, they moved me over to the dining room as part of a three-person crew, which took away some of the intense responsibility. And pretty much after another week, I started picking things up. By week four, I was much more comfortable and when the next guy finished his externship, they told me to take over his station and run it. For the next two months I was *garde-manger*. In English, *garde-manger* translates to "salad station." But in the French sense, you're responsible for all your cold dishes, including your cold appetizers, all your charcuterie, vegetable salads, leafy green salads, and maybe a little antipasti, if you're in a Italian restaurant. As *garde-manger*, I had two people below me, and I had to organize their prep and oversee what they were doing in the day.

At the end of my internship, I went back to the CIA to finish school and then the job hunt began. Finding a job in a good New York City restaurant is a nightmare. It's like trying to get a date but way worse. You want something from them, they want nothing from you, and you are constantly dealing with rejection.

You start by handing your résumé around to all the restaurants. If you're lucky, someone will read it and call you. Then it's, like, "Yeah, we kind of have a position open. You want to come see the kitchen? You want to come trail?" Sometimes you follow someone around and sometimes you stand and work at a station the whole day. Half the time they don't actually have a position, and you just spend the day working for free.

Sometimes you don't do anything. When I trailed at Per Se, I basically just stood for sixteen hours and watched everybody else work, which was pretty fucking boring, if you ask me. Sometimes you're there and it's a shit show and they're just, like, "I need you to do this, I need you to do that!" or, "Go up the stairs and grab this." Sometimes you're just with one person, usually the *garde-manger,* in which case they might let you pick a few herbs. But you almost never cut anything. It's usually pretty bitch work. Some of them will feed you, which is awesome, because it's kind of like getting to eat for free at a great restaurant. But some don't even do that.

The whole point is, you get to see the environment, to see the way the kitchen is run. As a beginning cook, you don't understand that. You look at the cooks and watch them cook and you don't see the bigger picture. You're not yet wise enough to know the right questions to ask. Like, "What are your bosses like? What is this guy like? Is he smart? Is he an idiot? Is this place organized? Do the prep guys know what they are doing? Are there schedules for the week?" That's what I would look at now, but back then, I had no idea what to ask.

My first full-time job was in 2006, when I went to work under

Chef Tom Colicchio, who founded Craft restaurants. Today, he has six restaurants, including Craftbar and Craftsteak. Tom's concept was very simple. He cooked in a New American style—proteins were mostly roasted with thyme, butter, salt, and pepper, which, at the time, was refreshing for his customers. People were happy to have an alternative to "fine dining." You know, French. Overdone. Molded into this mold and cut like that, blah, blah, blah. Tom's cooking was the complete opposite of all that. It was all very natural food. Craftbar was incredibly successful, and as the covers grew, so did the menu. Cooks kept leaving, and when they did, I moved up. To the point where during my first year I worked through all the stations and was eventually promoted to roasting meat and fish—the highest station for a line cook. But after two years, I found myself bored. It just sort of reaches a point where you think, "Okay, I've learned all I'm going to learn here." And you go. This was around 2008, right at the time when the economy turned sour. Everybody was closing. Nobody was opening. And if something did open, it was really, really lowbrow and didn't offer a lot of opportunities for someone like me who wanted to keep progressing.

I spent about a year slowly trying to find places to *stage*, and that led me to work with Andrew Carmellini at Locanda Verde. Whenever you start working at a new restaurant, you generally have to start at the beginning of the line as *garde-manger* and that was no different for me. Once again, I worked through all the stations. And then, two years later, he moved me to his newest restaurant, The Dutch, which is where I am today.

I started at The Dutch in the position of *tournant*, or as some people call it, junior *sous chef*. That's the guy you trust to cover everybody's ass and to whom you give special projects that might require more skill or attention. I was *tournant* for the first two months of opening and then got promoted to *sous chef.*

In a small house, the *sous chef* is kind of like your all-around guy. More of a multipurpose tool. In a larger house, you become more specialized. Because most fine restaurants are open late into the night, and because you don't want to keep the same people working there for more than eight hours at a time, there are usually two shifts, a.m. and p.m. My job at the Dutch right now is a.m. *sous chef,* which covers lunch and sometimes moves into the dinner hours. As a.m. *sous chef,* you're alone pretty much the entire day. You don't have reinforcements; you don't have backup management. It's just you and the morning-shift line cooks that do production and then do lunch shift. You're responsible for expediting during service, telling the cooks what's fired, and the waiters when to pick things up. It's your job to scrutinize every plate before it leaves the kitchen to make sure that what's about to be served to the customers is perfect. And if things get crazy busy, you physically have to go back and cook and plate and somehow figure out how to expedite the service.

So here's my day. At eight thirty a.m. I walk in the door, and okay, so I'm a half hour late, but I'm never out of here when I'm supposed to be out, either. I show up at eight thirty, and first thing I hear is, "This didn't come." Or "That didn't come" or "This is delayed," or "So-and-so is looking for this and we don't have any. What should we do?" A hundred questions the second you walk in the door. I do my best to answer what I can and try to immediately put out the little fires.

Next, I check in with the sending and receiving guys. The a.m. *sous chef* is responsible to make sure the raw food arrives at the restaurant. That, believe me, can be a bear. Say, for example, the fish purveyor doesn't show up with the fresh fish until eleven and eleven thirty is when you start service. At eleven, you're running around like an asshole making sure you can get the fish cleaned and portioned and ready for the fish cook. The cook can't do it, because at eleven he's getting himself set up with all his other shit. If it had arrived like it was supposed to at ten, he could have taken the fish and portioned it, but at eleven, he has to be ready for service. At eleven, if you don't have someone behind you, you're shit out of luck.

It's frustrating. When people don't send you exactly what you ordered, you start cursing. And you finally get them on the phone and they say, "Oh, well it's a hundred and fifty minimum delivery charge for a second run." And you're like, "Fuck you. You didn't send me what I ordered so now you'd better fucking send it . . . at no cost!" Usually they do, but you gotta be an asshole, you gotta kick and scream and fight. It can get exhausting.

And it's not just the quantity that you're responsible for. You have to check on the quality of everything that comes in as well. The sending and receiving team is supposed to do that, but at the same time you have to go behind them to make sure what's coming in is what you want. You can't just assume that it's good. So you spend pretty much every five seconds walking over to the hatch and sticking your hands in things and smelling stuff and tasting stuff. Especially in the summer when there's fruit to be dealt with. Fruit drives me crazy.

Then I start talking to the prep cooks. They do a lot of daily stuff, like setting up the *mise en place* for the line cooks. We make lists for them that tell them exactly what is needed that day, depending on the menu, and that gives us a lot of control without having to sit there and say, next step, next step, next step. The list keeps them going through the day, and when we need to, we add other things. We have a butcher

Monday through Friday who does meat and fish. He also takes care of pasta and he makes the dough for our ravioli and *rigatelli*. I go over his list with him and make sure he's produced what we need—and not too much and not too little. And then of course throughout the day, you go back and check out whatever he's doing so there's no surprise later on at seven o'clock at night when you find out that the ravioli looks like shit. You've got to catch it early.

Next up are the line cooks. I start with the *garde-manger*. The questions are general. "What are you doing today? What are your projects? What have you done so far?" When you talk to the "hot apps" cook, you talk more specifically about their project and how they're doing it, what time they're going to start it, when is it coming off the stove, and how they are going to arrange it. Cooking beets, for example. They cook beets pretty much every day. But beets come in different sizes, so some of the initial beet conversation is about when are they going to be done. "When did they go in? When are you going to start checking them?" "They went in an hour ago." "Did you separate the small from the medium from the big?" "Yes, yes, yes."

As you get higher up the line, with the more experienced cooks, you talk less. And you talk more in generalities. Managing people has taught me more about cooking than I learned as a cook. As a cook, I would try certain things and I'd figure out the best way to make things work. But to have to tell someone to do it, and to catch them before they do it wrong, you suddenly realize how many details are missed and lost over trying to make things consistent.

All this takes place in the morning, before the food service starts. These discussions will happen during service, too, but then they will be more about plating aesthetics or what their p.m. partner has to do and what they have left in the day to do. I'm teaching all the time. That is how kitchens were always run and that's how we run it at the Dutch. And that is why, as a young chef, you were willing to work ninety hours a week. Because you knew they were going to teach you, train you, and make you better than when you started. They were going to make you a chef.

I miss cooking so much. As *sous chef*, I don't get to cook very often and it sucks. I fucking hate it. I mean, what's the point of learning to cook if you don't cook later? I keep asking myself that very question. Your ambition is to be an executive chef, and what's the point of being a chef if you spend your entire morning in meetings and talking about numbers? And then you spend your entire evening basically yelling at everybody? There is no point.

Right now, I'm cooking vicariously through the other cooks, which can be good or can be extremely frustrating. Some people are so green that when you try to explain things to them, they just can't wrap their head around the concept. Teaching some of these guys takes a mountain of patience. Which, I admit, is not my strong suit. Right now I'm trying to show our *garde-manger* how to roast spring onions. One of the components in our pea salad is a roasted spring onion that is broken down into little petals. I'm trying to demonstrate how to get even browning, not using too much oil, and not cooking it too long, because when you overcook it and you pull down the outside layer, it just turns into a slimy, nasty piece of onion. Now the next time he does it, because I told him not to overcook it, now he's going to undercook it, and now it's practically raw onion with barely a bit of brown on it. You do this constantly and you do it with seven different cooks throughout the course of the day with different items; it can really try your patience.

Look, it's not like I wasn't ever in their shoes. I understand. There's so much to grasp for every cook. But when, for example, your meat cooks get it, when you see the meat come off the grill and it's evenly cooked, right on temperature, it's tremendously gratifying. It's like when you yourself finally understood it. You finally got what you were doing. There's like this epiphany. There was a year in my life when suddenly I figured it out. I knew how to cook! For a long time, it was recipes and ingredient by ingredient, this and that, this flavor with that flavor, and then suddenly it all transformed in my head.

As hippie as it sounds, you just kind of have to "feel" it. There is a sense of self-expression that comes through in food. That's why the exact same plate can look and taste completely different depending on who is behind it. Without self-expression, you don't get far.

When the service is over for the night, when the stressful time is over for everyone, that's when the fun starts—at least for the line cooks. They haven't been able to speak up all night other than to say, "Yes, Chef!" or "No, Chef!" So what do they do? They go out together after work—without you—and it gives them a chance to let off steam and laugh at that evening's "drama." You do have to laugh at some of that stuff. It's the only way to get through it. As a cook, I spent a lot of nights at the bar until six a.m., getting really drunk and the next morning being hungover and fucking up a lot of stuff and everyone, including you, thinking you're a fucking idiot.

I actually try not to yell at anyone unless they do something really stupid because it wasn't all that long ago that I was in their shoes. I usually approach the first time calm, with the idea that I'm going to teach them. I'm going to explain what's going on. But after the fourth time, it becomes, "You idiot! You know better! You've been taught this a million times!" And you start to lose it over a few fucking beets and you hate yourself and you hate them for making you hate yourself. If they're smart, they say, "Yes, Chef." If they start going into explanations, that's

FOOD AND THE CITY

when it gets worse and worse and worse. We're all trained that way. Every fucking one of us. It's "Yes, Chef" or "No, Chef." Period. There's no "maybe." There's no "But I was going to . . ." If you're unclear about what I told you, you can ask a question, but you have to say "Yes, Chef" first, meaning you know what I just said. As *sous chef*, you're talking all day long, so when someone suddenly wants to have a conversation, you get on their case with, "Listen, man. This isn't a fucking dialogue. It's a monologue! I'm talking. You're listening. Shut the fuck up."

And that's pretty much the way it goes.

Sandy Ingber

GRAND CENTRAL OYSTER BAR

In 1913, Woodrow Wilson was president, the Washington Senators' Walter Johnson began his string of fifty-six consecutive scoreless innings, the United States was on the brink of World War I, and the dazzling new Grand Central Terminal opened its doors. One flight below the main concourse, where glorious terra-cotta tiles lined the walls and marble columns connected the floor to soaring vaulted ceilings, the 440-seat Oyster Bar welcomed its first customers. While the architectural grandeur endures, executive chefs have come and gone. But for the past quarter century, Ingber has stayed put. It's a job he cherishes, but one that, he says, is not for the faint of heart.

B eing in the food business is only for the stalwart and resolute. It's a tough business. And if you get to a place of success, it's a huge sacrifice. The hours are incredibly long, you're on your feet all day, and you're working in cramped quarters. And it's hot. You can't imagine how hot those stoves can get. What you're sacrificing the most is a life. Ask anyone in this business. In the beginning, if you want to be a good chef, you have to put in so many hours. You have to work from a love of food. The ones who don't, don't make it. It takes more than talent. You have to have passion. Talent gets you to another level, but passion rules. I wouldn't say I'm the most talented person in the world, but I do have the passion. Even now, after so many years, it's the only thing that gets me up at three o'clock in the morning.

The Oyster Bar turned one hundred years old in 2013. Despite the name, a hundred years ago there were very few choices of oysters. That was true all the way up to the nineties, when we still had difficulty finding different varieties. Some weeks, we were lucky if we had four different kinds of oysters on our menu. But then came the late nineties and the explosion of the dot-coms and Wall Street going crazy, and suddenly a lot of people had a lot of money to spend. And they spent it. On all kinds of luxuries, oysters being one of them. Along with the demand, or maybe because of it, oyster farming became very popular and remains so to this day. By the year 2000, I had more than thirty different types of oysters on my daily menu. In the summertime, I sell about five thousand oysters a day here. And that's just on the half shell. That doesn't include pan roast or stewed. Over the year? Somewhere around two million.

I think it's safe to say that we have one of the busier kitchens in New York City. Walk into our kitchen in midafternoon and the place is like a roller rink—people constantly on the move, back and forth, in and out. We've got six line cooks and a couple of soup guys who do nothing but make vats and vats of chowder. We sell between five hundred and eight hundred cups of chowder a day.

Because we're in a commercial area, and of course with all these people coming and going through the station, we're busiest at lunchtime. Everyone wants everything immediately. (New Yorkers expect to be served a ten-minute piece of fish in five minutes.) Then multiply the cooking of each order by 1,200—which is how many people a day we serve. And that number increases to 2,400 people a day at holiday time. So, how do we do it? We do it. It's what we do.

My day starts at three a.m. I'm at the Fulton Fish Market in the Bronx by three thirty. I know what I need because the night before I've made up my menu and chosen the specials for the next day. I also know what we have in inventory and what we're out of—we call that the "86 list." The first thing I do when I get inside is make a complete turn all the way around the market—it's about a half-mile walk. I'm examining the fish from different vendors and finding the best prices. Then I go around the second time and place my orders. In a single morning, I'll buy about five thousand pounds of fish. It's all sushi quality, so anything I have left over from the day before is still super fresh. By tomorrow, whatever I bought today or yesterday will be gone.

The third time around the market, I pick up my invoices. Right now I'm spending around seventy or eighty thousand dollars a week on fish and shellfish. And add to that almost one hundred bushels of oysters. That's ten to twelve thousand oysters of varying kinds. Everything I purchased that morning goes to a drop-off area at the end of the building, where it's organized on pallets and taken to a truck that delivers it to us directly.

When I leave the market, I come here directly. The fish arrives soon after I do, so everything is ready to go when my workers come in. So now, we're at five a.m. The next hour and a half I sit in my office and do paperwork. Checking my invoices from the morning, planning for the week, and writing the menus. At seven thirty a.m., I come up to the kitchen and talk to my *sous chef* about the menu and what his responsibilities are for the day. At eight fifteen, I'm back in my office on the phone or on the computer answering e-mails. About ten thirty,

I start purchasing the produce and the groceries over the phone. Then I have two waiters meetings, one at eleven fifteen and one at eleven forty-five, where I clarify the daily menu and describe the specials and answer any questions. Then it's back downstairs until twelve thirty, when I'm ready to go into the kitchen to help expedite lunch until three p.m. I've now been at work for almost twelve hours—without a break.

I usually leave for the day around three thirty. I drive home to my wife and two kids, which takes an hour and a half. And I'm carrying enough paperwork to keep me busy almost the entire night. Dinner with my children is very important to me. For years, on weeknights, the only time I saw them was at dinner. When we finished eating, I'd go down to the basement to work, and my wife stayed upstairs watching TV or doing something else. When it was time to go to bed, she'd yell down, "Good night, honey." And I'd answer, "Good night, dear." And that was all I saw of her for that day.

It didn't make for a great relationship, believe me. I was there, but I wasn't *really* there. And then, three or four years ago, we moved the TV and a card table into our living room and now that's where we both sit. I'm still working, but I'm surrounded by the activity that's going on around the house. Sometimes I have to work harder at focusing on what I'm doing, but just to be able to look up and see my wife or my kids, that's perfectly okay with me.

Ghaya Oliveira

DANIEL

Born, raised, and educated in Tunisia, she was studying at the university toward a degree in economics, but after her second year, a captivating summer job at an investment banking company led her on the path to what she believed would be an excellent future. Instead of returning to college, she stayed on as a trainee, starting at the bottom. Six months after passing the stock trader's exam, she was working on the trading floor. "It wasn't as big as Wall Street. But it was big enough and fascinating to me."

Then, a year and a half into this "excellent future," her career was interrupted. She was twenty-four when the phone call came.

It was from my sister, who was single and lived in New York, telling me that I had to come to her. I had known earlier that she was pregnant, but only with the call did I learn that she had developed cancer during this pregnancy and couldn't take treatment for it until after the baby was born. As a result, after she gave birth to her little boy, her situation got worse. Now she was telling me I had to come right away. It was summertime. I took a month off from my job to come here and help her out. My mother flew in as soon as she found out. We did every-thing we could, but there was no way to save her. Before she died, she said, "Ghaya, I want my boy to live here, to grow up here. This is my dream and where I wanted to be all my life, and now it's my dream for him. I want him to stay in New York City." I said, "Do you know what you're asking me?" She knew.

There was no input from the father of this child. None. We didn't even discuss it with my parents. It was a big decision for me to take, but I said I would do it. How could I not? On her deathbed, she made my mom and me promise again to keep her son in New York and raise him here. This was a promise we agreed to keep.

My sister was an American citizen, so through a lot of lawyers we got legal guardianship of my nephew, and I managed to get a green card. My mother traveled back and forth, but because I was staying, I needed to find a job. In the beginning, I went to Wall Street to look around and see what was there for me. I wasn't fluent in English, and I certainly didn't know the New York stock market, so everywhere I applied turned me down. It would have taken a lot of time and money to learn, and those were the two things I didn't have. Time was impos-sible because I was in charge of a baby, and although I had brought some money with me, it too would soon run out. I had to do some-thing. Fast.

My father had a friend here in the city who owned a pretty nice-sized restaurant. I went to see him and asked if I could be a waitress. He offered me a job in the kitchen. "Are you crazy?" I said to him. "My parents will kill me!" Being a cook back home is for the lower classes. What I didn't realize was that the job wasn't even as a cook; it was as a cleaner. He sat me down, and he said, "Look, Ghaya, whatever you can get right now, just take it. It's not so easy to get a job in this city, and this is the only thing I have to offer you."

I started by cleaning the front of the restaurant. But every day, when I could, I was watching the cooks and every day I was more impressed by what they were doing. When I asked to work in the kitchen, he agreed. And he made me a dishwasher. I wasn't complaining. I was just working. At a certain point, it didn't matter to me. Taking out the garbage, being a dishwasher, scrubbing down the walls, cleaning. It was fine. But true to my nature, I wanted more. To learn something new. So after a while I asked if I could work as a cook.

He said I could be *commis chef*. That's the person in the kitchen who does the things that no one wants to do, like peeling, cutting, things like that. I liked the idea, because all the chefs come to you and give you all these detailed things to do and I thought it would teach me something. But it was messy and painful. I was standing all day long with my hands in the water, washing things like spinach and shrimp. It got to be too much for me. And the truth is, I never really liked the place, so I left.

I found a position in a restaurant on the Upper East Side that was owned by Plácido Domingo. The chef was a terrific Mexican guy. I was the only girl in the kitchen, and it wasn't easy for me, but they let me do pastries, and I was happy there. And then one day, I came to work after my day off to find a sign that said the restaurant was temporarily closed. I knocked on the door and the manager answered. He apologized for the situation and said he had a place to send me that he was sure I'd like just as much. "It's called Café Boulud. They speak French there, Ghaya," he said. "It's perfect for you." He had already set up an interview for me.

I had never heard of Café Boulud. I thought it was just another French restaurant. I had never heard of Daniel Boulud, the chef/owner, either. But I agreed to try it. The year was 2001. My nephew was three years old. I had been at this for three years, and I was just attempting to fit in somewhere. I went over right away. Looking through the door of the restaurant, I saw immediately that it was a different level from the places I had worked before. It looked beautiful. Very classy. I thought, "Oh my God! What am I doing here?" The manager took me straight to the pastry chef, who blinked at my résumé—I think he threw it in the garbage—and sent me downstairs to change. From there, he took me to the basement kitchen to "pipe *macarons*." "What is a *macaron*?" I'm thinking. "What are these green things?" I wasn't even in the kitchen. Nine sheet pans were on this low table outside the kitchen, and I stood there in the hallway just piping out macarons onto all of them. When I finished, he came back down and asked, "Can you start tomorrow?" "Yes, yes!" I said. "Of course!"

Tomorrow came. I don't know why but I was so scared. Probably because I took things so very seriously. I was supposed to be there at six a.m. I knew that the first train that runs by the station where I live is at 5:40 a.m. I woke up at four, got dressed really quick, and got on the train. When I arrived at the restaurant, I ran downstairs and got changed into my whites. I didn't even look at the time, but I knew it was still early because it was dark outside. I took the stairs up two at a time, and there is the chef, standing in the kitchen, glaring at me from afar. He said, "Did you look at the time? It's 6:07!" I couldn't even speak. "When I tell you to come in at six, you are here at six sharp! At your station. With your apron. On!"

His name was Remy Funfrock. He was the executive pastry chef at Café Boulud. As a person, he's not someone I want to meet for coffee but I always had great respect for him. He was an artist, and he was tough! An old-school chef with really high standards, who, lucky for me, became my mentor. It's thanks to him that I'm here right now.

Nothing satisfied Chef Funfrock. He looks at anything made with the wrong shape or texture, even barely, and he throws it away and tells you, "This is garbage! Do it again!" Things fly through the air when he gets upset. And when he yells, he splashes spit. So don't get too close.

My second week with him on a.m., I thought, "I can't take this anymore." It wasn't the hours. It was the pressure. On a.m. duty, you have to learn, prepare, produce, execute, and be ready at twelve noon sharp with everything, towel wiped on the table, standing by for service. This is no joke. You don't have time to breathe, eat, or sleep. And I had this little baby at home. If you saw me, you would say I looked like a dead person walking.

The end of that second week, I showed up in the kitchen at six a.m. sharp, still in my street clothes. Chef Funfrock looks me up and down and he says, "So?" He knew something was wrong. "I'm done," I said. "It's too much." He said, "Ghaya, I will say this to you only once. You want to become something? You finish what you started. You want to learn? You stay. You don't like it? Then leave—and I don't want to see you anymore."

Well, you know when that bubble goes off in your head? I had something like that, like an epiphany. I was, like, "What the hell am I doing? Am I crazy?" I ran downstairs to the locker room, threw on my uniform, ran back up, and apologized. He didn't even acknowledge me at all. So I started working. Then he turns around and says, "You're very late, you know." I didn't even answer. I just got my stuff going. It was terrible, but that was the moment. If I didn't take it, that was it.

Whenever I could, I worked from six a.m. to ten p.m. I stayed late to learn more, to see what the p.m. people were doing. All of them went to cooking school; they are all from the CIA, French Culinary. I was nothing at the time and really wanted to be at that level. It was very hard, and I used to ask them just to give me anything, I'll do it. Time didn't matter to me. I got married right when I started working at Café Boulud and every day I would come home crying. But I just kept going. My mom was here, so she was helping care for the baby, and so was my husband. He's a great guy. He and my mother were very patient with me. I see cooks try to get into relationships, have partners, and it's so difficult for them. Before, I used to say if you're not married already in this business, forget it, you won't be able to do it. But then I did it. I was one of the lucky ones.

Café Boulud was my school. It taught me everything. I started as *commis*. Then I was promoted to pastry cook. That meant I was responsible for production and service—that is, preparing your doughs, your *bases-anglaises*, making *mise en place* for your service, getting ready for lunch or dinner. As a pastry cook, I had two chefs over my head, the executive pastry chef—which was Chef Funfrock—and the pastry *sous chef*. The executive pastry chef creates and designs the pastry and the *sous chef* executes the chef's creation. *Sous chefs* supervise the team and make sure everything is clean, organized, and ready for service. Toward the end of my stay at Café Boulud, I became Remy Funfrock's *sous chef*.

And then, after six and a half years, in 2007, Chef Daniel opened Bar Boulud and promoted me to executive pastry chef. Bar Boulud is a bistro with very simple bistro-style desserts. *Coupe glacée*, which was just three scoops of ice cream, and tarts, which we served on a plate with *crème anglaise*. Slowly, Chef Daniel allowed me to begin developing my own style with these desserts. I agree that the classics are imperative, but people already know the classics, so you have to give it a little twist, a little extra something surprising. So my tarts took different shapes, different looks. The *coupe glacée* also was more developed. As I got more freedom to work with the products, I became more and more creative. I loved every second. It's as if I was on drugs making desserts. There were no limits.

To me, every dessert has a story. I used to dig in and think, "What's the *mille-feuille* story? How did it come about? Who created it?" I went through every classic and tried to find the story behind it. What's the story behind the apple? The apple was like the Garden of Eden. What can I do if I want a golden apple? How can I make it golden and present it as a myth? That's how my head spins when I think about things. I like to work with fruits because there are always long stories behind them. And I like to serve the fruit as it is, but make it look different. So I'll poach it, for example, or roast it.

It's very important to me, that you, as a diner, have a full fruit or dessert in front of you. A lot of pastry chefs today are reducing their desserts on a plate. They give you a little powder and a line of sauce, and voilà! They call it "molecular cuisine." I call it watching food literally disappear from your plate. Molecular cuisine can be great, don't get me wrong. It's innovative. But as a little touch on your plate. Not the whole A to Z. You don't want to do biscuit, mousse, *coulis*, or fruit only as a two-inch line of powder on a plate. And that's what some pastry chefs are doing today. Everything is a dot. What's that all about?

Things were going along great for me at Bar Boulud. I had been there four years when I learned that Chef Daniel was planning to open a Mediterranean restaurant, Boulud Sud, right around the corner from Bar Boulud. The two are attached through a hallway. Then one day, Chef Daniel came looking for me. "Yes, Chef?" He said, "Ghaya, this new restaurant is for you. This is your position. It's Mediterranean cuisine. You're the perfect fit."

We had an excellent relationship, Chef Daniel and I. I met him for the first time when I was working at Café Boulud. When he came in, I heard his accent, but I didn't know who he was. He would come in and ask Chef Funfrock about the new desserts. He opens the freezers, looks at what's inside; if there's anything new, he tries it. He goes around and says hi to every single person. He remembers the higher-up people as well as the cooks. If he's never met you before, he will give you five minutes and stay with you, focus on only you, just to know where you're from, which school did you go to, how did you end up here? Always with a big smile. He does that with everyone, including interns. It doesn't matter to him who you are.

The day I met him, he was shaking everyone's hand and someone told me he was the executive chef. I was at the pass, doing service, and he introduced himself. I said, "Hello, Chef. How are you?" He asked how long I had been there, where I had worked before. I was speaking in French to him, so it was a little different because it was easy for me to express myself. He asked my name, and I told him "Ghaya." The next time he comes in, he calls me "Maya." And I never corrected him. One day, after his books came out, I asked him to please autograph one book for my mother and the other for me. He said, "Of course." In the first book, he wrote, "Dear Maya" and I said, "Chef, my name is Ghaya." He said, "Oh, I'm so sorry. Why didn't you ever correct me?" I said, "It's okay, it's not a problem." For two or three years he thought my name was Maya. I still have it scratched out on the book today.

When Boulud Sud opened, I worked as the pastry chef for them both—Boulud Sud and Bar Boulud—at the same time. Boulud Sud, the Mediterranean-inspired restaurant, was great for me because I had even more freedom to use spices and real flavors in the desserts. I used all the flavors I grew up with. Although I wasn't a cook in Tunisia, these spices speak Mediterranean to me: Sesame, orange blossom, jasmine water, geranium, ginger. This is where I debuted my favorite dessert, which I call Grapefruit Givré. It's a real construction. You start with an empty grapefruit shell that you fill with grapefruit sorbet. You then press the sorbet against the sides to make a thick, bowl-like lining. Inside that, you place grapefruit pieces, followed by homemade grapefruit jam, and fill it to the top with sesame foam that's like a light mousse. Into that you tuck some pieces of rose *loukoum*—a kind of a gummy rose candy. I add some halvah, which is sesame paste crumble that's been baked earlier, and then cover it all with a disk of caramel lace orange *tuile*. On top of that goes a heaping pile of halvah hair that looks like cotton candy. And it's done. It's still my favorite, and we're still serving it at Boulud Sud and now also at Daniel.

After I was two years at Boulud Sud, our corporate pastry chef, Eric Bertoia, came to the restaurant. Eric opens the Daniel restaurants around the world. He travels a lot. He singled me out, and I thought there was a problem. He looked very serious. "Sit down, Ghaya," he said. "We need to talk." He had his hands on my shoulders the whole time and he said, "Ghaya, Daniel wants you to be the executive pastry chef at Restaurant Daniel." My eyes went wide open and I couldn't say anything.

I always wondered what's next for me, but I never thought it would be this! Restaurant Daniel? It's a completely different world than any other restaurant. It's rarefied. The highest of the high. I knew I wasn't ready to work with the best chefs in the world. I was sure I wasn't good enough to be part of this team. So immediately I said, "No." He pressed on my shoulders harder. "No? Why do you say no?" Then he said, "I'm going to say this again. Daniel wants you to come to Restaurant Daniel as the executive pastry chef."

I needed some time to breathe, and I told him so. He said, "Ghaya. You have to say yes! I came in to see you personally, just to hear those words from you. I wasn't even going to call, I was just going to put you straight in." Suddenly, my nerves got the best of me, and I started laughing hysterically. I knew how much more was coming, how much more I would have to do. To me it was like restarting at another level. I told him, "Between you and me, it will of course be a yes, but please, Chef, give me some time to process it."

The first thing I did was call my husband, and I asked, "What do you think?" He said, "Are you crazy? Of course you can do it!" He didn't know what it would take, how bad it would be, and that he wouldn't see me anymore. He said, "Just do it, we'll figure it out. You reached that level. It's waiting for you. Just go for it."

Chef Eric came in the next day and said, "Okay. You don't have to worry anymore. Daniel's looking for someone else." He was trying to mess with me. I looked at him and I said, "Okay! Yes!" He turned around and said, "Seriously? Are you joking?" I said, "Of course not, Chef. It's an honor for me. But I'm still a little in shock." From the day he told me until I met with Chef Daniel two weeks later, every day I was scared and biting my nails off, for no reason.

When Chef Daniel and I finally got together, I will always remember the big smile he has on his face. He's like part of my family; that's how it is with him. He said, "Ghaya, there's no one else here. This is your position." When I heard that from him I thought, at this point, at this level I'm appreciated. He thinks I'm that good. I said, "Thank you very much, Chef. There are no words for this." He said, "You are a hard worker, you're faithful, you're honest." He kept saying that kind of thing and I didn't want to hear it anymore. I didn't think it was true! My head was somewhere else, thinking this is impossible. I still could not believe it until the day I arrived here eight months ago and put my apron on for the first time.

That first day I wandered around, trying to understand the system. It's a completely different system than all the other Daniel restaurants. This one has one hundred and forty seats, and a bigger team. I have ten people working on two teams, a.m. production and p.m. service. These teams were already in place when I came in. When you're the new person who lands in a team, no matter what your level, it's very difficult. They have their system already, and they know what they're doing. You're the one asking the questions.

My first priority was to connect with everyone, and know everything about him or her. That's how I am. I need to know where they live, how they think, where they are from, how long their commute is, how they sleep. That way I know how to deal with them. I report to the executive chef, whose name is Jean François Bruel. Creatively, though, I'm on my own. That is, I don't have to get my desserts approved by anyone. What I'll do is, I create a new dessert for the night, I always give it to the executive chef to try. Then, I send it out for a night as a special that's not on the menu, to see the feedback. The captains are the only connection we have between the customer and ourselves, and if you ask them to, they'll come back and tell you what the customers thought, and how they liked the taste. After the feedback, you adjust, fix, and add what you need to. You never see the customer, but you can also tell what they think of your desserts by looking at their plate when they're done. When *le grand chef pâtissier* Pierre Hermé came to eat here last week, the captain made sure to bring the plates from his table when they were finished. I was very happy to see those plates were empty.

Sometimes, when it's quiet and I have a minute to myself, I look back at where I was when I came to this country. When I think about it now, every time I fell, every time I got hurt bad, every time I had the worst time of my life, it was a life lesson to me. I've seen it all in New York, went through all the rough times. I was here during September 11, my sister passed away here, I was in charge of a little boy who was eleven months old when his mother died and is now fifteen and at a school for gifted children. It was difficult for me to speak English, to deal with people, to know where I am. I've seen and been through all of it. People were tough with me at work. But those were good life lessons and a good beginning. I'm happy I went through all of that. I don't regret a thing. New York is a tough city, but it's my city. I'm a New Yorker now, and I will stay here for the rest of my life.

John Greeley

THE "21" CLUB

A former speakeasy during Prohibition, the "21" Club opened for business on New Year's Eve 1930 and immediately became a celebrated place to dine. Thirty-three years later, John Greeley was born. And thirty-three years after that, he became the youngest chef in the restaurant's history. An artist and a skateboarder, Greeley spends his leisure time artistically re-creating skateboards of the past.

Boyishly handsome despite his gray hair, he is in his early fifties. But that doesn't stop him from thinking ahead. When he retires, he says, his goal is to be somewhere down by the ocean with a little skateboard shack and a taco stand attached to it. Very low key. "I'll have one guy with me working the stand. I'll show him how to make tacos and then I'll kick back and watch people sailing by on my skateboards. That," he says, "will be a life."

As a kid, I always wanted to be an artist. So, when it came time to go to college, I went to New York's School of Visual Arts. But after two years, I decided what I wanted even more was to get out of the city and live by a beach. I transferred to a school in Savannah. For extra money, I worked in a restaurant called 45 South, where I became an expert at grits and shrimp and other Southern foods. I liked it so much that after graduation, I started thinking about culinary school.

At the time, my dad was an advertising executive at Grey. I went to work with him one day, and he introduced me to Sara Moulton, who ran the executive dining room at *Gourmet* magazine. Sara very generously gave me a list of chefs from fifteen New York restaurants and told me to send them my résumé and to use her name as a reference. I'm sure her name didn't hurt, but I was still amazed to get three immediate responses. One was from Alfred Portale of the Gotham Bar and Grill, one from Charlie Palmer at Aureole, and one from Michael Lomonaco, who was at "21." Thirty years ago these guys were major players at the hottest restaurants in the city—and they still are to this day.

I went to see them all, and Michael offered me a job on the spot. I didn't know what to say, so I told him I was looking at some other restaurants and I'd get back to him. He said, "Listen to me, John. These guys are going to put you on *garde-manger* for two years. Do you want to be slicing tomatoes for two years? Come to me and I'll put you on the hot line right now." I'll never know what he saw in me that day. It certainly wasn't my résumé. I'm big, and maybe I looked like a strong person who could deal with a lot of lifting and carrying, but whatever it was, I agreed. And that's how I ended up here.

Chef Lomonaco wasn't kidding. He did put me on the hot line, but I was the lowest of the low. I was *entremetier*, the vegetable cook. And true, I didn't slice tomatoes, but for a good year all I did was cut and sauté other vegetables. And mash and dice potatoes. Lots and lots of potatoes. French fries. Potato chips. You name it. For nine months straight, nothing but potatoes. You know what? It didn't matter. The line at that time was made up of all young guys from the CIA. All very macho. We had a great time. And I remember thinking how glad I was that I didn't end up at Grey's, or some other place where you sit in an office all day reviewing files and having meetings. Here it was more like, "Oh my God, we're running out of striped bass!" "Who has the *crème fraîche?*" People sprinting from floor to floor. Fire blazing through the grates. Pots and pans banging against the metal stove. It was non-stop action! I loved it then and I love it now.

I also was partial to the late hours. The other places I worked introduced me to the subculture of night cooks: stay late, go out and party, wake up late, and do the same thing again the next day. My buddies would ask me, "How can you deal with working every single night?" I said, "What am I missing? *Law & Order* reruns? What do you do? Watch TV and go to sleep. I wake up, I go to the gym, go to a museum, go out to lunch, go to work, and after work, I go out with my friends! What's not to like about this? It's awesome!"

I worked under Michael for twelve years, eventually moving through all the stations and ending up as meat cook, which is the most coveted station of them all. From there, he made me *sous chef,* one step under executive chef. And then, in 1995, the restaurant was sold and he left. The new owners brought in a couple of interim executive chefs who came as fast as they went, and then one day, they called me in and offered me the job. I was thirty-three years old—the youngest executive chef in "21"'s eighty-four-year history.

That was seventeen years ago. It's pretty rare for a chef to last this long. But then it's pretty rare for a *restaurant* to last this long. There are probably a number of reasons why "21" has outlasted all the other places, but our iconic stature is surely one of them. We're as much a part of New York City's history as the Empire State Building, or taking a carriage ride through Central Park. Sure, we've changed through the years, but we never changed so much that we lost our way. I realize that now, but in the beginning it was hard for me to understand. As a young chef, I wanted to change everything. I'm a creative person, and I don't necessarily fit the mold of someone who's comfortable in the safety of tradition.

In the old days, "21" was known for its "classic" European-style service. Everything was done tableside upstairs in the main dining room. Dining theater at its very best. Captains in tuxedos pushed the *gueridons* to the table, opened them up, and sliced your roast beef in front of you. If you ordered Dover sole, they'd come tableside with your fish in a shiny copper pan on a burner and bone out the sole while you watched. Nobody does that anymore, including us. Our décor, on the other hand, despite our adding a few new spaces, has remained pretty much the same. And we still require men to wear jackets in the dining room.

Currently, I'm looking to attract a younger clientele, which means updating some of our menu choices. Our famous chicken hash has changed probably four or five times since I've been here. When I started here, we poached chicken and cherries and covered them with béchamel sauce. Now we're using Mornay sauce with Parmesan cheese and placing the dish under a broiler. Same thing with our hamburger. My burger today tastes just like a steak, because I use only steak cuts of meat. And sure. The price went up. It's thirty-two dollars today. But people still order it like crazy.

We try to be farm-to-table, too, which I think can sometimes go too far. I was talking to my *sous chef* last week and I said, "What do you think? Should we order farm eggs?" And he said, "Chef, aren't all eggs from a farm? What makes this so special?" He's right, of course. All eggs start from a farm. And so does all produce. Where else are vegetables ever raised but on a farm? And where do they go if not from the farm to the table?

Every night a parade of diners streams through our kitchen because it's the only way to get to the wine cellar, which is a private party room that accommodates twenty people or so. The room used to be part of our original wine storage area, which was behind the kitchen, so nobody went there except the staff. Now, though, people passing through get a real fly-on-the-wall look at our kitchen dynamics. Between the mike bellowing orders and the guys transporting huge trays of food up or down the back staircase and the line cooks dancing around each other trying not to step on toes—there's a lot of action. Years ago when I was a line cook, Whoopi Goldberg came in for dinner. She wanted to learn how to make *pommes soufflés,* so they sent her over to me and I gave her an apron and showed her how we do it. Don Rickles came through right about that same time, cracking jokes as usual. On his way back from the wine cellar, he heard me expediting the service and he came up behind me: "You! Boy! Are you the chef?" "Oh, no, sir. Not yet." So he looks at one of the grill guys and he goes, "Make him the chef! You hear me?" And he walks out like he owns the place. I'm not sure who they thought he was. But they did make me the chef . . . eventually. I met Bill Clinton when he was president and came in for dinner with Hillary. The Kennedys have been here, too. Actually, I think other than George W., every U.S. president since FDR has dined under our roof.

These days I relax by cooking at home for my family. It's crazy, because we're only four people and I'm so used to ordering food for hundreds at a time that, well, I've been known to overdo it a bit. My wife'll be the first to tell you. I kept track once and I realized that I'm spending fourteen hundred dollars a month on food just for my family, not counting going out to restaurants. What the hell am I spending all this money on? I buy tons of food on the weekend, cook it all up, and my wife just throws it out. I have five different smokers in my backyard, so I might make three or four racks of ribs, of which my wife eats two. Ribs—not racks. The rest? Grill-to-garbage-can.

My son is seven, and with his eyes closed, he can tell you what's in just about any dish I make. My daughter, who's eight, eats quinoa, short ribs, and every vegetable under the sun. She's been doing it her whole life. But she'll have friends over and they say, "I don't eat this, I don't eat that." And they turn up their noses at all the good stuff. When I asked one of them what she *did* eat, she said, "I only eat popcorn and chicken nuggets and cookies. My mom lets me." Welcome to the future.

Toni Robertson

MANDARIN ORIENTAL

The wine room of Asiate restaurant, with its sixteen-foot-high picture windows, is on the thirty-fifth floor of the Mandarin Oriental hotel. I'm waiting for her there, at a long table that runs down the center of the room. She's a few minutes late, but I don't mind. I'm completely mesmerized by the breathtaking views of Central Park, and by the continuous yellow blur of taxis weaving their way through traffic on the streets below. On the wall behind me, a thousand bottles of wine sparkle as if they were polished just ten minutes ago. A glistening tree branch sculpture hangs from the ceiling.

She arrives, wearing a black chef's outfit with the hotel's logo emblazoned in gold near the collar. An ex-member of the U.S. Air Force, this small woman with dark hair pulled back into a tight ponytail speaks softly as she apologizes for running late. She hasn't been in New York all that long, but her reputation is well known. She was the first female executive chef in the history of not one but two countries—South Africa and Singapore. And she has won some of the culinary world's most prestigious awards.

I was born and raised in Mandalay, Burma. I have six sisters, five of whom are doctors, as are my parents. I'm clearly the black sheep in the family. Growing up, even though we were middle class, we always had a cook. I loved hanging out with her in the kitchen because that's where the action was. The cook would say, "Okay, Toni, if you're going to be hanging around, you're going to make yourself useful." And she'd give me the garlic and the onions to peel.

We left Burma when I was fifteen. The country wasn't stable, and for us, being of Chinese blood, it wasn't safe. We ended up in Chicago. From the time we arrived in this country, I always said that because they took us in so readily, one day I would pay them back, and I did. When I graduated, I enlisted in the U.S. Air Force for four years. With all those doctors in my family, I felt comfortable signing up as a medic. I was lucky enough to be stationed at a hospital in a little town called Spangdahlem, Germany, which is where I became infused with my love of cooking. I worked the night shift in the emergency room. So at two or three in the morning, whoever was around would show up and we'd all cook and eat together. We often found old copies of *Bon Appétit* and *Food & Wine* lying around in the waiting room, and we'd use them to create something delicious.

Spangdahlem is an hour or two by train from Paris. In an effort to eat at as many different restaurants as I could, every opportunity I had, I took the train to somewhere I'd never been. I literally ate my way through Europe; it was fantastic. I'm certain that those experiences were central to my decision to one day become a professional chef. But there was a problem. In an Asian family, cooking, and in fact working in any service industry, is not a face-saving occupation; it just isn't done. My parents wanted me to be a doctor like my sisters. Or if not that, then a housewife. Anything other than a chef. But this was what I wanted. And even knowing I was disappointing them, I pursued it.

Once I got out of the military, I returned home and enrolled in culinary school in Chicago. When I graduated, I applied to the five best restaurants in Chicago, one of which happened to be the dining room at the Ritz-Carlton hotel. At the time, the French chef Fernand Gutierrez ran the kitchen. Of all the places I interviewed, he was the only one willing to hire me. I was the only woman on his service, so initially he gave me the option of what I considered (and he probably did too) "girl" chores. That meant working in the pantry doing salad or doing pastry. Pastry is too exacting for my taste—you have to measure everything and do it all by the book. So I opted for salad, where I believed I could be more creative.

Did I say creative? That's a joke. No sooner had I signed on than they sent me to the dungeon to wash lettuce for the whole hotel. Every day, for six months, I washed lettuce. Nothing else. Just lettuce. My hands were freezing and my fingers numb all the time. But I didn't complain. I kept at it and I waited. In six months, a *garde-manger* position became available and I moved into the "cold" kitchen, making canapés, salads, and appetizers. I was still cold, but at least I wasn't wet all the time.

And then, one day, I got my first real break. Chef was looking for someone to help him bone chicken and I just happened to be in the right place at the right time. I volunteered, and the next thing I knew, I had tiptoed my way into the "hot" kitchen—the only female cook on the hot line. That was a real milestone, because the perception at that time—even though a woman cooks at home—was that as a career job, being a cook was man's work. Sure it's physical, it's grueling, and you're constantly on your feet, but what difference does it make if you're male or female? In my kitchen today, 50 percent of my line cooks are female. Before long, I became a *saucier*, which, in a French-style restaurant like the Ritz-Carlton, is the last station before *sous chef*. In a matter of four years, I had gone from washing lettuce to *saucier*, which is amazing— and very lucky for any cook, and particularly for a woman.

From Chicago, I began my world travels, always working at different hotels. The Beverly Hills Four Seasons hotel recruited me to be executive *sous chef* at their restaurant, and from there I went to the Grand Wailea in Maui, and then to the Palace hotel in South Africa, where I scored my first executive chef's position. That was exciting, because it was the first time in the history of that country that a woman held an executive chef position. I followed that job with a stint as executive chef at the five-star Pan Pacific hotel in Singapore—another first for a female in that country.

And then it was time to come home. Anyone in this field knows, if you move too far away from the United States, you lose what's going on. So when, in 2005, the then three-year-old Mandarin Oriental in New York offered me the position I hold today, I was thrilled. Even though I must admit, at first the thought of being here scared me. Really, what did I know about New York? That it's an international hub with big business, and big money? Yes. That people know incredibly good food here? Yes. That great chefs are made in this town? Yes. Last question: Am I good enough to be here? In the end, that didn't matter. It was love at first sight and I wasn't leaving. There's nothing like New York. Nothing in the world.

There is a vast difference between working as an executive chef in a freestanding restaurant and in a hotel. In a freestanding restaurant, the concept is set and the chef has only the restaurant to take care of.

A steak house is a perfect example. You come in to work, and you cook steak. Next day, you cook steak again. Next day, same thing. Sure, you change the menu once in a while, but it's still a lot of repetition. Come to work, cook maybe two hundred covers, and at the end of the day, you're finished. You close the doors and the next day you start all over again. It's like *Groundhog Day*. My job is never over. I can never say, "Done! Closing! It's midnight. Shut the door. Tomorrow we start again!" No. I'm here twenty-four hours. Or at least I'm accountable for twenty-four hours. Seven days a week. Twenty-four/seven, the buck stops here.

As hotel executive chef, my purview includes anything and everything that has to do with food. This means menus, budgets, purchasing, and staff for every one of our food-related venues. And there are a lot of them. Let's start with the smallest area: The minibar. We make sure it's stocked with the food and drinks a guest might like, and if there's something special they require, we add it. Our cocktail lounge on the thirty-sixth floor serves bar food. Then there's room service. Say an international guest checks in at midnight and he's hungry for breakfast. Or an Asian with jet lag wakes up at two in the morning wanting a Chinese snack. We're on it. We're always filling personalized requests. This month is Ramadan, so I'll provide large and early meals for the Muslims, who celebrate it by fasting between sunrise and sunset. A Hollywood film star checks in and she's preparing for a movie role that requires her to be on a 1,200-calorie diet. We happily accommodate her. We cater business parties and banquets. And then there's Asiate restaurant, which is the star of our hotel, and which, like any freestanding restaurant, is open to the public for breakfast, lunch, and dinner. That's all our front-of-the-house dining.

But as important as it is, the back of the house is equally as significant. Four hundred employees work here around the clock, and it's up to me to keep them fed when they're here. They eat in a large employee cafeteria downstairs. We provide food for them, plus all the policemen from the street who work this area. It's always good to invite in the cops, so that if anything happens and we call, they respond quickly. Those guys love our food and they're here a lot! Because I'm a New Yorker, I don't drive. But if I did, I don't think I'd ever get a ticket.

Even though mentally I'm never really off duty, I have a life and a family I go home to at night just like everyone else. And when I get home, again like everyone else, I'm hungry. My colleagues in the kitchen at work wonder why I don't eat there, but I'm picky with my food. I like to cook for myself. Depending on what I'm craving, I generally do something really easy. If I'm craving pasta, I'll have a pot of spaghetti going on and I'll sit and enjoy it after work. That's my downtime. That and, believe it or not, running marathons—of which I've completed six in my eight years in New York.

Jeb Burke

NEWS CORPORATION

After high school, he traveled the world for three years, doing oil exploration in the Northwest and living on small islands along St. Barth's, until his father told him the time had come to get serious about life. "I thought, 'Okay, I'll be a chef,' and I enrolled in the Culinary Institute. I did my externship alongside Bobby Flay at Joe Allen's on 46th Street. Like me, Bobby was a young kid, trying to figure out what he wanted to do in life. We were line cooks together, and good friends. He went on to become this famous celebrity chef with his own restaurants and TV program, and I'm happily ensconced in the board-room at News Corporation. Two guys who clearly ended up just where they wanted to be."

It's been an amazing ride. While I was training at the CIA, who would've thought I'd end up sailing around the world on some glorious, private luxury yachts within the first month of graduation? Or that I would end up as the corporate chef for one of the largest publishing magnates in the world? But here I am.

My first job out of cooking school, I flew to Ladue in St. Louis County, Missouri, to work as a personal chef for an elderly gentleman, his wife, and his ninety-eight-year-old mother. Two months later, the three of them got into the backseat of their Rolls-Royce stretch limo, I hopped onto my big motorcycle, and we made our way to West Palm Beach, where we boarded their hundred-foot yacht. From there, we sailed to Cat Key, off the coast of the Bahamas, where we lived and I cooked for the family. Eventually, the family went home and I moved on to other boats. For the next two years, I cooked and sailed up and down the East Coast to Halifax, Nova Scotia, and then across the Atlantic to Brest, France.

Two gentlemen who were big into real estate in Florida owned one of the ships I cooked on. They both got seasick whenever the boat went out to sea, so they never traveled with us. They'd tell us where to go, they'd fly there and would meet us at the port. When the boat was tied up in the marina, they lived and entertained on it. But before we untied the lines, they got off, climbed aboard their private jet, and flew to the next location. Which meant we crew had the boat to ourselves. We had ski boats, Jet Skis, and scooters. All of this amazing stuff that we could use at will. It was a great life for a twenty-year-old. But how long can you keep it up?

During my time at sea, I kept in touch with some of my classmates from the Culinary Institute. One of my buddies worked as Rupert Murdoch's personal chef. He asked me if I'd like to work with him at the corporate headquarters in New York City. New York sounded great to me, and I figured it was time I jumped off the boats. So I joined him.

We worked together for about a year, and when my friend left to open his own restaurant, Mr. Murdoch asked me to stay on board. That was twenty-one years ago and I'm still here.

All this time, I never wanted to move on to a big restaurant. Sure, I've dreamt about it on occasion, and in fact I've been offered several opportunities to open restaurants or go to private clubs. But that was not for me. Most chefs I know work evenings, holidays, and every time their children are off from school. I chose to stick with the corporate world so I could be a good husband and a dedicated parent to my two young boys. They don't stay young very long.

I've seen so many changes here over the past two decades. When I first started working here, my day began at six thirty a.m. We did a continental breakfast for whoever might want it, and a hot lunch for the executives. That was it. Day's over! But as the company grew, so did the responsibilities of the food staff. We've become a much bigger operation today. We have eight full-time cooks, chefs, bartenders, and stewards, and fifteen to twenty part-timers who come in as needed. Which is often, because we cater screenings for Fox Paramount two or three nights a week in our in-house twenty-five-seat movie theater. We do cocktails and hors d'oeuvres prior to the screenings, and desserts and coffee at the end. We cover the Fox Sports hospitality suite on the second floor, where we do a lot of entertaining for the NFL, the NHL, NASCAR, and baseball.

Our floor is a real rabbit warren of dining rooms. Mr. Murdoch's private dining room seats four people. The next one down seats six. Dining room three holds maybe eight to ten, and four holds twelve to fifteen people. Our A, B, C, and D dining rooms can accommodate anywhere from ten to thirty-five people. The dining facility is exclusive to the top executives. Mr. Murdoch, of course, and his inner circle—his sons, James and Lachlan, and Roger Ailes, who's president of Fox News Channel. He's got a great sense of humor, Mr. Ailes. He'll call down and request a fried chicken sandwich or a hamburger, and he'll say, "Jeb, if my wife calls, tell her I ate the fish today."

Every day I try to have a different menu for the executives. Early in the morning, my *sous chef* and I look for the freshest fish, fruits, and vegetables available that day, and from that we put together the luncheon choices. Once the food is on hand, we start preparing. Before you know it, it's lunchtime in one or more of our dining rooms. When the guests arrive, I put on a fresh chef jacket, walk into each of the dining rooms, greet our guests, and offer a verbal menu. There's always a fresh fruit or vegetable juice, a fish, poultry, some kind of meat, and pasta. We have vegetarian options if someone requests it. We serve anywhere from two to fifty people a day. Yesterday, we served twenty-five. Today, it's quiet. Mr. Murdoch will be in with two guests and a couple of the other executives, and that's it.

One of the great things about being a chef in a corporate environment—at least this one—is that in terms of the quality of the food we serve, we get to use the best of the best ingredients. And as a result, we create great food. Because we're not a moneymaking operation, we don't have to follow any budgets or any restraints like a lot of these big hotels and restaurants, where the executive chefs have to worry about money at the end of the month. Not to have to cater to a bottom line is a huge pressure-lifter. When I go out to pick ingredients for a meal, I'm like a kid in a candy store. To have such free rein is truly a chef's dream. Another perk is how many interesting people we get to cook for. They're continually streaming in and out. For example, when dignitaries from Saudi Arabia visit us, they travel in very large groups. They bring friends and family and their own heavy security. Sometimes they even bring in people who are filming the visit. On those days, we might have twenty-five to thirty people showing up for lunch.

I've cooked here for a number of our former presidents. Bill Clinton is the coolest. He's very engaging and seems to truly enjoy interacting with everyone. I said to him one day, "I heard you have a great appetite, Mr. President," and he said, "How'd you hear that?" I said, "I just heard a rumor saying you loved food." "Well, you got that right, Jeb," he said. "What do you have for me?" Very outgoing. He always asks me questions: How many kids do I have? Where am I from? It was a real pleasure to cook for him and get to know him. Mayor Ed Koch, our ex-mayor of New York City, was another politician who would come in here all the time and chat with me and my staff. He was a unique and flamboyant guy, and everyone loved when he came in for lunch.

When I go into the dining room at lunchtime to present the menu, for confidentiality purposes and just because it's expected of me, I keep my blinders on and never listen or pay much attention to what anyone is saying. Sometimes if there's a high-power meeting going on and they're talking numbers and stocks or any company business, we're not even allowed to walk into the dining room. Mostly, though, I come in and welcome them, I tell them what we're serving, ask if they have any dietary restrictions or restraints, and explain that we can try to do anything they would like. If they engage in conversation, like President Clinton, I will engage. If it's a very, very quiet kind of meeting, I offer the food choices and make a quick exit. I know instinctively when to talk and when not to. And I never ask for autographs or take pictures with anyone. Never, never. My friends always want to know, "Why don't you have a photograph with these celebrities?" My reply is, "If I did that, I would not have lasted here for twenty minutes, let alone twenty years." That's the corporate facts. There's absolutely no doubt in my mind about that.

Luísa Fernandes

ROBERT

This is the story of a Portuguese woman who followed her dreams through peace and war, Africa and America, marriage and divorce. Grit, guts, passion, and drive all rolled into one small individual who struggles with the English language, but who makes herself perfectly understood in her restaurant's kitchen. And nationally as well, if you want to include her first-place prize on the Food Network program Chopped.

I am a person who has always known what I wanted. And I am a person with dreams. Not one, but two. My first was to be a nurse. Always I have this in my soul to help persons in need. My second dream was to be a chef. I am very lucky. I got to do both dreams.

I grew up in a small town called Monte Real, which is outside of Lisbon, Portugal. I got my nursing degree there—my first dream—when I was twenty years old. My first job was in a psychiatric hospital. I stayed there a few years, but I saw this is not enough action for me. So I became an operating room nurse working with orthopedic surgeons. This was the time of the wars in Rwanda and Sudan. From my home,

I would read how very bad things were there, and that these countries were desperately in need of nurses. So I volunteered to join Médecins Sans Frontières—Doctors Without Borders. They needed surgical nurses badly. Right away they sent me to Sudan. Everything is so rudimentary there. It is such a poor country. No helicopters, no water, no hospitals, no food, no medicine. No nothing. The Red Cross provides medicines and tents and people to work with, but they can't get these important things to the most desperate areas because it's too dangerous to travel on the ground. The only way in is by helicopter or plane. And with no landing fields, you have to parachute in to get the supplies where they are needed. As soon as I saw people doing that, I said, "This is for me!" I was thirty-six years old at the time, but I wanted to become a parachuting nurse.

I went to school for a year to learn. My first assignments were in Angola and Kosovo. We went up thirteen thousand feet, jumped out of the plane, and opened our parachutes at one thousand feet. Always we were carrying a load of supplies with us, and almost always we jumped at night, when it's safer, because the radar can't see you. In all, along with a dozen or so engineers, nurses, and doctors, I made 347 jumps. Was I scared? Of course I was scared! But feeling scared is a good sensation in your body. It's like a war between you and you. It means you have to tell yourself to be stronger. It's no different from working in the operating room when people are brought in after an accident and limbs are missing or every bone in their body is broken. You see this and your body goes into panic mode, so it immediately secretes adrenaline. Then the battle is between you and your panic, and you must not let the panic win. Take a deep breath. Do something. Make decisions right away to save your patient. Same thing in war. Everyone is scared. When I was jumping, I saw men with a thousand jumps behind them and still they are sometimes scared, too.

Even as a nurse, always the part of me that is a cook comes with me. In Rwanda, while I was assisting with surgery, I also taught the mothers to cook for their families. I showed them how to find fruits and greens and to make food from them. These people weigh seventy-five pounds a person. So skinny. So dried up. Right away I am thinking, "I want to feed them." All the time. All I can think about is, "Get them some nice food. I don't care how."

This passion for feeding people has been going on since I worked my first job at the psychiatric hospital in Lisbon. In that place, they would bring the food for the patients in a cart with two pots and some bread. I looked in each pot and I couldn't say if this is the soup or the main course. It all looked the same. Just mashed together. So I went to the director, and I said, "If you are feeding the patients fish and rice and beans and cabbage, why the guys in the kitchen don't do a good job?" I'm twenty-one years old at this time. Looking still like a kid. And the director stares at me and he says, "What are you talking about?" I said, "If you're spending money on chicken and rice and cabbage and beans, why the guys in the kitchen mix everything up like a soup? It's disgusting! Why don't you use the same rice and for the same cost, make a good rice dish? Take the chicken and fry it?" And the guy says, "Okay, Nurse. I'll think about it."

So one day he tells the head nurse, "The young nurse Luísa comes and tells me this and this and I agree with her. Our food for the patients is like the jail." The chief nurse gives me permission. I go to the kitchen and I give them recipes for protein and vegetables and pasta. I ended up with a gold medal because I did a good service, not just as a nurse, but because I did a good job as a cook! Always the cook things come into my life. Always. Wherever I am.

So now comes how I became a chef.

I worked two years with Médecins Sans Frontières before I returned to the hospital in Portugal again as an operating room nurse. But remember, I had two dreams. Dream one is be a nurse, and the second is to be a chef. I have these two wars in me. And what is the natural thing? To do both. In 1998, I took another risk, and with no professional culinary experience, none, I opened a little restaurant, Tachos de São Bento, in Lisbon. Right away it was a huge success. It was full all the time and won some very important awards. But no matter how busy it was, I never quit my nursing job. I worked days in the hospital and nighttime in my restaurant, which was open only for dinner. I was happy. But not completely.

Here is my third dream, which I didn't talk about before. It's going to New York City. This dream is with me since I am fourteen years old, in 1969, when I saw on TV that the American men go to the moon. I knew then that America is a country like no other. I also saw on TV a movie with Liza Minnelli. And I remember after that movie saying to my mother, "I am going to New York City. I want to live there." And my mother tells me about Al Capone and she says, "No! Is too far!" I stormed out of the room and I yelled back at her, "You say no, but one day I go!"

Years passed. I had been through the wars, opened my restaurant, gotten married and divorced, had two children. And the whole time New York City was in the back of my head. Then, when my children grew up with homes and jobs and didn't need me anymore, I realized it was time; it was now or never. In 2004, after a good five-year run, I closed my restaurant in Lisbon, retired from the hospital, left everything behind, and headed to New York City. I was almost fifty years old.

Seven days after I got here, I found a job as a pastry chef in a Portuguese restaurant in the West Village. I believe in God. And I believe this was meant to be. Just the day before, the pastry chef in the restaurant quit. The owners right away made me the visa application. So I'm now in New York for seven days and already I have a job and a visa in the works. This is okay. But my dream is not complete. I'm working in a Portuguese restaurant but what I want is an American restaurant. I have now a Social Security number. I want American restaurant! I want America, America! Again everyone tells me I'm crazy. I have everything, they say. But I don't have everything. I wanted American restaurant. And I found.

The restaurant was called Park Blue. It was on 58th Street in Manhattan. They knew about Tachos de São Bento. They tried me out and they gave me a job as *sous chef*. It was an American restaurant that served American cuisine. Oysters on the half shell, tuna tartare, eggs Benedict, hamburgers. It was wonderful. I loved cooking American food and I wanted to know more, to keep getting better as a chef. I bought a million books. I read old menus. I studied all the time when I was not working. And with the money I earned, I went by myself for dinner at Jean Georges. I went to Daniel. I bought a book by Alfred Portale, chef of Gotham Bar and Grill, and I became a regular customer at his restaurant. I went at lunchtime when is not so expensive.

While I was *sous chef* at Park Blue—which had a Michelin star—the chef was let go and I was hired as executive chef. And now it's all perfect. I am in New York. I am at an American restaurant. I am an executive chef. I was so happy. Our kitchen stayed open until three in the morning, so chefs from other restaurants came in at nighttime. They relaxed, took a glass of wine, ate something, and went home. I met everybody. Chefs from Jean-Georges. Gordon Ramsay. Marcus Samuelsson. I became myself a little famous.

And then . . .

Like happens so much in New York, after I was working as executive chef for two years, the building our restaurant was in was sold, and the new owners decided to tear the whole thing down and put up a new one. Park Blue shut down for good. Am I out of a job? Yes, I am. But not for even a single day. I knew so many good people and I got hired right away by another restaurant. And then another and then another. And then I learned from a good friend that Robert—a most beautiful restaurant on the top of the Museum of Art and Design building on Columbus Circle—was looking for an executive chef. After I make an interview and have the test and another food test, I got the job! And here I am today. Luísa Fernandes at Robert. On top of the world!

Even though I so much love America, I can never forget my Portuguese roots. I have instituted Portuguese night at Robert where the whole menu celebrates the food from my country, and I organized Portugal Day in Central Park. This is the third year and it's going strong.

One day, Jorge Sampaio, the past president of Portugal, was in town for a meeting at the United Nations. He came up for dinner by himself. He never told anyone he was coming, and I wasn't even here when he showed up. I was home. My reservations person called me and she said, "Chef, in the restaurant right now is the president of your country! He has come just to meet you!" I said, "Oh my God. You're kidding!" I took a cab and in ten minutes I'm in the restaurant. I run into the back, put on my whites, and come out to his table like I have been there all along.

I sat down with him and I asked why he didn't tell me he was coming. He said, "You know, I'm a simple person. I go everywhere and I don't say who I am. The only reason I told the woman up front was because I wanted to meet you and I knew you would come out if you knew I was here. I wanted to say thank you for being an example for everybody in Portugal." This is one thing I cannot explain to you in words my pride that this man, the ex-president of my country, came to my restaurant in America to meet me. I can't say ever how much that meant to me.

PART V

The Party Line

In the gospel of Sally Quinn, the veteran Washington hostess and author, there's only one reason to throw a party. And that's to enjoy the hell out of it. "If you don't care about having fun," she opined, "then have a meeting."

And if you do care about having fun, I might add, then have a caterer. Please.

These days, someone's got to worry about accommodating the lactose-, fructose-, gluten-, and/or nut-phobic crowd. And whether describing the first course as "farm-to-table *petite mâche* and micro-heirloom tomatoes in a *fleur-de-sel* fairy-dust vinaigrette" when a) both mâche and tomatoes spent forty-eight hours on a truck in Milwaukee between farm and table; and b) the *sel* came from Morton's, can be justified with poetic license. And even if it's true that kale sorbet is the new kale salad, as your second cousin's food-critic friend insists, does it really have to make an appearance on the dessert buffet?

Aside from such questions of culinary correctness, there are other, larger matters to resolve. The overall menu planning, for one: What's the right balance between crowd-pleasing and *au courant*, familiar and exotic? Or, for another, navigating the juncture of social event and social media. When, for instance, is a wedding cake still a wedding cake, but better—better tasting, better looking, and more to the point, better for/on Instagram?

Exactly. Leave that kind of worrying to the experts; it's all part of their job description. They know how to deal with fussy eaters, escape the scrutiny of the Food Police, and create YouTube–ready food bites for attention-seeking clients. They also know what's in, what's out, what's so out it's about to cycle in again, and what might never return. Take the triad of caviar, lobster quenelles, and oceans of Cristal, which had its last big moment back in the Reagan era—with no sign of a reprise to date. And that's because the availability of "real," i.e., Iranian or Russian, caviar is nil; most hedge-fund baby billionaires are unlikely to know what a quenelle is; and a single bottle of Cristal, about $150 in the 1980s, goes for $750 today. But it's also about the shifting patterns of collective taste. As with haircuts or architecture or child-rearing, so it goes with party style: Things change.

Once upon a time—say half a century ago—the nonnegotiable prerequisite for a career in high-end catering was to be fluent in French. "Menu French," that is. If you had any hope of rising to the top—say, banquet manager at the Plaza Hotel—the phrase "ice cream" disappeared from your vocabulary, to be replaced by *"crème glacée."* Mastering the art of French menu-speak wasn't just about getting and keeping the boss's favor, either; it impressed clients, who in turn wished to impress their guests by demonstrating their sophisticated knowledge of haute cuisine—and, *bien sûr*, no cuisine was more *haute* than French.

"No formal menus existed in those years," remembers Herb Rose, himself a former banquet manager at the Plaza and Pierre hotels, and now, at eighty-two, an éminence grise of the bespoke party-planning circuit. "You'd sit down with the client and talk about what we could do, and if they asked for fruit salad we'd nod and say, 'Very good.

Macédoine de fruits frais au Grand Marnier.' But all that has changed drastically. Now you present them with a variety of preprinted sample menus, all in English, with elaborate descriptions of the food and what each and every item will cost. There's no mystery to it anymore."

At today's parties, there's the food, and then there's the *presentation* of the food, and lately the importance of the latter equals, and sometimes eclipses, the former. Consider those new canapé platters with built-in lighting. Yes, designed by lighting specialists, and so visually arresting that the canapés themselves don't even register—a good thing if they're not up to snuff. The vogue for live-action food theater extends to oyster-shucking bars and sushi bars manned by their respective experts, working to order. Way more entertaining than just grabbing a prepared piece of California roll off a buffet table.

But back at that party. One thing you *will* want to grab if you find it, probably on a butlered tray, is a glass of water. But not just *any* glass of water (and please, not coconut water; it's *over*). According to my confidential source—a member of the catering crème de la crème, I assure you—the "It" drink of the moment is birch-tree water. You heard it here first.

Chris Edmonds

THE PIERRE HOTEL

For the past eight decades, the Pierre Hotel has been catering high-end events for private clients. Edmonds is one of the banquet managers who have been making these social events happen for twenty years. He looks the part. Tall, thin, and somewhere in his forties, he's dressed in a bespoke suit, perfectly starched collar, subdued tie, and highly polished shoes. He leads me to the hotel's tearoom, which is accessed from the hotel's entrance by walking down a long, gilded passage that takes you past the banquet spaces. For me, it's a trip down memory lane. I have not been to this hotel since my daughter, and then my son, were married here.

Everyone thinks of a wedding as one of the most high-stress events of a lifetime. But it doesn't have to be. The key is organization. And after eighteen years of doing this, that's become one of my strong suits. Our weddings go off like clockwork. Literally. It's really all about making and keeping your time line. You do that, you're home free.

By the time I meet the bride and groom, they've already seen our event spaces and decided to hold their wedding here. My first task is to introduce them to our menu, and we start talking about some choices. That's also when I get a feel of what the crowd will be like, how many people they're planning to invite, and any special things I need to know about the guests. At our next meeting, we have a "tasting." The kitchen puts together five or six appetizers, five or six entrées, five or six desserts, and a selection of wines to try. We'll sit together and eat a bit of each, and from that they'll choose what they want to serve. Next, we sign the contracts. So far, so good.

We may talk on the phone a few times in between, but I generally don't see them again until the day before the wedding, when they show up for the rehearsal. Normally, the rehearsal dinner is held at a different venue, but the wedding party comes here first. For the next hour or so, we rehearse the processional and recessional, and determine where members of the bridal party are going to stand or sit, and then we send them on their way to the dinner. That night, which is almost always the night before the wedding, we give the bride a room upstairs so she can sleep here if she wants to. It's hers the next day as well.

The morning of the wedding, I come in at about ten o'clock, check in with the bride, and check with the kitchen to make sure my guys have delivered some amenities to her room. I'll check to make sure that the wedding gown has arrived and that it's safely in the bride's room. That day, the groom gets a room for himself and his groomsmen, so for him, we'll send up an assortment of beers and sandwiches.

Next, I turn my attention to the party rooms for the ceremony, cocktails, and dinner. I check on the florist to make sure they're not only setting up but also cleaning up as they go, make sure they're positioning their centerpieces on the tables in the dining room as well as the cocktail buffets. Meanwhile, the dinner tables are being set by my house staff. Around three o'clock, I talk with the bride and groom to learn who'll be making speeches and when. Who'll be greeting the guests when they first come in? Is there going to be a father-daughter, mother-son dance? Once I get this information, I go to the office and type up a time line, making copies for the chef, the captains, the bandleader, and whoever else might need it. The time line includes a minute-by-minute report of what should be happening and when, from the time the ceremony begins until it ends. The idea is to make sure the minute the ceremony is over, the waiters are ready for the incoming guests.

If the ceremony is over at seven, cocktails will go on for the next hour. That's generally when I summon the bride and groom and the parents and take them to see the reception room. The lights are low, the candles lit, the flowers overflowing. Somehow that first view of the ballroom is always breathtaking. I love to see the look on their faces when I open the doors. They light up! Imagine getting to experience this feeling every week. This has to be the best job in the world.

Around eight, we invite the guests into the ballroom, and after everyone is seated, at around eight twenty, the bride and groom are introduced for the first time as husband and wife. At that point, I signal the bandleader to begin playing music. They have their first dance, and then if it's a Jewish wedding, they go into a hora, which really gets the crowd going. From there, everyone sits down and we start serving the first course.

I'm pretty much around the whole evening—checking in with the bride and groom, reminding them that they can have anything they want. When the cake is served, I show them exactly how to cut it, and then step out of the way so the photographer can get the "feeding the wedding cake" picture. At the end of the night, we send up a package of memorabilia to the wedding suite. It will have the top of the cake, which we've boxed, along with any presents, leftover programs, menu cards. And if it's a Jewish wedding, the tallis, the broken glass, and the kiddush cup.

Does every wedding run smoothly? Generally, yes. Have we had any disasters? Of course we have. Not major ones, thank God, but people are human and there are always times when that human element comes into play. And sometimes that human element can get pretty bad. Those are the ones you don't forget. Like what happened recently. We were setting up for a six o'clock wedding. The bride and groom were upstairs in their respective rooms. It was beautiful outside, snowing lightly. At three p.m., I was in the dining room checking on some last-minute things when the maid of honor came downstairs to find me. She said, "Chris, the bride is calling off the wedding." I said, "What are you talking about?" She told me that, at the last minute, the bride decided she just didn't want to go through with it. I said, "What about the party?" And she said, "Nope. She doesn't want the party, either. Just call the whole thing off." And that was it.

I felt terrible. The table settings were beautiful; the florist did a fantastic job. The place was glorious. And of course I felt awful for the bride and groom. Who knows what set it off? We're never privy to any of that stuff. As the guests arrived, we had our people stationed at the door to tell them, "We're very sorry, but the wedding has been canceled. The bride and groom will be in touch." The band packed up and went home, and we were left to break down this astonishingly beautiful room. We called City Harvest, an organization that provides food to the needy, and we told them to come and get the food. I'm sure there were a lot of homeless men and women who didn't understand what the story was behind their feast, but I'm equally sure that they enjoyed it. For everyone else, though, it was a real shame.

Before you head into this type of work, you really have to give some thought to whether or not you want a career that's going to take you away from everything. Well, maybe not everything, but you do miss a lot of life. The absolute first requirement, if you have a family, is an understanding and patient wife and children. You're here so many hours, and most often these are the hours that your children are home. So you miss a lot of their growing up. But you can't sign a client on, work with them through the entire buildup, and then say, "I'm sorry, I have family to get back to. Someone else will be covering me during your wedding."

I knew what was ahead of me eighteen years ago when I signed on to do this. I was never the kind of guy who could take being stuck behind a desk every day, or behind a computer. Despite having curveballs thrown at me all the time, I find this work so meaningful. I actually like resolving problems. When people tell me there's a problem, I say, "It's not a problem. It's only an issue that needs resolution." And we don't just do weddings here. We have parties and banquets for major organizations—both society and business—as well. So it's party time any night of the week! Now, how many other jobs would let you watch people enjoy themselves like this?

One of the requirements for what I do is: You have to have a little ADHD. Or a lot. Because you're always moving, and you often have to change gears on a dime. Thinking about what's going on now, what's going on the next day. You have to be three or four steps ahead. You have to learn to ask a lot of questions because being informed puts you in a better light and sets you up for a fantastic event. You have to speak quickly, react quickly, and be prepared to put out fires, because you're always doing that. Oh, and while you're at it, don't forget to smile.

What are the trade-offs? On balance you get some pretty amazing perks. We recently did a wedding for the daughter of an extremely affluent family. They hired Stevie Wonder—one of my all-time favorites—to sing. He always has a little prayer meeting backstage with his people before he goes on, and because I was there, they invited me to join them. So there I am, eyes closed, standing in a circle shoulder to shoulder with Stevie Wonder. You're talking perks. That, to me, was fantastic.

I adore music and, yes, I get a little star-struck in the presence of a famous musician. But it's funny; movie stars just don't do it for me. Maybe because I don't have time to go to the movies. And I don't watch a lot of TV, so I don't know who the latest stars are. But the truth is, I don't know who the latest rock stars are, either. Just ask my kids. Lady Gaga came in a few years ago and I didn't have a clue who she was. It was terrible. I have two children, twelve and nine. I came home and I told them, "Oh, this woman named Lady Gaga was at the hotel tonight." And they're like, "What? Lady Gaga? Really? Wow! Dad, you don't know who that is?" And then I told my niece; she started carrying on, "Oh my God! That's crazy! That's crazy!" And I'm standing there scratching my head. "Okay, okay. Who is she, already?"

Tony Bennett performed here a couple of times. Now, *him* I knew.

Lulu Powers

"It's really small," she says while leading me inside her midtown Manhattan apartment. She indicates her kitchen/classroom, which she had described to me earlier as two feet by two feet. It's actually more like four by five. Powers is blond, with sparkling blue eyes and more energy than the whole U.S. hockey team; it's easy to see why one city is not large enough to contain her.

I was a kid when I took on my first private chef job. I was sixteen years old, in Nantucket with my family for the summer, and working part time for a woman named Sarah Leah Chase in her gourmet food shop called Que Sera Sarah. I manned the counter and helped in the kitchen. One day, Richard Menschel, a New Yorker with a home on the island, came into the shop and asked Sarah if she knew of a private chef who could help him out over the summer. Sarah suggested me. He called me, asked me a few questions, and hired me over the phone, never asking my age. So when I showed up at his door, he took one look at me and said, "You're Lulu?" I'm small and blond, and with my hair in a ponytail, I looked even younger than I was. I'm sure I was not at all what he expected, but he agreed to try me out.

The family lived in a great old stone house with huge formal rooms. The third night I was there, I'm in the kitchen cooking when suddenly I heard a buzzer go off. I ran into the dining room yelling, "Mr. Menschel, there's a fire! It's in the house!" He said, "No, Lulu. That's how we call you in from the kitchen." They had a buzzer on the floor underneath the dining room table which, when you stepped on it, called forth whoever was in the kitchen. I had never seen one of those before. But you know, I was sixteen.

At the end of that summer, I went back to high school, and when I graduated, I moved to the city. I attended college here, and while I was in college, I started catering dinner parties for anyone who asked me. At one of these parties, one of the guests—a very, very wealthy man— called me aside and told me there wasn't a single person working in his home who could cook worth anything. Did I have any suggestions? I offered to teach his house workers in my apartment—never mentioning that my kitchen was two feet by two feet. He sent me three women to start and I taught them the best I could, considering they spoke Spanish and I spoke none. And, typical of the New York mentality, I don't think we had done more than two lessons when I got calls from other people with housekeepers. Soon I was running a little school for a bunch of women from different households—and, I should add, different countries. All in my tiny apartment with its very tiny kitchen.

It was hysterical. The limousines would drive up and discharge the women in front of my building and I'd buzz them in. I did a six-week program where they would come once a week for the day. Most of these women didn't speak English either. But as best I could, I taught them basic recipes, I wrote the recipes down in these little books. I took them to Fairway Market and showed them how to shop. Personally, I think they couldn't have cared less, but they went along with it, smiling away. At the end of the day, the drivers would come get them, and I would send them home with the food they had made.

In 1994, I decided to move out to Los Angeles. I left New York with a suitcase, a tennis racquet, and a plan to write TV sitcoms. I decided that once I hit L.A., I would be finished with my cooking career. And I was. Until out of the blue, one day I got a call from Sigourney Weaver wanting to know if I was available to work for her as a private chef. "Wait a minute," I said, "don't you want to taste my food?" "Oh, yeah," she said, "sure. I'm staying for a while at the Four Seasons hotel. Why don't you bring something over here tomorrow at six p.m." I made a swordfish dinner with a tomato basil orange salsa. I made fancy jasmine rice and broiled zucchini, and I put Saran Wrap over everything and presented it to the hotel's concierge. Sigourney called me an hour later and told me I was hired.

Sigourney is a New Yorker at heart, but she was out in L.A. for work. From the Four Seasons, she had moved into a rented house in Bel Air. I continued to cook for her, but I didn't do it at her house. Mostly, her driver picked up the food from my house at ten a.m. for lunch, and then came back and picked it up at three for dinner.

After that, I became bicoastal. Shuttling back and forth from New York to L.A. to New York. I cooked privately for Madonna in L.A. She had a macrobiotic chef but I would do stuff, too. I have to say, she is an inspiration. I think she's awesome. She's the hardest worker. You see her in action, you can't help but be inspired. She let me do what I did and she did what she does. She's Madonna, you know? What's left to say?

One day, when I was back in New York, I got a call from Jeffrey

Steingarten, who was writing an article about private chefs for *Vogue* magazine. He wanted to interview me for the piece. No sooner did the magazine hit the stands than I got a phone call from Herb Ritts—one of the biggest fashion photographers of his time. I worked for him part time in both L.A. and New York for fifteen years, and I think that was when I really came into my own as a chef.

We had some pretty amazing times together, Herb and I. The one that stands out most in my memory began with a phone call on a Friday morning at seven thirty a.m. It was Herb, telling me that he was having a guest that night and he wanted me to do these cute little Cornish game hens. I said of course I would. I hadn't told him that two days earlier, I received a call from the White House asking me to cook for President Clinton. At first, I thought that call was a joke, you know? It was right around the time of the impeachment trials and maybe someone was being funny. But the woman said, "You were highly recommended by the Blue Ribbon Society"—that's this little WASPy society I had cooked for earlier—"and we would *looove* for you to do this luncheon. It's to be a hoedown. Barbecued chicken, real simple. For the president and the press corps. At a private residence."

I hadn't told Herb yet, because it wasn't confirmed until late that Friday afternoon. So that Friday evening, I get to his house, and I walk in the front door to find him busy showing his photography to this woman who I saw only from the back. The two of them subsequently came into the kitchen as I'm washing my hands, and Herb says, "Lulu, I want you to meet my friend." I turned around and it's Monica Lewinsky! He was shooting her for *Vanity Fair* magazine. Running through my head was, "Oh my God! Who am I going to call first?" No one can say they cooked for Monica Lewinsky and the president in the same week! And yet, there I was, an hour later, standing in Herb Ritts's kitchen, talking to Monica Lewinsky about Martha Stewart paint colors, like two old girlfriends.

The Clinton luncheon was for thirty people. He was unbelievably charming, and it turned out to be a real success. Six months later I saw him again at a party for Rock the Vote, which I attended with a friend. There were fifty people waiting in line to be photographed with him, and when he saw me coming, he stepped aside and said, "I know you! You're the caterer that made the amazing brownies." I had made these caramel fudge brownies the day I cooked for him and he remembered. I got the same feeling being around Bill Clinton as I did from Richard Gere. That chill when you're in the presence of someone really special. Yes, I cooked for Richard Gere, too.

Lest you think this job is all about hobnobbing with movie stars, politicians, and masters of the universe where everything always comes off perfectly, it's not and it doesn't. Disasters happen, too. But it's how you get through them that separates the proverbial men from the boys. And, if I must say so myself, I am a master in my own right at doing that. Sink or swim, I'll swim any way I have to.

I learned how early enough. At my very first catering job. It was to be a big buffet party for a couple at their home. The woman had told me specifically when she hired me that her husband loved this special turkey made only by HoneyBaked Ham. For the luncheon, she said, we should provide everything, except she would get the turkey, which we were to put out on the buffet along with our spread. My staff and I arrived at her home five hours early because I was a little nervous—okay, I was a lot nervous—this being my first party and all. I had hired some boys I knew to help me. When we arrived, as I was putting things away, I noticed that in the refrigerator is this huge thing wrapped in foil, which I figured was the turkey, so we started sliding in our prepared foods around it to keep them cold. Five hours later, we were all set up and right on schedule with the guests due in thirty minutes. The hostess came over to me and said, "This is all very beautiful, Lulu, but where's the HoneyBaked turkey?"

Oh my God! The turkey! I checked the refrigerator and it was gone. I ran outside to ask if anyone on my staff had seen it, and one of my guys goes, "Shit, we ran out of room for our stuff in the refrigerator, so I just threw it in the guesthouse freezer! I was going to take it out and put it back in the fridge when the party was over!"

I ran to the guesthouse garage where the freezer was and pulled it out. Then I got hold of my bartender, Michael Weiss, and I said, "Jeff put the fucking turkey in the fucking freezer! Five hours ago! You've got to help me defrost it!" I knew we couldn't put it in the oven because it was already cooked and it would dry out in no time. I didn't yet have the experience I have now, to just pour hot chicken broth over it for a while. At the time, all I could think of was the shower. We would steam it in the shower! Mike's, like, "You want me to get in the fucking shower?" So there I am with Mike, it's thirty minutes till showtime, the shower is running, and both of us are leaning into the steam from the shower trying to defrost this twenty-pound turkey and trying to stay dry at the same time.

It actually worked! It did! And he's, like, "Man, I've seen it all now."

So, that was my first catering job. There have been well over a thousand since then. I've had my share of flawless successes and, of course, a few mini disasters along the way. But nothing scares me anymore. And that's the feeling I want to impart to my clients, particularly those who get nervous before a party. I tell them fear is like fire. You can either cook with it or let it burn you. And then we go into the kitchen.

Burt Leventhal

NEWMAN & LEVENTHAL

KOSHER CATERERS

High fives for anyone who recognizes his calling at the age of six. That's how old Burt Leventhal was when he attended a cousin's wedding in Brooklyn. "The name of the place was the Quincy Manor. I still remember the address: 289 Quincy Street. I don't remember what happened last week, but I remember that. I also remember being unable to take my eyes off a man in a tuxedo who was running around doing all these party things. I asked my mother, 'Ma, what is that man called?' She said, 'He's a hall keeper.' I said, 'That's what I want to be when I get older.'"

Almost eighty years later, he still is a "hall keeper."

It's really astonishing how a small, first job can turn into a career—particularly if it starts when you're fourteen years old. I'm one of seven children. We weren't a wealthy family, and by the time I reached my fourteenth birthday, my parents told me I needed to bring some money home. We lived around the corner from a catering facility in

Brooklyn, so I applied there and they hired me. My job was to stand at the door as the guests arrived and hand out escort cards, which told them what table they would be seated at. For that, I got three dollars a party. Once the guests were all inside, I bussed tables for the waiters and they chipped in a quarter apiece, so I made an extra couple of dollars that way. And then I found if I moved the escort card table close to the checkroom counter, I could help the checkroom lady, and she would give me fifty cents. Put it all together, I'd made an extra two dollars, so I wound up going home with almost five or six dollars per party. In those days, I felt like a millionaire. Don't forget, we're talking 1948.

I stayed until I was nineteen, during which time I learned every part of the catering business from vacuuming to polishing the dance floors, cooking to cleaning the kitchen. And then I was drafted.

America was between the Korean and Vietnam wars when the army called. My records showed I had some cooking experience, so they sent me to cooking school for four months and then to Schofield Barracks in Hawaii to cook for the 25th Infantry Division. It was just a matter of time before I was put in charge of all special events at the officers' club. I'll never forget, one Friday night at Shabbat services in the chapel, I ran into Chief Warrant Officer Halpern, who said, "Officer Leventhal, my kid is thirteen and I want to give him a bar mitzvah party. Can you help me out?" It was a challenge—considering we were on an army base in Hawaii—but I did it. I made gefilte fish out of mahimahi. We had matzo ball soup and chopped chicken liver. I'm pretty sure it was the first bar mitzvah on or around that Hawaiian army base. And it well may have been the last.

On discharge from the army, I joined Newman Caterers, an established and highly reputed New York glatt kosher caterer. At the time, I was twenty-six and Mr. Newman was sixty. In the first year, I increased the business threefold, which is how "Newman Caterers" became "Newman & Leventhal." Mr. Newman retired not too long after that, but I kept his name on the masthead because he had such an amazing reputation and because at that point everybody in the industry knew Newman & Leventhal. Even today, we're repeatedly selected to collaborate with some of the best restaurant people in the world, including Daniel Boulud, and Todd English, and Danny Meyer. We've worked with and for them on galas for organizations such as the Israel Philharmonic, Shaare Zedek Medical Center, the Elie Wiesel Foundation, and many, many more. We've also catered for presidents and prime ministers and our share of celebrities. Why us? Maybe because I'm such a perfectionist. I won't accept anything second rate, whether it be food or products or staff. It has to be top of the line, all of the time. People know and like that.

The rules of keeping kosher are fairly simple. One: No shellfish or pork products may be eaten. Two: You cannot mix meat products and dairy products at the same meal. Not on a plate or in a pot or pan. This law comes from a single paragraph in the Torah [Exodus 23:19]: "Thou shalt not cook the calf in its mother's milk." Glatt kosher is a little more restrictive. "Glatt kosher" catering means that the catering company observes the Sabbath—which begins on Friday at sundown and ends on Saturday at sundown—and all Jewish holidays. There are certain rules and regulations for kosher caterers. The strictest one is: You cannot cook on the Sabbath. So for example, if a client is planning a Saturday bar mitzvah luncheon, the food has to be cooked on Friday before sundown. The cold food is no problem, because you make it and it goes right into the refrigerator. But because you're not allowed to turn on a stove on Shabbat—another rule that comes from the dictum that the Sabbath is the day of rest, and turning on the stove is considered work. So if you are serving hot food at that Saturday luncheon, the hot food gets cooked before sundown on Friday and put into a heating cabinet, where it stays hot all night long.

Here's another challenge kosher caterers face all the time. Let's say you're kosher, but you want your party at a hotel that's not kosher. For that party, we have to turn that hotel's kitchen into a kosher kitchen; it's a process known as "kashering" the kitchen. Before the party, we send in our crew, headed by a *mashgiach*, who is trained to work with them to ensure there will be no mixing of meat and dairy—not even on a countertop. First, they clean the kitchen thoroughly with steam and soap. Then, to remove any traces of nonkosher food, they burn out all the ovens, which means lighting up all the stoves to the highest point and just letting them burn for a while so that anything that's left is burnt to a crisp. The way the kosher law reads is, if anything that's left in there is not fit for a dog to eat, that oven is considered kosher. Next come the stainless-steel counters. In all hotels today, everything is stainless steel, so kashering the counter is done with live steam. You wipe it down first and then steam it. To ensure that the dishes have no trace of nonkosher food on them, we bring our own china and silverware. Glassware is considered neutral because it's nonporous and it can't hold any remnant of any nonkosher food. We bring in all our own pots and pans and our own china, and the kitchen is ready to go.

Sometimes the timing can get tricky, especially if the event is on a Sunday and the hotel is having an event Saturday night—which is more often than not. We wait until the event is over, and then we send our crew in, sometimes at one or two in the morning, because the process can take up to five hours. The supervising rabbi—the one that certifies that everything that has been done is kosher—will come in around six on Sunday morning to make sure it's all within the code.

There used to be a commercial for Levy's rye bread where they said, "You don't have to be Jewish to love Levy's." Well, you don't have to be kosher to call Newman & Leventhal, either. Years ago, we did a banquet for the American Irish Historical Society, which took place at the 7th Regiment Armory on Park Avenue. Over a thousand people attended. In the past, this group always had their events at the Waldorf Astoria, but that particular year they were honoring President Ronald Reagan, and the date they had reserved at the hotel didn't suit his schedule. So they asked the Waldorf banquet manager to suggest an alternative. He said, "The only company I can recommend that I know for sure will do an outstanding job is Newman and Leventhal. They're kosher, but you'll never know it." It was a magnificent affair. We didn't serve shrimp or lobster, but the food we did serve got some of the best comments we've ever had. And why not? A perfectly cooked filet of beef, whether it's kosher or not, is still a perfectly cooked filet of beef.

This business keeps you young. At least it keeps me young. Because if you keep working, you don't have time to think about what's age appropriate. Friends ask me all the time, "Burt, when are you going to retire?" I tell them, "Never." Two of my friends retired. A year later one of them wound up in a nursing home, the other one died. I want to keep my mind going, keep it alive. Do I get tired sometimes? Sure. Who doesn't? Especially on the weekends when we've had eight and ten parties. But retire? Me? Not on your life.

Sylvia Weinstock

SYLVIA WEINSTOCK CAKES

New York's Cake Diva. Leonardo da Vinci of Cakes. Grande Dame of Butter Cream. Flower Fashionista. She's been called it all. And those are just a few of the talent-related words describing this slight, gray-haired woman whose oversized glasses have become her trademark, and whose cakes, it has been said, are worth marrying for. Life seems always to be on fast-forward for Sylvia Weinstock. It doesn't pay to mention which celebrity she's baking for this week because by next week, she'll be on to the next one. Suffice it to say her star-studded client list reads like a Who's Who *of American entertainers, sports figures, and hedge-fund guys. But if you happen to be none of those, she'll be just as happy to see you. She'll bake you anything you want, too, but wedding cakes are her first love and always have been.*

"After the bride and groom, the cake is the most photographed symbol of any marriage celebration. I mean, you'll never see a wedding album with a picture of the bride and groom feeding each other a slice of roast beef . . ."

I grew up in a tenement, in an area of Brooklyn called Williamsburg. Williamsburg is so chic these days, you can't get in there. But as a kid growing up, I couldn't get out of there fast enough. I left home to go to college and became a teacher. In those days of yore, if you were a woman and you wanted to work and didn't want to be a secretary or a nurse, that was your only option.

In the early 1970s, my husband and I built a country house near Hunter Mountain. Everyone in my family skied except me, so while they were out, I baked. And I baked. And because I ended up with far more desserts than my family could possibly eat, I sold the extras to the local restaurants. I made strudels and tarts and brioches and apple pies and layer cakes, and I would come home with four hundred dollars from the weekend. As a teacher, I was earning forty dollars a week. Well, you didn't have to be a math genius to realize what was happening. That's how fast my career as a teacher was over.

In those days, Hunter attracted a great many chefs: Luminaries such as André Soltner of Lutèce and Jacques Pépin and a whole slew of people whom I invited for dinner and who would critique my desserts. André introduced me to pastry chef George Kellner, who ran a guesthouse near our country house, and I became his apprentice. And then happily into my life came the Upper East Side baker William Greenberg, who said, "Your cakes are delicious, Sylvia, but if you decorated them with flowers for weddings, you'd have a business." So I learned to make sugar flowers that looked incredibly real, using a special formula that lets them dry hard and keep for days. That way, I was able to stockpile them. Which was key.

I created my first wedding cake for my daughter's friend. This girl worked in a food shop and before the wedding, she put the cake on display in the window. As luck would have it, a chef who worked for

New York's biggest society caterer, Donald Bruce White, saw it in the window and told his boss about it. In no time flat, Donald started ordering cakes from me. Within weeks, guests who attended his parties started calling me directly. And that was the beginning of Sylvia Weinstock Cakes.

One of the things that put me in the forefront of this business was this: When I started, if you wanted an over-the-top beautiful cake, it took so long to decorate, that by the time you served it, the cake itself was stale and dry. Conversely, if you wanted a delicious, moist cake, it didn't look like much. So I figured, by combining both, we would have a great product. By preparing the sugar flowers and other decorations in advance, you could produce a magnificently decorated cake in twenty-four hours. So I hired a group of women to do the sugar figurines ahead of time, and we could then bake the cake, fill the cake, ice the cake, and decorate it, sometimes in one day. We still do that.

The second reason I think I did so well had to do with just plain good fortune. We were in the right place at the right time. People had money in New York City in the eighties and nineties, and they spent it. They gave great parties and everyone wanted only the best for their guests. For people like me, success rested on being in a major city like New York. You could be the best and most artistic baker in the world, but if you don't have a clientele who can pay what it costs to create these highly labor-intensive cakes, what does it matter how good you are? I know my cakes are expensive. But they're not unreasonable when you consider the quality. My prices start at seventeen dollars per person and can go up to over thirty dollars. But we are in New York City. When I go uptown to one of the nice restaurants or hotels and I have a drink, with tip and tax it's twenty dollars a drink. And I need two drinks.

One mother of a bride called me and said, "Look, I can't afford that price, but my daughter loves your cake. She really wants it at her wedding. Can't you reduce the price?" I said, "I'm so sorry, but I'm giving you the very best price I can." "Oh, Mrs. Weinstock," she said, "you're a mother. You know what it is to want to give your daughter everything she wants." I said, "Hold on, just a minute. I do not believe in giving my children everything they want. I don't think anyone should have everything they want. There should always be a little piece that you don't get, that you yearn for."

I go out of my way to do anything I can to please my customers, but I'm not going to give things away. I've had a couple of very well-known people who worked their way around to inquire if I would do it for free for the "publicity," or just for the "honor" (their word, not mine) of making their wedding cake. I always say, "Sure, I'll do it for free. But only if you come down and talk to my seventeen employees and ask them to give up a week's salary to create your cake. If they agree, you've got it for free." Nobody ever took me up on it.

Like everything else bright and beautiful, creating a wedding cake is a process. Every one of our cakes begins with a consultation. For me, dealing with my customers, 95 percent of whom are terrific, is the best part of my job. I'm a people lover and I'm curious by nature, so I want to know all about them. What they do for a living; if it's a bride and groom, how they met. I like to know if it's a first marriage, a second marriage. When it's a second marriage, I like to know what went wrong in the first. I ask the worst questions. It's true. But I get a kick out of knowing who they are, what their taste level is, and what they want. I tell them, if they can dream it, we can make it.

The next step is to discuss what the cake should look like. How many people it is to serve. What kind of design they want. How many tiers. How elaborate. When the design is approved, we move on to the delicious part. How it should taste. Every couple has the opportunity to design their own wedding cake. They pick from almond, carrot, angel food, yellow cake, and lemon—or anything else they might request. Next up are the fillings: chocolate mousse, caramel, vanilla, lemon pistachio. Blood orange, lemon, raspberry, mocha espresso, Key lime, and coconut. And then we talk about the design, which is really important because they'll always remember it.

When the wedding date nears, my whole team gears up: The bakers, the flowermakers, the carpenter, the icer, and the transporter. (And people wonder why a slice of cake is so expensive.) First, we start on the cake itself. Baking the cake is the least of it. It takes only a few hours to bake, chill, fill, and frost a cake. It's constructing the cake and decorating it that involves all the man-hours. The sugar flowers alone can take weeks to create. We never know in advance how many we're going to need. We just keep placing them until it looks beautiful to us. That could mean hundreds and hundreds. Each flower is individually handcrafted, petal by petal, so it might easily take one artist a week to create a hundred roses.

The carpenter's job is to make the infrastructure that the cake is built around. They do this with wooden or even steel dowels, depending on how tall the cake is to be. We've made them up to six and seven feet tall with no problem. After we complete the cake, we have to get it to where it's going. These cakes are sometimes five tiers high, so it's a delicate process. We have specific people we've trained to deliver our fully decorated cakes to the local hotels and clubs. When the cake goes out of the state, it goes by van or truck. Or in the cargo hold of an airplane. If I'm on the plane with it, I tell the pilot he's got a wedding cake in cargo. "Don't brake too hard," I say. "Glide onto the runway!" Think he appreciates me?

I've been at this almost forty-five years and I've watched things change over that time, and sometimes I need to remind myself of what's real and what isn't. I came from a very simple background. My husband and I were very poor when we were first married. Today I'm living in a world of absolute luxury. I sell luxury, and I sell fantasy and it's wonderful to do that, but I'm afraid that that has become so important to so many people that reality doesn't exist for them anymore. Sometimes values surrounding a celebration can get so blown out of proportion, especially as the date nears, that I have to remind myself and often others: We're not talking about world peace here. We're talking about a piece of cake.

PART VI

Front of the House

It's not just about the food. Or the prices or service or location. Or even the buzz quotient. What makes a restaurant win and keep customers also has to do with how the place makes you feel— consistently. "Ambience" doesn't fully describe it. Nor does "mood" or "vibe." Possibly because this quality I'm trying to pinpoint is, well, unpinpointable. The voguish "umami" might work if we were talking about taste, but we're not. Maybe the closest we can get is the Latin phrase *genius loci*: the spirit of the place. It's the thing that keeps you coming back even if getting there is tough and even if the food isn't the most dazzling. It's the thing that outweighs all the others in the where-to-eat-tonight calculus.

What you want most from a restaurant experience, sometimes or all the time, is a sense of coziness, of being at ease among strangers— the feeling that you belong there as if it were home. And when you get that feeling, you can be fairly certain that someone at "the front of the house," visible to and interacting with the customers, is the source. This person might be an owner, host, manager, captain, even a waiter; whoever it is, he or she conveys that elusive *genius loci*.

One such case in point is Jonathan Parilla, the night manager at Cafeteria. If you happen to be familiar with only the daytime scene at this casual, comfort-food joint on 7th Avenue in Chelsea, you're probably rolling your eyes right now and thinking, *"What scene?* It's a glorified diner!" And that's exactly how I responded to friends when they told me that I should talk to Parilla for this chapter. "Obviously," said one, expressing the general sentiment, "you've never been there at three a.m." Which was true. So I called Jonathan and he suggested I show up three days later, at the end of his shift, around eight a.m.

Wanting a sneak peek, I got to the restaurant just after six a.m.; it was still dark outside. I was about to enter when two creatures of the night, eyes bloodshot and arms around each other, made their exit. Quite the odd couple: a short, scraggly-bearded guy in a head wrap à la Stevie Van Zandt, and his tall, distinguished companion, wearing a nicely tailored navy blazer. (Musician and manager, maybe?)

Inside, the place was in full swing and softly aglow from what seemed to be a million tea lights on the tables, the bar, and everywhere else in this sleekly modern space. Near the front door, two men in jeans—one of whom turned out to be Parilla—huddled over cups of coffee. Soon a third man, in drag, joined them. He wore a gorgeous black suede jacket, flared at the waist, with multiple zippers around the neck, a floor-length dark-colored skirt, and a pair of six-inch-high black leather stilettos; not to mention a full face of makeup (Addams Family dark lipstick, at least two sets of expertly applied false eyelashes), and an upswept hairdo. I would later learn that he was Markus Kelle, a fixture of the New York party scene and Cafeteria's nighttime door host. This was when it occurred to me that I might appear conspicuous—a straight woman sitting alone at the tail end of an all-night revelry who was doing nothing but staring at the clientele, like an FBI agent trained to look oblivious—and decided to order a large breakfast.

I waited until seven thirty to identify myself to Parilla, at which point he led me to a table at the far side of the restaurant, where we settled in for our talk. It didn't take long before he was summoning a waiter over and telling him to fetch the special house dessert for me to try. With two fried eggs, hash browns, bacon, juice, and toast still undigested, I now faced a platter of batter-fried Oreo cookies, a small tumbler of coffee-chip ice cream, and a vanilla shake in a shot glass. But if you think I said, "Oh, no thank you," to this spread, then you don't know me at all.

As I stuffed myself a second time, some of the remaining night-time customers stood up from their tables and started filtering out, but not before stopping at our table. They all knew Parilla, and they wouldn't dream of leaving without saying good-bye. He was and is their connection to the restaurant. That's when I realized that during the midnight-to-eight shift, Jonathan Parilla *is* Cafeteria. He may not be the owner, but he clearly owns the night.

Ed Schoenfeld

REDFARM

From the time he was a young man, Ed Schoenfeld claims, he wanted to be a culinary feinschmecker—the Yiddish term for "an authority." He has more than realized this dream. In the food world, he's been described variously (and sometimes simultaneously) as a creator, maître d', master host, performance artist, restaurant maestro, auteur, director, and walking encyclopedia of Chinese food. No surprise. After all, this guy has been behind the development of some of New York's most beloved and innovative restaurants of the past forty years, starting with Uncle Tai's, which opened in 1973 and quickly received four stars from the New York Times. *Then came a slew of others, including Café Marimba, Vince & Eddie's, Chop Suey Looey's Litchi Lounge, Jack's Fifth, Thalia, Our Place, Shanghai Tea Garden, City Eatery, Pig Heaven, and Chinatown Brasserie. Not all of them are still around, but in their time and place, all were hits.*

Today, with people milling about outside, waiting for a table in his bucolic-themed, no-reservations, newly opened Upper West Side restaurant, he table-hops with the same energy and enthusiasm he's been known for his entire career. Dressed in his typical uniform of suspenders and thick-framed glasses, and sporting a bushy Santa Claus beard, he is greeted as an old friend by one customer after another. In fact, everyone in town seems to know him—and vice versa.

W hen I was a kid, I went to a goyish private school. On Friday they would let us off early. Because my parents were working, I would go to my grandmother's house, just hang out with her and watch her cook. Grandma Goldie, who was married to husband number three and living in Brooklyn, cooked Shabbat dinner every Friday night. At first, I just watched her as she made everything from scratch—gefilte fish, blintzes. Like that. Eventually, she let me work with her. I got so into it and so good at it, by the age of ten or eleven, I was able to work four frying pans at the same time.

And I've been cooking every single day since then.

In junior high, I was often invited to go out with the family of one particular friend. He was a little bit dorky, so his parents would tell him to invite somebody and they would take us to a really nice restaurant. Even at that early age, I loved the whole feel of a nice restaurant. The ones I went to with my parents were limited. They would never even *think* of going to a French restaurant because, one, they wouldn't spend the money; two, they wouldn't get dressed up like people did in those places; and three, I think they were intimidated. My folks were middle-class, intellectual Jews, so going out to dinner meant we did what any normal Jews did on Sunday night—we went to a local Chinese restaurant for spare ribs and shrimp with lobster sauce.

Somewhere around the age of seventeen or eighteen, I started thinking about what I wanted to do with my future. One of my favorite pleasures every week was going through the *New York Times* food section and reading restaurant reviews by Craig Claiborne. That got me thinking I might want to write about food and cooking. I knew I didn't want to be a chef. Rather, I wanted to be a food authority. So I needed to learn as much as I could about cooking.

I signed up for cooking lessons with a woman named Grace Zia Chu, a wealthy seventy-year-old Mandarin lady from Shanghai who was the wife of a general under Chinese Nationalist leader Chiang Kai-shek. If you wanted to study Chinese cooking in New York City, she was the doyenne. At the same time, I was also making some money and so I started going out to eat at the four-star Shun Lee Dynasty. Ultimately, I learned to cook the same dishes from Grace Zia Chu as I was ordering from Chef Wang and Chef Lee at Shun Lee. The dishes Grace taught us how to make tasted good, but the dishes the chef made at Shun Lee tasted fucking *awesome*. Which was when I realized: There was a lot that these professional chefs knew that Auntie Grace was clueless about.

And there was a good explanation for that. It turned out that Grace didn't really know how to cook because she never had to cook. Her husband had been close to Chiang Kai-shek, who made him the Chinese ambassador to Moscow. At the Moscow embassy, she had chefs who cooked for her. So when you came to study with her, you got this great lady, this great taste of culture, and food served on beautiful plates with incredible chopsticks. But if what you were after were tricks of the trade or a deep culinary knowledge on how to cook superb food, she didn't know any of that. In fact, she was lucky to be in this country at all, and that was only because she was the wife of a diplomat. Otherwise, before 1968, if you were Chinese, it was extremely difficult to come here. The first wave of Cantonese people came to work on the railroads in the 1800s and when that project was finished, the only ones who could stay were those who were married to an American or were part of the embassy staff, or on an education-based visa. The vast majority of Chinese people could only come to visit. And that included the great chefs of China.

I've always been fascinated by what happened to the great chefs. Before the Communists took over China in 1949, high-end cooking was strictly for the elite. The best chefs didn't work in restaurants; rather, they served members of the Chinese aristocracy. They basically worked for benefactors just as an artist would work for a patron in Europe during the Renaissance. Budding young chefs would apprentice themselves to a master, and after years, if you were good, you became a master chef yourself.

When Mao Tse-tung took over, one of the elements that really changed was the food culture. There would be no more fancy cooking. How could there be? The necessary ingredients were no longer available, and the behavior itself was socially unacceptable. But even worse was the way Mao's followers went into people's homes and took their pots and pans, knives and stoves, and every metal object that they had so they could melt them down to build railroads and airplanes.

That left the people to cook only basic foods in communal kitchens where everyone ate from the same pot. It also meant that good Chinese chefs were no longer able to practice epicurean cooking. And as a consequence, younger chefs were no longer trained. And so on down the line. Until the mid-1960s, when the U.S. immigration laws changed and wealthy Chinese people, who had earlier immigrated with their chefs to Taiwan, were allowed to come to America. And they brought their chefs with them. The best of these were the old-school chefs who had learned to cook before the revolution. A group of them ended up opening restaurants on the West Side of Manhattan, where they adapted their food to the Western palate. This was known as Szechuan food, and these restaurants popped up all over the city, alongside the already established Americanized Chinese restaurants that I went to with my parents when I was younger.

Much to my parents' chagrin, when I turned nineteen, I dropped out of college. I became a New York City cabdriver to support my cooking habit, my culinary dreams, and myself. I started devoting myself to learning Chinese food and everything around it full time. In my quest to visit the great restaurants of the sixties and seventies, whenever I got enough money together, I went to Europe on an eating tour. By the time I was twenty-five, I had managed to make it to every three-star Michelin restaurant in France.

After a couple of years of writing and cooking on my own almost every day, I decided it would be much more my pace, rather than critiquing restaurants, to get personally involved with them. I started by arranging Chinese banquets for my friends at some of the more authentic restaurants in Chinatown. These banquets became so popular, I decided to make a business of it. One day, after a Szechuan meal at a wonderful restaurant, I made a halfhearted joke to the owner, David Keh. I said, "If you ever want to open a fancy mainstream restaurant in midtown, and you're looking for someone to do that with you, I'd be interested in the job." As luck would have it, he took me up on my offer. Together, the two of us spent nine months creating Uncle Tai's Hunan Yuan Restaurant.

When Uncle Tai's opened, they gave me the host's position. They dressed me up in a blue polyester tuxedo with fake suede lapels, a ruffled blue shirt, and a bow tie. I felt like a real bozo, but I did it. Don't get me wrong. It was thrilling. Here I was, this twenty-three-year-old Jew from a New York City private school and the only white guy in the room, working right alongside a bunch of people who had just jumped off the boat from Taipei. I, who had never worked in a restaurant a day in my life, found myself at the front door of this amazing Chinese restaurant. After being open for a mere two weeks, Uncle Tai's received a four-star review from the *New York Times*. Chef Tai deserved every one of those stars. He was a superb cook. He also was part of the generation of chefs who had learned to cook in China before the revolution.

I was with the Uncle Tai group for three years, and then I got stolen away by the Shun Lee restaurants, where I worked as a captain and then as a consultant, helping them open the restaurant that is currently across the street from Lincoln Center. By the end of the eighties and into the nineties, I was full time at creating and operating new restaurants, including the city's first gourmet Mexican restaurant, Café Marimba. Plus more Chinese restaurants than I can count.

Of course it was only a matter of time that I'd want to open my own restaurant. With my kids grown, I was finally able to take a chance or two economically. That's when I came up with the concept of RedFarm, which I described to potential backers as a farm-to-table restaurant that used only local in-season fresh produce. If you look at Japanese food, you think of it as clean and healthy. If you look at Chinese food, you think sweet and salty, oily and sugary and, in some cases, not so clean. RedFarm would be Chinese food with a Japanese-food sensibility.

With the backers in place, I started my search to find a great chef. I had met Joe Ng ten years earlier at a restaurant in Brooklyn. Even then, I recognized him as a particularly talented dim sum chef. He has learned his craft so well that if you ask him how many dumplings he has in his repertoire, he'll tell you a thousand. When I interviewed him, I asked what his vision was for RedFarm. He said his plan was to take foods that were regular parts of his classic repertoire, and present them with a visual twist. He said, "You know how, in a restaurant, you sometimes glance at someone else's plate to see what they're eating to decide if that's what you want to order? I want to create food that, when the waiter is taking it to another table, the customer sees it and wants it for himself." His creativity and flavors blew me away. So we hired him.

Our idea was to serve food with a sense of humor, items that literally make people smile. Like our Katz's pastrami egg roll. Or our Pac-Man dumplings. Those are shrimp-filled dumplings shaped like ghosts with little faces on them, arranged in a line on a plate, at the end of which is a circle of sweet potato with a wedge cut out, looking like Pac-Man ready to gobble them up. And that's RedFarm in a nutshell. It's about coming to this very small, very tight, and very cacophonous space where people practically sit on top of each other, enjoy great food, and have fun. We're replacing dinner and a show. For us, dinner *is* the show.

Miriam Tsionov

CHEBURECHNAYA

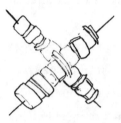

She's all of nineteen. She was born in Israel, where her parents settled after fleeing anti-Semitic violence in their native Uzbekistan. After her parents divorced in 2002, Tsionov came to America with her mother and sister. Now she's working as a waitress at her uncle's restaurant in Rego Park, Queens. With the lunch rush over, she's ready to explain just what Bukharan kosher cuisine is all about—and which dishes here are customer favorites. We settle into a corner table, she studies the menu for a few minutes, and starts to point them out: A sesame-seed-coated, pumpkin-stuffed pastry called samcy; *a garlicky carrot salad,* morkovcha; *fried turnovers known as* chebureki. *"It's all good," she insists. "Ooh, and if you like your lamb testicles skewered, you've come to the right place."*

Everyone's always watching the waitress. And because I'm the owner's niece, there's even more pressure on me. My uncle has high expectations. If something goes wrong, it's always *my* fault. There were times where I fought back and said, "Stop putting the pressure on me! I'm not the only waitress here." But he doesn't hear me. So mostly, I just take it. Where's my choice? I have to help out making money for our family.

Cheburechnaya is kosher Bukharan. Rego Park, all the way to 108th Street, has a big Bukharan population. I can tell if someone is Bukharan. The way they talk and the way they behave. I can pick them out of a crowd. They see a Bukharan girl, immediately they have a fiancé waiting for her. "Are you Bukharan?" I say, "Yes." "What's your age?" "Nineteen." "Let me get your phone number." I usually give it to them. Mostly, though, nobody calls.

I love all the different nationalities that come here to eat. When I see that you're a new customer, that's it. I'm the girl for you. Americans are the best. They're fun, spontaneous, and definitely more patient. They have that understanding bone. I like the Asians, too. They're gutsier. You'd be surprised at how many of them try our specialties. Things like lamb testicles, and sweetbreads, brains, hearts. Americans? Not so adventurous. But there's always that one daring American that'll try the testicles. Especially when they come in a big group. Someone will look up at me and say, "I'm up to trying anything." I'm like, "Really? Can you look at number forty-seven for a second?" (It's lamb testicles.) "Why not try that?" And he'll go, "Uh, maybe not today."

I have befriended so many of our customers. They say, "If you're not here, Miriam, we're not coming back. You make this restaurant what it is." That makes me feel good. And heaven knows, I need those good feelings when things get tough around here, because this job can be very hard—physically and emotionally. There were many times where the pressure got so bad, I wanted to just hang it all up. Like one night, I had a table of people sitting at the window, a party of fifteen or twenty people. The hostess of the group said to me, "Just keep

bringing food, little by little, and I will let you know when to stop."
They ordered a lot of different varieties of kabobs and we were serving
them slowly but continuously, the way she wanted. At some point, I
brought her a few more skewers on a platter and put them on the table
like before, and she suddenly starts yelling at me, "I told you to stop
serving!" I said very politely, "No, you didn't. You told us you would
let us know when to stop." "Well, stop. We don't want these." "I'm
sorry," I said, "these skewers are cooked so you have to take them."
She started yelling at me, "You take them back." Now everyone in the
restaurant turns around.

My mom was having dinner in one of the booths, and I ran over to
her and burst into tears. I said, "I don't want to work here anymore!"
She goes, "Everyone's looking at you, Miriam. Pull yourself together.
You can't just walk out. Where you gonna go?" That was such a bad
night for me. And did they even leave a tip? No. They did not.

Tips are not included on the bill in this restaurant. It doesn't matter
if you are two people or twenty, thirty, one hundred, tips are not
included. We work for tips, which is fine because on a good night, you
can make a hundred and fifty dollars, just like that. Americans and
Russians generally leave 20 percent, depending on the service. But
some customers don't tip at all. Like the Tajiks and the Uzbeks. They
don't tip because in their country, waiters get paid salary. So when they
come here, they think we get paid salary. But we don't get a salary. And
we're not allowed to tell the customer that.

Doing this work has made me realize so many things. When I go
to a restaurant with my mom, say, and I see that it's busy and my food
comes out slow, as a waitress myself, I cut the staff some slack. My
mom will say, "Why are they taking forever? Why is it so hard to bring

me a salad?" So I tell her, "Give the poor guy or girl a break. We're not the only people here." Sometimes when service is really slow, I complain to myself. But I say nothing. I could never treat somebody badly—or not leave a tip. I couldn't. I want to say to them, "If you mess up, that's okay. I mess up myself. Don't worry. I feel your pain."

Jonathan Parilla

CAFETERIA

He saw on Craigslist that Cafeteria, a sixty-seven-seat, open-all-night diner, was looking for an overnight manager. Having been there often himself, and as a participant in the New York City social scene, he thought the position was tailor-made for him. He explained to the owners that he already had a name on the party circuit and that if he got the job, his legions of friends would follow him. "That was my selling point to the owners. And it sold me right into this amazing job."

As the overnight manager, I come in at midnight and don't leave until eight the next morning. The place is already in full swing when I get here. The ceiling lights are off, the banquettes lit up, candles everywhere. Of course we still have the standard diners here at midnight—you know, the ones who might be found at any city restaurant. But as the night progresses, the crowd begins to change. When the bars and clubs close in the early-morning hours, the coolest people start drifting in here; people who aren't ready for the night to end yet. Being where we are—in Chelsea—you would expect us to be gay-heavy. And we are, I'm not going to lie. But what gives this place such a great late-night vibe is the way we mix all kinds of people together to create a perfect storm. It's that mix that makes Cafeteria the place to come in the wee hours of the morning.

Don't think for a minute that this just happens, though. We plan every bit of it. We literally curate the room. You know how when you curate an art exhibit, you take things that you think will go well together? Well, we work on the same principle. It's like we're putting on a stage play here every night. It's all very *Grand Hotel.*

So how do we do it? Well, we start with our regulars who come in all the time. They're these fabulously wild, eccentric people, as well as Wall Street bankers, professional athletes, movie stars, and people famous for being famous. As the night progresses, we add performance artists, doormen, DJs, restaurant owners, club owners, and post-clubbers. Then—and this is the fun part—we fill in the empty spots in the room by picking and choosing from the crowd waiting on line outside. It's the people from that crowd who really contribute to the show. And in many cases, they *are* the show.

They don't have to be famous or beautiful for us to invite them inside. If they have the personality we're looking for that particular night, we bring them right in. Some nights we're in the mood for young people. Or people in crazy dress. Or foreigners, or short people. Or all of the above. You never know. And that's because until we see who's already inside—we never know either. If we decide we need, say, some people from middle America to balance all the New Yorkers, we'll ask who in line is from Iowa, and we'll bring them right in. I think of them as "Middle Earth people." You know, they're not L.A., they're not New York, they're not Chicago. They're usually fun and funny. You might think that they would be a little shy in these strange surroundings, but *au contraire*. They're the first to get up and sing a song. If we've done it right, we end up with an eclectic mix of people that would be hard to duplicate anywhere else. Everybody really has fun—and that's why they all keep coming back week after week, year after year.

We have two kinds of gatekeepers on the overnight shift—security and hosts. The two security guys (we never call them bouncers—God forbid!) are stationed outside at the front of the line, to filter the crowd. If someone looks too drunk, too brash, too abrasive, too rowdy, too underdressed, or if there are just too many of them, security will let them know that "Maybe tonight is not your night." If they refuse to move, then the guys look to one of us to come out and speak to them and we'll invite them kindly to come back another time.

While security manages the outside line, it's the door host who decides who comes in and who doesn't. Who fits where; who will sit where; who will be seated next to this table that will get along. Who we're going to put in the back. Who we can skip up the list to look better at a certain table. The host I work best with is Markus Kelle. When I came to work here, I brought him in specifically because he knows all of New York and vice versa, and because he has the perfect personality and smarts for this job. And he's very, very funny.

Markus is six foot three and he dresses in drag. But not tacky drag. He has a fabulous flair and a style all his own. He wears only the finest clothes, always false eyelashes, full makeup, and great jewelry. He's one of the most famous doormen in New York. He sizes up the room and then he goes outside and talks to the people on line. It's his knowledge of the right people to let in, his toughness at the door, and his looks that make him so outstanding. You need a certain sophistication to work here and Markus has it. And you have to be tough because you're forever dealing with those crazy characters who won't take no for an answer.

We get our share of celebrities here. More than our share, if you ask me. Susan Sarandon is always here. So are Cyndi Lauper, Bruce Willis, and Julianne Moore. We've had Lorraine Bracco from *The Sopranos*, Queen Latifah. They walk in and nobody even looks up. New Yorkers are so used to seeing celebrities around, they couldn't care less. The tourists spot them, sure, but they're too afraid to approach them. I think they're just happy to be in the same room, breathing the same air. Frankly, half the time, not even the tourists notice these people. Unless, of course, they're sports celebrities like Alex Rodriguez or Derek Jeter. Knicks players are here a lot, too. There's no missing those guys when they walk in.

One New Year's Eve, Mariah Carey—one of our biggest fans—was playing at Madison Square Garden. Suddenly, her handlers texted us to say she's on her way in with a small party. We were already packed. We have a lounge downstairs, so I got everyone out of the lounge, and found him or her places to sit upstairs. When her limousine pulled up, we brought her in through the side door. Being Mariah, I thought she'd appreciate the privacy. But no. She walks into the dining room in this white, gorgeous fur-trimmed gown and starts waving at the customers. The entire place went crazy. We escorted her downstairs. I ran upstairs, lowered the music, ran back down to the lounge, and asked her to sing, which she did. Her voice, even from downstairs, reverberated throughout the whole restaurant. It was one of those rare nights where everything is perfect. New Year's Eve, Mariah Carey. Just a perfect night.

David McQueen

From across the table at one of New York's most beautiful restaurants, thirty-eight-year-old McQueen tells me he is a waiter/sculptor. It's a classic New York combination, he says. When I ask why not call himself a sculptor/waiter, he says it's because one makes money and the other doesn't. "I care deeply about my career here, but would I leave it tomorrow for the right opportunity to make my studio practice economically viable? Absolutely. While I'm at Gramercy Tavern, though, this is my vocation—100 percent."

He's actually not a waiter anymore, having been promoted to captain eight years ago. And he is a serious sculptor, with works in several New York art galleries.

My advice to someone who wants to become a waiter is this: You need to acknowledge that waiting on tables is a servile act and make peace with that. You can wait on your guests with a tremendous amount of self-respect and recognize that, if you do it right, what you are giving to these people they may never get again. It feels good to make someone happy. That's where the beauty in the profession is. But if you never get past the serving part, if you attach your dignity to that, it can become a really destructive influence.

At Gramercy Tavern, the front-of-the-house hierarchy is: Captain, front waiter, back waiter, or runner. If the captain wants to, he can play all parts, including seating a guest, pouring water, bringing bread, clearing and resetting the table. Every restaurant is a little bit different, though. Some are much more specific as to who does what, and generally the captain is responsible only to see that everything gets done. But here, what the captain does that no one else can do is greet the guests, explain the menu, take an order, and deliver the check. The front waiter enters the order into the computer, brings and clears the *amuse-bouche*, manages the timing of the table, and makes sure it's ready for the next course, which includes placing the silverware specific to what you have ordered and sometimes placing the plates of food on the table. Our runner's primary focus is to pick up the food in the kitchen and bring it to the dining room. There, the front waiter, or I, will place it in front of the guest.

There's a saying that in any restaurant, service and food can salvage each other. If one is great and the other lacking, you'll still go back. But I think it takes more than just food and service. A restaurant needs ambience. And it needs energy, which, to me, is the most crucial component of the four. And that energy can be brought to a restaurant only through hiring the right people. Danny Meyer—who owns this restaurant and a number of others—has a corporate philosophy. It dictates that we seek out two specific characteristics before we hire an individual: Emotional intelligence and skill, at a divide of 51 percent emotional intelligence and 49 percent skill. The thinking behind this is that a skill can be taught. That is, you can learn to recognize the difference between a chardonnay and a sauvignon blanc—in fact we have classes all the time for just such reasons. You can be taught how to serve something properly, or which piece of silverware to set down with which dish. What we *can't* teach is work ethic or self-awareness or emotional awareness—those make up the 51 percent. You either get it or you don't.

In this business, you need to know how to access someone's feelings and respond in a meaningful way. It's about recognizing unsettling situations and putting the guests at ease from the start. You'd be surprised how many times this comes into play. For example, say a guest decides he's waited long enough for something he ordered, so he starts to feel he's been forgotten. He might start looking around and eventually he's so on edge that he seeks out anyone who comes by and asks them to check his dish in the kitchen. And he may be right— maybe he ordered fish and everyone else at his table ordered meat and that guy who is roasting meat has only six burners and can only cook so much at a time. Or maybe there is some other complication in the kitchen. If a waiter picks up on that, he or she learns early on to come to the table and say, "I understand your food is taking a long time and I want you to know that you are not forgotten. I just spoke with the chef and he tells me it will be ready in six minutes." As soon as you say that, the mystery goes away. They've been acknowledged and know that it's all okay. But first you have to learn to recognize the situation.

Here's another example: Let's say a table is set for five people. The first couple arrives and sits down. I greet the table with the wine list in hand and say hello, and the first thing they say before we have any conversation, is, "We're waiting for three more people." I already know that. There are five chairs there. But I recognize that they are concerned about being rushed along without their friends being there. They feel they're going to be asked to make decisions they're unprepared to make because their party is incomplete. They haven't given me a chance to acknowledge that they are waiting for three more. So now, the first thing I say to an incomplete party to put them at ease is, "I see you're waiting for your friends. Can I offer you a drink in the meantime?" Recognizing these situations, though they're not stated outright, takes emotional intelligence. Knowing how to solve them is the skill. That's the 49 percent.

Like everything else, things keep changing in the restaurant business and you can never rest on your laurels. In 2008, the economy tanked, and restaurants closed left and right, especially at the high end, because people were unwilling to spend three hundred dollars for dinner. Either their corporate accounts couldn't or wouldn't tolerate that, or they no longer had that expendable income. As a result, everyone at Gramercy worked extra hard to ensure that if you are coming here for dinner, that you get the best possible food and service. We want you to come, but we also want you to return. Some of our guests come a few times a month; some come a couple of times a week to sit at the bar. Two lovely couples have been coming in every year for their anniversary for the past twenty years. They fly in to New York and spend their anniversary weekend in the city. And that's great. But then we also get the opposite end of the spectrum. Those whose relationships break up.

There was a two-week period here where three couples broke up over dinner and that affected me greatly. As a kinetic sculptor, I create many pieces that have to do with relationships, and one of my pieces, which consists of two lighthouses staring at each other, was born from that two-week period. From a server's vantage point, you can absolutely see it when it's happening. There's a very specific trajectory that's revealed when the couple has reached a point where there's nothing left to say; it has all been said. Of course they could trade lies about trying again, but they both know that's not going to happen, so they just stop talking. Sometimes they sit there like that for a half hour, not talking to or looking at each other. Maybe there's a silent reach for a hand and retraction and looking away again. It's a torturous moment to watch. I want to sit down with them and tell them, "It's okay to go home. As soon as you leave, you get to start looking for something new that will make you happy. Because right here, what's existing in this moment is driven by a lack of potential." I want to say that, to help them, but of course I don't.

When you've been here for ten years like I have, you become an expert on reading body language. The body language of a dissolving couple is totally different from that of the long-married couple. They, too, might go through the meal not talking to each other, but that's just because they're happy in their silence or they've simply run out of things to say.

Alexander Smalls

THE CECIL

Daylight floods his Harlem apartment, an eclectic space crammed with old and new mementos from a well-traveled, well-lived life. There are treasures everywhere, but I can't stop looking at the walls of a narrow gallery that spans the three front rooms. They're lined from floor to ceiling with photographs of family members representing multiple generations, and of friends, famous and not so famous—singers, musicians, writers, and poets.

His name belies his stature. He is tall and hefty, with a buoyant personality as large as his physique. His deep, rich, baritone voice is well suited to a gifted raconteur, which he is, and to an opera singer, which he was. His storytelling, Smalls believes, is in his genes, passed down from his grandparents. "They leased land for livestock and would take me with them to the slaughterhouse when I was young. We'd bring back the meat to their house and spend the afternoon in the kitchen making sausages. And while we were doing that, they would tell me stories. This oral history is how my siblings and I understood where we came from. Nobody was interested in writing about who we were, and oftentimes, who could write?"

My grandparents were the children of slaves. I grew up in the South, in an area known as the Low Country. Low Country spans across Charleston, Beaufort, and Savannah, a region heavily influenced by West Africa. When the African slaves came to America, they largely came to places like Charleston, which, aside from New York, had the largest slave market in the country. A lot of my heritage, the stories and the rituals of West Africa, came along with those migrating blacks.

The dawning of Sunday was ritualistic in my home. We woke up early and dressed for church, and my mother would start her preparation for Sunday dinner, the absolute best eating ever. It didn't matter what you had during the week. Come Sunday, you could always expect a feast. If it was summertime, we ate on the side porch, under the shade of big oak trees. My mother made a panful of hot buttermilk biscuits with fresh butter and sorghum. Potato and macaroni salads, fresh creamed corn, fried okra, and some kind of roast followed that. If we were lucky, we could get some dumplings out of the deal as well.

Of course no one used the expression then, but ours was definitely a farm-to-table home. Our extended family lived on a triangle of connecting lots. My grandfather lived at one point, Uncle Jo lived at the second, and we lived at the third. A path connected these houses, and if I was clever enough—and fast enough—I could time it where I would have two breakfasts, two lunches, and two dinners. Needless to say, no grass could ever grow along that path.

As a kid, I had an enormous gift for music. When that gift became obvious, my aunt and uncle took me in hand and guided my musical education with laserlike attention paid to who I was and who I would become. My mother had her own ideas, but on one thing they all agreed: I was not going to suffer the rough roads, the misguidance, and the difficult bumps that are prescription for a number of African American males growing up, particularly in the South. So music became the foundation of my expression. As I learned to play the piano, I developed as a vocalist as well. I was only eight years old when my uncle introduced me to opera. I got hooked on Joan Sutherland and Marilyn Horne doing duets on *Ed Sullivan,* and afterward, I would literally stand in front of my mirror and imitate the singers. If it was a male and female duo, I'd throw a shirt on my head to be the female and I would sing in my high voice, and then throw it off and sing like the man.

As time went on, I spent more and more of my time in voice training, eventually ending up at the Curtis Institute of Music in Philadelphia, one of the best music schools in the country, if not the world. When I started winning competitions, my fate was sealed. I set out to be the first major African American male opera star, a privilege that had been denied up to that point. African American women were considered exotic, so there was always a place for them after Marian Anderson broke those barriers. But the African American male? Not yet there.

When I was in Philadelphia, the Houston Grand Opera gave a performance of *Porgy and Bess* at Philharmonic Hall. I auditioned and was hired for the chorus. I traveled with that production throughout the States and in Europe, and when it was over, I stayed abroad. While singing and studying in Europe, I was also cooking my ass off. All of my performing friends flocked to my house for Sunday dinner until one day I realized that entertaining them was becoming more important to me than my music; in fact, my singing jobs in Europe were petering out. That's when I decided to come home.

Here, suddenly, everything I had done abroad careerwise meant nothing. I was in my late twenties by then and I had to audition all over again for every role. It was like starting from scratch. And a rude awakening. My skin color was a big problem. There were no African American male superstars in opera. When I was in *Porgy and Bess*, I remember looking at all of these middle-aged men of color, some with grandchildren, who were still saying, "When I make it." I was, like, "Don't let me be this person who doesn't realize that his time has passed." When the last audition I did turned out to be for a very minor role, I went back to my apartment, had a big glass of red wine, and decided I was done. I couldn't afford to have other people decide my fate or what my legacy would be. From that moment on, I would own my own stage, even if it meant selling hot dogs in Central Park. It was the most sobering moment of my life.

Because cooking and entertaining are so important to me, it seemed only natural that this would be my new career path. I was living in a large loft downtown and entertaining small and large groups all the time. Soon enough it dawned on me that I'm doing again just what I did in Europe. I not only needed to get these people out of my house, but it was high time someone else bought *my* dinner for a change. And that's when I opened my first restaurant, Café Beulah.

Talk about naïve. I don't know what I was thinking! The only thing I knew about the restaurant business was what I had learned as a singing waiter one summer in Tanglewood. I knew nothing! I wrote a semblance of a business plan, went out and tried to raise money. Fortunately, I had a lot of friends in high places, and in an excellent show of confidence, they were all happy to help. I went to Percy Sutton, who used to own the radio station WBLS as well as the Apollo Theater and is regarded as one of the deans of the African American evolution in Harlem. I went to Toni Morrison, the writer, a good friend who loved my food and came often to my New York soirées. I went to my friend Kathleen Battle, the opera singer, who also was happy to help.

We hit the ground running. From the moment we opened the doors in 1994, Café Beulah was a success. The timing could not have been more perfect. People were discovering that restaurants were more than just a place for a great meal. There was an entertainment factor built in. You found a new place and you reported it to the world either on the Internet or through Zagat's, and so your diners became your PR department. I picked the perfect downtown location. And we had a wonderful menu that introduced New Yorkers to what I called "Southern revival cooking with Low Country notes." It was the food of my childhood, a fusion of French Creole, African, and the Far East. We served a lot of seafood and game, but with a regional character all its own. Diners loved the food; that was never in question. And the place was always packed. In fact, everything was right on target—except for the fact that I had no idea how to run a restaurant. And I kept running out of money.

A big part of the problem was my role in the restaurant. I started out as the chef, but people ended up coming into the kitchen to hang out with me while I cooked. Well, you can imagine how that worked out. To socialize and broil a steak to a certain level at the same time is rarely well done (if something can be rare and well done at the same time). This is when I understood that I should be "the guy up front," and let someone else do the cooking. But even that didn't help. As busy and as popular as Beulah was, and despite some great reviews, in five years we ran out of money and had to close.

There were so many reasons for our demise. For one, we had a difficult time turning tables, which meant that instead of two or three diners in a chair of an evening, we had one. People wouldn't vacate their

tables. Imagine if you have Julia Roberts at one table, and Catherine
Deneuve sipping bourbon at the bar, Jane Fonda, Glenn Close, Debbie
Allen, Jessye Norman, and Kathleen Battle sitting around you, would
you want to leave? Literally, I had to go around and plead with them, "I
need your table. I'll buy you drinks at the bar." But nobody listened to
me. We closed in January 1997. I subsequently opened and closed two
smaller restaurants, and that's when I started traveling.

On my return from one of my trips, I got a call from Richard Par-
sons, a longtime pal who was the former CEO of Time Warner. Richard loved the restaurant business, particularly nightclubs. He had
always wanted to own a jazz club, and we set about looking to make
that happen. One day, while looking for real estate, I stumbled upon a
building on the quiet corner of 118th Street and St. Nicholas Avenue in
Harlem. The building had been the historic Cecil Hotel, but it was
now Section 8 housing, otherwise known as single-room occupancy or
SRO. Not exactly the environment most people would think to put a
new and upscale restaurant in, but to me it was perfect. And in a dual
stroke of luck, in that same building but around the corner, was a running jazz club called Minton's. Minton's is the home of bebop, the foundation of modern jazz. Monk, Dizzy, Bird, Charlie Christian, Hot Lips
Page. All these guys performed there on a regular basis.

In 2009, Richard and I bought the space where The Cecil is now. In
the process of developing it, Minton's became available and we bought
that, too. It was thrilling for both of us to think we could bring this
legendary jazz club back to its former glory. In its time, Minton's had
been the most elegant club in town, with white linens and everyone
dressed up. We decided to continue that legacy by installing a house
jazz band and pairing it with authentically American food that was
reflective of the jazz image.

On the other hand, opening The Cecil allowed me to realize a dream I have always had. I had always wanted to learn about, celebrate, and re-create the food of the African diaspora. The "African diaspora" refers to the groups of people throughout the world that are descended from slaves who were taken from Africa and transported to distant places such as the Americas, Europe, Asia, and the Middle East. To learn about the food they made, I traveled to the countries where they landed. Using Africa as my base, I followed the slave route to South America, Europe, Asia, and the Caribbean. In each place I discovered new foods that fused African roots with flavors and foodstuffs of the newly inhabited world.

I based The Cecil's menu on what I learned from those trips. Many of the dishes fuse Afro/Asian/American culinary techniques and flavors. For example, a Brazilian *feijoada*, which is a traditional meat-and-bean stew, now includes lamb *merguez* and oxtail. In a nod to the Orient, we created a whole section of rice bowls with a choose-it-yourself protein, or a Chinese chicken sausage. Our specialty dish, which emulates the all-American Southern fried chicken, is actually a cinnamon-scented fried guinea hen, which we serve on top of a bed of charred okra. Other hybrid American dishes include benne-seed-crusted Skuna Bay salmon with scallion grits, corn, and house-made kimchi, and gumbo consisting of smoked chicken, Gulf shrimp, crabmeat. The ambience of the restaurant is meant to showcase the diaspora as well. Masai wallpaper covers the walls, and a picture of an Afro-Asian geisha graces the rear wall. Even our music is influenced by the connection between Africa and the landed countries.

So much has gone into creating this moment. I wanted to say something authentic, honest, and inspiring about the tragedy of slavery and people uprooted; to show the other side of something so horrible that bears beauty. I am trying every day to do this through the culinary experience. It has been a gamble, no getting around that. But for me it has also been a gift that happens only once in ten gathered lifetimes. When you are so absolute in your conviction, you have very little time to debate or measure if people are going to get it. I was basing the success of this multimillion-dollar project on the fact that people would both understand and love what I do. The Cecil is no little venture. A lot has gone into making this huge statement on the corner of 118th and St. Nicholas. But I felt like, if I were allowed to explain my motivation and my passion, people would understand.

And if they didn't? If they didn't, and if I gave them something undeniably delicious that kept them coming in and back, then the hell with all the rest of it. That works for me, too.

Nino Esposito

SETTE MEZZO

With his thick silvery hair and perfectly tanned complexion, he looks like a dapper impresario from some Italian film. He's a motorcycle enthusiast who takes off once a year to ride across the country with his buddies. "People say my face never ages. I tell them it's not Botox. It's from riding my motorcycle into the wind."

My father, who was a maître d' in Italy, always told me not to go into the restaurant business. "You won't ever have a life," he said. So when I married an American woman and moved here from Sorrento, what did I do? I went into the restaurant business. What else can you do if you don't speak English?

I started as a busboy at Elio's, a very popular Italian restaurant on Manhattan's Upper East Side. I was so good at bussing, Elio promoted me to waiter. Well, you know, every waiter dreams of owning his own restaurant. And I was no different. A group of us at Elio's used to talk about it a lot and we coincidentally all decided to leave at around the same time. Don't get me wrong. Elio was a great guy to work for.

And we made good money in those days. But it was the late eighties, when things were booming, and that just seemed like the right time to go out on our own.

I partnered with Gennaro Vertucci—a fellow Elio's waiter—who, after twenty-seven years, is still my partner. Our plan was to open a small restaurant, just the two of us. In those days, if you were a nice-looking guy and you spoke English, a lot of Jewish people would come and say, "Hey, I got some money. Let's open a restaurant!" But if you say yes, you can't do what *you* want because now you have partners. Even if they're silent partners, the place still isn't yours. So Gennaro and I pooled what we had, which wasn't much, and we opened Vico's on Second Avenue and 83rd Street. It was tiny—only a thousand square feet—and it could fit only twelve tables at the most. But it was ours.

Because we were so small, we knew we had to stand out in some way or we'd quickly be eaten up by the more established places. Fortunately, that location was in an area where good Italian restaurants were few and far between. We also decided our décor would be unique. Whereas most Italian restaurants are wood paneled and dark, we did all white, all open, lots of plants and skylights. We also created a different type of menu. At that time, most Italian food was locked into the heavy cooking of the 1940s. Our food was simple and of good quality. As it turned out, just as we opened, the *New York Times* published an article about how healthy the Mediterranean diet was— which was exactly what we had planned to be our menu all along. Lots of olive oil, fish, and light fare.

All those undertakings combined to make us a huge success. From day one there were always people standing outside, waiting for a table. I didn't know who half of them were, but I learned in time that they often included John Eastman, whose sister Linda was married to Paul

McCartney; Steve Weiss and his wife, Donna Karan; and the architect Charles Gwathmey. People who were considered big celebrities, to us were just customers.

Eventually, people started complaining about the wait, so we decided to expand. One of our customers who was in real estate took us to see a space for a second restaurant. Gennaro and I walked inside, loved it, made a deal, and in 1989, our second restaurant, Sette Mezzo, was born. Sette Mezzo was basically a spin-off of Vico's, which was still going strong, but Sette Mezzo was better looking and much bigger. And again, we were knocking it out of the ballpark. Once again, we had fortuitously found a great location. The restaurant is one block over from Park Avenue, and at the time, there were no restaurants there. Today there are four on our block alone.

What you hear a lot about Sette Mezzo is that it feels "clubby." We didn't plan that, believe me. It just happened. What gives it that clubby feel is that the same people keep coming back again and again. Sometimes once a week and often more. New Yorkers like to see and be seen by people they know. To them, this place is an extension of their dining room. We know these "members" on sight and they know we know them, so that's a bonus as well. They know they don't have to make a reservation one or two weeks in advance. That we'll always squeeze them in, even at the last minute. Is that fair? I think so. If you have people who come all the time, why wouldn't you go out of your way to accommodate them? The Newhouse brothers and their families show up almost every Sunday. Rudy Giuliani comes often. So do Ralph and Ricky Lauren. The late New Jersey senator Frank Lautenberg was a good customer for years. Shouldn't they get some credit for their loyalty?

Reviewers have called our food "pedestrian." They claim our prices are "over the moon." But we say: Why change something that works? And in any case, we don't really agree with that assessment. Maybe ten years ago we were overpriced, but right now, we're average for New York City. Wherever you go, if it's a nice restaurant, you will spend fifty to seventy dollars per person or more. We always buy top-quality food, so you pay for that. And we have an outstanding staff, so you pay for that, too.

If you ask me what I find the most difficult challenge in this business, and what's probably the reason my hair has turned gray, I'd have to say it's seating. When you're in this kind of atmosphere, where almost everyone who comes in knows everyone else who comes in, you're eventually going to get a good-table/bad-table situation. Personally, I don't get it, because the food is the same no matter where you sit. But people care. And some of them *really* care. To the extent that they put you on the spot and you don't know what to say. If they ask to sit at a certain table, I might have to say, "I'm sorry, it's booked." So they say, "What, Nino? I'm not a good customer?" "Yes," I tell them, "you are. But these people are, too." I hate having to come up with excuses. Absolutely hate it.

At Sette Mezzo, the three tables in the front when you walk in are the most desirable. Sometimes we set up four there, but that's the absolute most we can do. Those front tables can and often do seat eight, nine, ten at a time. Then you walk down two steps and there are more tables there. And that's considered okay, too. But after the middle area and toward the back—well, let's put it this way: Someone told me once, "I'll never sit in the back. That's Siberia!" "What's the difference?" I'll ask them. "The food is coming from the same kitchen! The sauce is from the same pot!" But they'll have none of it. Up front, you're eating with someone else's elbow in your plate. This is better? I guess so. They want to be there and that's where they want to be!

We have a few little tricks we use when we absolutely have to. For example, if you're one of our regulars and we know you're coming in with three people and we want to keep a three-top empty for you, we put a top over a table for three to make it into a table for six. Then, when people come in for a table of three, we don't seat them there because it's set up for six. And when *you* come, I take the top off and set you up for three.

I still work six days a week. I'm here from eleven to three. I go home to rest, take a shower, and I'm back at six until close, which could be eleven or twelve. It's not easy to keep a marriage with these hours. There are problems if you're never around. I've been lucky because my wife is strong enough to understand. Also, she enjoys what we've been able to afford, because like me, she came from nothing. She married a waiter. Now we are in a better position financially, so it paid off. But it hasn't been easy.

I think the fact that Gennaro and I were struggling kids has been a strong influence on the way we run this place. We're not just managers at the door saying, "Welcome," and leading people to the table and that's it. When we're really busy, and our staff is under tremendous pressure, we're right in there helping to clear the tables. Twenty-seven years later I'm still working the dining room like a waiter. And I'm good at it, too.

PART VII

Pairings

SYNERGY

Syn-er-gy "sin er je"

/ˈsɪnədʒɪ/

noun (pl) –gies

Definition: The creation of a whole that is greater than the sum of its parts.

Also called **syn-er-gism**. The potential ability of individuals to be more productive or successful as a result of a merger.

Word origin: mid-nineteenth century; from Greek *sunergos* ("working together").

Sun ("together") and *ergon* ("work").

Alessandro Borgognone and Daisuke Nakazawa

SUSHI NAKAZAWA

Two men, both in their early thirties, brought up on two different continents. One on North America, one on Asia. One with an idea, the other with a dream. One bold and brash, the other quiet and retiring. Two jigsaw pieces that shouldn't fit together, but with a little help from Google Translate and a lot of conviction, do just that. A year after their first face-to-face meeting, they are partners in a small restaurant that earns a coveted four-star review. If this is not a New York story, I don't know what is.

It's a wintry Thursday afternoon, around three. Fast-talking and thoroughly self-confident, Alex Borgognone is all over the still very new restaurant, simultaneously consulting with his staff, picking up a scrap of paper he notices on the floor, finishing a call on his cell phone. Finally, he takes a deep breath and joins me at the gleaming white marble sushi bar, which, he tells me, he has specifically designed as a backdrop to "the real art we're presenting here, the sushi."

While Alex and I are talking, Daisuke Nakazawa is downstairs in the kitchen, preparing for the evening's service. There, unlike the buzzing hive of activity upstairs, all is calm. No music plays. No one speaks. His assistants are deeply absorbed in preparing an octopus and tending to a raft of sea urchins. When Alex and I finish our conversation, Daisuke comes upstairs. He and I repair to a table in the rear of the dining room. On the opposite side of the room, several staff members are having an informal meeting. Nakazawa's English is, by his own admission, still quite fractured. My Japanese, on the other hand, is nonexistent. As we talk, both he and I occasionally have trouble understanding each other. When this happens, we both turn helplessly to those seated across the room. Sometimes they can assist us, but mostly they just throw up their hands and laugh.

Alessandro Borgognone

In 1993, my dad bought his first restaurant—a little pizzeria in the Bronx, which he named Patricia's after my mother. When I joined him, even though I had attended culinary school, I chose to make my career in the front of the house. Cooking is a lot of work, and when you're in the kitchen, you never get to see anybody. I much preferred getting dressed up and mingling with the diners.

From a little pizzeria, we built Patricia's into a small neighborhood restaurant with great Italian food. Business was excellent and we quickly outgrew the space. So, when we got the opportunity to purchase the building next to us, we grabbed it. The new Patricia's was much fancier than the old neighborhood joint, which made a lot of our regulars from the old place feel uncomfortable. As a result, we lost 50 percent of them, which meant we had to work a tremendous number of hours to get that back. And that meant I would come home really late every night. One particular evening, I rolled in at one in the morning. My wife, who was already fed up with my bullshit, said, "I never see you anymore! Your children don't see you. Nobody sees you!" I retorted with my usual: "I love you. Let's watch a movie together and work things out." I turned on Netflix and we chose a subtitled documentary called *Jiro Dreams of Sushi.*

The documentary was about Jiro Ono, an eighty-five-year-old sushi master from Tokyo, who is considered one of Japan's national treasures. It highlights this man's ten-seater sushi bar, which is downstairs in the Ginza subway station and is so popular, it's next to impossible to get into. The documentary follows Jiro, his son, and his three apprentices as they go through their day. One of the apprentices stood out for me because of his backstory. For eleven years, this man had been toiling with barely a glance in his direction by the master. He had tried, unsuccessfully, over two hundred times, to make a perfect egg custard, *tamago*, which would elicit Jiro's endorsement. When finally Jiro nodded his approval, the apprentice literally broke down in tears. The camera captured the whole scene. I was truly moved—and fascinated.

As someone in the restaurant business, and as someone who has trouble sitting still, I'm always thinking of my next move. So when I saw this, I thought, "Fantastic! I could open a sushi restaurant with one of these guys at the helm!" My wife goes, "Don't get any ideas, Alex." And I'm busy thinking, "What an amazing idea!" I knew I didn't stand a chance trying to entice Jiro or his son to America, but I thought this senior apprentice—the one who made the egg custard—just might say yes. I reran the movie and learned from the credits that his name was Daisuke Nakazawa.

The next morning, I went directly to Facebook. There were many Nakazawas, but only one with the first name of Daisuke. The photo was of some young children. I took a flyer and I wrote a letter, telling him all about myself and what I wanted to do. I included my telephone number. I then went to Google Translate to convert it into Japanese. And I sent it off.

Two weeks later, I got a phone call from the 206 area code, which is Seattle. I had truthfully forgotten about my letter until that moment. It was Nakazawa, explaining in broken English that he was now living in Seattle making sushi at the restaurant of his friend Shiro Kahiba. I explained as best I could that I wanted to open a sushi restaurant in New York City similar to Jiro's, but with a different spin on it for the American palate. He told me—as best he could—that he had the same idea, that it was his dream.

I was very surprised that no one else had thought to call him, but they hadn't. For me, the stars were really aligned. I was simply in the right place at the right time. I sent him a ticket to New York, and with the help of a translator, we got to know each other over a three-day period. Over the next few months, we continued e-mailing, and on Valentine's Day, 2013, I brought him back again. This time we started putting things together.

We did most of the planning on that second visit. For the restaurant, we chose an 1100-square-foot space. It was a horrible wreck that had formerly housed a hair salon. But I loved the block, which was quiet, quaint, and perfect. You don't find many tree-lined blocks in the heart of the West Village, so we said, "We'll take it." When I told Nakazawa I would be done building our restaurant in three months, he said, "I don't think so, Alex." And he laughed. But I've learned since then that Daisuke is always laughing.

As I predicted, it took us three to four months to construct the restaurant. But what was really time-consuming was everything else. The staff, the food, and most important, creating a concept that we both envisioned. Here we were, an Italian and a Japanese guy, from totally different cultures, who could barely communicate, but who respected each other and shared a single goal: To create a restaurant that had the most amazing sushi and was different from every other sushi restaurant in the city.

And we did just that. One way we stand out is through what we call "theatrics." That is, providing a bit of a performance in every dinner. That's Nakazawa's role every night. Did you ever see anyone receive a live tiger shrimp on her plate? That's the unexpected. That's the theatrics. The *uni*—that is, the sea urchin—that he brings out is practically still in the cocoon. The sea scallops are still fluttering when they arrive in front of you. All that really does make a difference. By visually seeing that process, you're creating something that not a lot of restaurants do. Most people are not so adventurous as to bite into these things. But if it's placed in front of you, and Nakazawa is standing right there, smiling and watching, you have no choice. You're going to try it.

Daisuke is always smiling. In most sushi restaurants, the chefs are so humorless. If you go to Masa, the guy won't say two words to you. That bothers me. When I go out to dinner, I don't mind spending money, but I want to have a good time. And some of these guys take themselves so seriously. Nakazawa, on the other hand, greets everyone with a huge smile the minute they walk in the door. While he's working, he engages with the customers and they love it.

He loves it, too. He talks to them. They take "selfies" with him. They have fun.

Sushi Nakazawa opened for business on August 22, 2013. At first, we kept it very quiet to give us time to get our feet wet. Then we unleashed the opening by sending a one-line e-mail to the *New York Times*, and to the two biggest foodie blogs, *Eater* and *Grub Street*, both of which bring you up-to-the-minute info on what's going on in the food world. The line we sent them was simple: "Daisuke Nakazawa, apprentice to Jiro Ono, is opening up a restaurant at 23 Commerce Street." That was it.

Our website was up and running and my intention was to create a mailing list based on people who called or e-mailed for reservations. I figured that would be the start of our PR campaign. But within the first day after the word was out, people saw that single mention on *Eater* and *Grub Street* and called or wrote us to make reservations. I got well over two thousand requests! Such is the power of the Web. Such was the power of that movie! Almost all of the callers left their names, numbers, and e-mail addresses and how many people to reserve for. It's now a year later and we've been booked solid ever since.

I attribute our success to a number of factors. Being at the right place at the right time never hurts. And okay, I do take credit for grabbing Nakazawa, bringing him here, and creating a place for us. The rest? It's all the incredibly talented Daisuke.

And Pete Wells.

The *New York Times* review just blew the lid off everything. I was pretty sure they would eventually come to review us. At least I hoped they would. And I knew that Pete Wells was the reviewer, but that's all I could have told you about him. He doesn't book under his name, and you're not supposed to know when he's here. According to his review, he sat in the dining room and at the sushi bar. I never recognized him and neither did anyone else. The first we knew he had been here was when the paper called to clarify a few things. That's when we were certain the review was coming. But to wake up one morning to find that Pete Wells has just given your restaurant four stars? Let me tell you, there are absolutely no words to describe it. None.

Without that review, we would probably have been just another restaurant. It was in his hands to give us two, three, or four stars. If we got two, we would be like every other restaurant. If we got three stars, we would be special. But at four stars, we are amazing! Outstanding! That puts us in a league with only five other New York restaurants that currently have four stars—Le Bernardin, Jean Georges, Eleven Madison Park, Del Posto, Per Se, and us.

I carried over a lot of what I learned at Patricia's to this restaurant. From a little Italian pizza place to a four-star sushi restaurant, things aren't all that different. People want amazing service no matter where you go. What we did there, how we made people feel really comfortable and how we developed an amazing clientele that kept coming back is the same philosophy I brought here. Service is of paramount importance to us at Sushi Nakazawa. When you walk into a Japanese restaurant, how many times can you say you have had the most amazing service? Try none. I hand-picked every one of our front-of-the-house people. Stealing a few, I admit it, away from different restaurants that I really loved. And I worked hard to bring out the best in every single one of them. My role, as front-of-the-house guy, is to do just that. To worry about my staff, myself, and what we are doing here. And I go forward with that. Keeping this the best sushi restaurant in America is my goal right now. My only goal.

Daisuke Nakazawa

Twelve years ago, when I was twenty-three, I came across an ad Jiro Ono put in the Tokyo newspaper. He was looking for a junior apprentice to help him at Sukiyabashi Jiro. Of course I knew who Jiro was. Everyone in Tokyo knew Jiro. He was an old guy with a ten-seat sushi bar downstairs in the Ginza district subway station—and he served the best sushi in Japan. Jiro was already famous when he put the ad. But not like now. Now he is a movie star. Now the whole world knows Jiro. I made an application. And I was chosen to be his junior apprentice. He has three apprentices—two juniors and a senior. It was a very happy day for me.

When you apprentice to Jiro, you learn to make sushi but you don't actually *make* sushi. Only Jiro does that. And his son. Apprentices work in the kitchen. They prepare the ingredients. They set up things for Jiro. For the first three months, I washed the produce and obeyed and said, "Yes, yes, yes." You never talk back to a sushi chef. And you never, *never* talk back to Jiro. After a few years, I was allowed to handle fish—cleaning and scaling. But it was still more years before I got to go behind the sushi bar and directly assist Jiro and his son. But still only assisting. Never making.

The restaurant is tiny. Just a counter. There isn't space for more than two people to work from that counter. The rest of us worked in the back making rice and heating the seaweed and taking care of everything else he needed. Jiro is a perfectionist. Every grain of rice and every sheet of seaweed had to be perfect every day.

One day, some people came in to make a movie about Jiro-san. They set up cameras in our restaurant. That day, I was making *tama-*

goyaki; it's a sweet egg custard dish served at the end of the meal. I had been making this dish for months and months, and it never was ever good enough for Jiro. All I want is to please him. That's what I work for. But two hundred times in a row, he rejects my *tamago*. And then, on the day the cameras are there, Jiro finally says, "Okay," to me. At last, he approves my *tamago*! It made me so happy, I cried that day. And they put my tears in the movie.

I stayed with him for eleven years. But in 2011, Japan had an earthquake and then a tsunami. I was afraid for my family to stay there anymore. I had three kids at the time—I have four now—and I was scared for them and for my wife. I wanted to come to America. I told Jiro, and he gave me his blessing. He said I had learned enough. I was ready to become a *shokunin*—a man who makes sushi. The only person I knew in America was a man named Shiro Kahiba. He was one of Jiro's apprentices who now had a restaurant in Seattle. He came back to Tokyo every summer and he would stop in to say hello to Jiro. I wrote him to ask if he remembered me and if he'd consider giving me a job. Shiro is in his seventies now. He said yes, he remembered me, and he hired me.

In Seattle, I learned to speak a little English. Also, I learned how to make sushi with Western fish. I was with Shiro for two years when I got an e-mail from a man telling me in this strange Japanese that he saw me in the Jiro movie and he wanted to open a sushi restaurant in New York with me as the sushi chef. I didn't answer for two weeks because I needed help to understand his letter. And when I understood what he was saying, I thought, "This man is crazy! Why does he want me? He doesn't even know me!" I didn't think he was serious, but I got someone to help me call him. We e-mailed back and forth using Google to change our words to each other's language. And then, he sent me an airplane ticket to New York so I could meet him and learn his ideas. I went, because this was what I always had in mind—my own sushi restaurant in New York City.

I met Alex in New York. I saw he is around my age and learned he owns a restaurant in the Bronx. We spent some time seeing New York City and we talked about the sushi restaurant. It all sounded good, and he was a very nice guy, but I still wasn't sure he was serious. Finally, he said if I would be part of this restaurant, we could call it Sushi Nakazawa. *My name!* That was what did it for me.

On my second visit, we saw a shop he had picked out. We made our plans and I believed for the first time that this really was going to happen! We signed the contract for the space together in February, and from that day I knew it was a great decision for me. I thought this gives me the best opportunity of my life.

From the day we opened in August, every seat in the restaurant is filled. It's very cool. Meeting the people. Being able to do whatever I want behind the sushi bar. Being the boss and the teacher. The sushi in my restaurant is only 10 percent like Jiro-san's sushi. I use many of his techniques but in a different way. I'm creating for America now. For American taste, which is different from Japanese.

We serve a twenty-course tasting meal. The menu is *omakase,* which means I choose every day what we will be serving. We order from here and overseas, so what we make depends on what comes to us that day. Sometimes it's *sawara* (Spanish mackerel) and sometimes *amaebi* (fresh Hood Canal shrimp). Some days we get sockeye salmon, which we smoke over a bed of hay. We get fresh scallops from Maine and serve it still moving. That's how fresh. Our *o-toro* (tuna-belly hand roll) gets wrapped in nori (seaweed) from Tokyo Bay.

My day is always the same. I come in to work around eleven thirty a.m. I go into the downstairs kitchen where my three helpers and I prepare for tonight's meal. It's very quiet downstairs. No talking. No phones. Only work. We first open boxes of what has come in earlier to see what we have. Today, we got a four-hundred-pound tuna that we will cut into fatty, medium fatty, and lean pieces. We crack open the sea urchins, portion the smoked bonito, skin the octopus, and start the *tamago*. By six, we are ready to begin service.

At Sushi Nakazawa, I am the one training the apprentices now. I work hard like Jiro, but I'm completely different. I tell my guys always, "Good job." Sometimes Jiro might tell you "good job" but to get just that, you had to work so hard. So much pressure. Another way I'm different. He is very serious all the time. Never smiles. I like to have fun. In Japan, they want just good-tasting sushi. In America, they want good taste but some entertainment, too.

I don't know if Jiro ever thinks of me, but I think of him all the time. Every so often I write a letter to him in Japan and tell him what I'm doing. I don't hear from him yet, but I don't care. He's almost ninety now and probably still making sushi. I'm sure he's too busy to write me back.

Connie McDonald and
Pam Weekes

LEVAIN BAKERY

In 1995, Connie McDonald and Pam Weekes opened Levain Bakery, a minuscule subterranean establishment on West 74th Street. Outside on the sidewalk, the steadily moving line is peppered with both locals and tourists who have been lured down into this cozy alcove either by the intoxicating aroma wafting out onto the street or by the ubiquitous media buzz that continues to surround it, even after twenty years. The shop offers a creative display of rustic breads and cakes, but once the customer makes it to the counter, it's a good guess he'll come away with at least one of the warm, gooey, hockey-puck-sized, walnut-chocolate-chip cookies that are undeniably the bakery's crown jewel.

How many do they sell a day? That's top secret. "People ask us that all the time," Connie says, "and I say, 'a lot.' Then, they'll try to guess. So I say, 'When you come in with your pay stub and show me what you make, I'll tell you how many cookies we sell.'"

Connie McDonald

Before moving to New York, I traveled all over the country working in resorts, waiting tables, and teaching tennis. While I was enjoying myself, my father kept reminding me how extremely successful my brother was on Wall Street. He "suggested" I come to New York and do the same thing. So what do you do when you've grown up obeying your father? You get on a plane.

After a few false starts, including a stint at a Long John Silver's restaurant where I dressed up as a pirate and delivered fried fish to the customers, I made my father happy; I got a job on Wall Street as a broker's assistant. Problem was, I was terrible at it. I was cold-calling people, trying to sell them stocks I knew nothing about. And why did I know nothing about these stocks? Because I never showed up at the meetings. They were too early in my day. I was busy training for a triathlon!

I've always been really active physically. When I was a kid, I played golf and tennis; I swam on the club swim team and swam in high school. I started skiing when I was three. One day I was talking to a friend and he said, "I swim at this really nice pool in midtown, you should try it." The next week, I signed up and showed up in my polka-dot swimsuit; I didn't have another suit because I just didn't have money then. It was old and really ugly, horrible. I walked in, checked everything out, and saw this group in the pool.

They were in the fast lane and I was fascinated watching them. I hadn't swum in years and I just got in on the slower side and swam a couple of laps. Eventually I started swimming with the faster group. One of the women in that group was Pam Weekes. I didn't know her all that well but someone told me she was looking for a roommate. Well, I was too, so we decided to room together. This was in 1987. During that year, there was buzz about people doing triathlons, so we decided to try it. We were already swimming and running and racing with our bikes, so this was a natural.

But it wasn't a natural as far as my boss at the brokerage house was concerned. When everyone else would get there at seven for the morning meetings, I would saunter in at nine, hair still soaking wet from the pool. I wasn't fooling anyone. In those days we all had desk phones. If I wasn't there on time, my boss would pull the receiver from my phone and I had to go into his office to ask for it. That lasted a few times, and that was the end of my job.

While working on Wall Street, I supplemented my income by catering small parties, which I really enjoyed, so when I got fired, I enrolled at Peter Kump's New York Cooking School, which is now the Institute of Culinary Education. It was a small, very cool place. You went there for six months, at the cost of six thousand dollars, and that allowed you to come out and get a job for six dollars an hour. I did my externship at Amy's Bread, where for ten hours a day I shaped bread dough. Boring? Absolutely! But I loved being in the surroundings of a bakery. There was just something about it.

In 1994, I signed on as pastry cook at a tiny restaurant called One Fifth Avenue. It wasn't very successful. The owners spent a fortune renovating it, but the customers stayed away. I don't know why, maybe because they didn't have a liquor license. In a last-ditch effort, they fired the chef, and we were all speculating about who the next chef would be. One afternoon, I was standing in the pastry area when the side door opened. I smelled cigarette smoke and heard the sound of heavy boots clomping down the hall. Suddenly, this tall, skinny guy in a black leather jacket swaggers in and I'm wondering, "Who is this?" It was Anthony Bourdain. He sauntered downstairs to interview for the position and came back up with the job. Tony was—is—a great guy, but even he couldn't save the restaurant. It was clear our days there were numbered. Is a pastry chef with no diners still a pastry chef?

Right around that time, the *New York Times* published an article that said practically the only good thing about One Fifth Avenue was the bread, which they called "amazing." Well, this being New York, people immediately started coming in to buy the bread and take it home. We still had no idea what the future held for Tony or the restaurant. But I had an idea what it might hold for me. And maybe for Pam.

At the time, Pam had a really good career going, working for the designer Norma Kamali. I asked her what she thought about going into the baking business together. We had always talked about wanting our own business, but the time was never right. Now, because I had a great relationship with Tony and with the restaurant's owner, I felt safe putting this proposition to them: I would continue working in the restaurant's bakery but I'd go off the payroll. My partner, Pam, and I would turn the restaurant's pastry area into a wholesale bakery business, and in exchange for using their kitchen, we would give them all their baked goods for the restaurant for free. It was a win/win for everyone. How could they say no?

Pam took a leave of absence from her job and we started doing wholesale bread out of the restaurant kitchen. We put samples together and brought them around to different restaurants. I was such a nervous wreck. I didn't want to hear if someone didn't like our product, so I would drop off the samples and run away before anyone got a chance to tell me. Eventually, we got a couple of really good accounts and then a few more and a few more. Well, you know how things go. One good thing leads to another, and the accounts kept mounting. One of us would bake and the other would deliver. When restaurants started asking for two deliveries a day, we hired a delivery guy. Our first employee!

We knew nothing about being in business, but we decided even though we were still working out of One Fifth, we should at least have a business card. A good friend, who was a graphic designer, volunteered to make us one. "So," he said, "what's the name of the bakery?" "The name?" I looked at Pam. "Oh God, Pam. We don't even have a name!" I gave him a bread book, which he perused, and at one point his eye got stuck on the word "*levain.*" It's French for a sourdough starter. He wrote it out on a small card, and he said, "Look how perfectly that fits over the word 'bakery'!" Well, the last thing we wanted to be was "Pam and Connie's Bakery," so Levain Bakery it was.

The busier we got, and the more space we usurped, the less happy they were with us at One Fifth. We knew we had to get out of there. And that's when we opened the 74th Street store. It was a challenge to open a small business. Banks wouldn't lend money to two thirty-five-year-old women with no business background, so we financed it all ourselves by going to people we knew. I think the banks were also turned off by our chosen location. We weren't exactly moving into a prosperous neighborhood. It was 1995. The Upper West Side was mostly rent-stabilized buildings. There were a lot of drugs and no good food. Our bakery wasn't even on the street level. You had to walk down a short flight of steps to get in the front door. We put as many lights as we could outside because when we first started, we were working around the clock, and people were sleeping in our stairwell. At the time, it was the wholesale accounts that kept the money coming in, but we were also making and selling bread to walk-in customers.

And of course we sold "the Cookie."

It's a chocolate-chip-walnut cookie that has been described as resembling a very warm, very delicious hockey puck. Call it what you will, it is not only our signature pastry, it has truly changed our lives. How we came to make that cookie is a story in itself. Back in 1988, when we were on the triathlon team and training for the Ironman race, we biked, swam, and raced almost daily. And every day, the rigors of training left us feeling depleted and starved by the end of the workout. We knew we needed something to sustain us, both during and after our rides. Today, there are so many amazing power bars available, but back then, the only things on the market were those gross bars that, after a short time in the sun, got so mushy you could wrap them around your handlebars.

So we decided to make a cookie just for us that would be our replacement for power bars. We made it big, like around six ounces, so we could tuck it into our bike shirts as we rode, pull it out when we felt the need, and eat as much as we wanted. It was substantial enough that it wouldn't fall apart if you ate it on the go. Whoever we shared these cookies with, loved them. So it was only natural that when we opened our bakery, in addition to all our breads, we would bake and sell these huge cookies. Customers raved. In 1997, Amanda Hesser wrote an article for her "Temptations" column in the *New York Times*, saying "the most divine chocolate chip cookies in Manhattan" were at Levain Bakery on the Upper West Side.

Well, let me tell you, when the *New York Times* discovers you, you are on the radar. It doesn't take long before the Food Network comes knocking. Which in our case happened very soon after the article appeared. We were on the Bobby Flay *Throwdown* show, which we won with our chocolate-chip cookie. Also on that network, Rocco

Dispirito called our dark chocolate chocolate-chip cookie the best thing he ever ate. An article in the *Huffington Post* was called "25 Foods You Have to Eat Before You Die." Our cookie took the number one spot. And you know what's next. Eventually, it's only a matter of time before Oprah finds you. Don't even *ask* what that amounts to.

Today, there are still lines outside the door all day long. We never advertise or solicit press or TV. Our success has been strictly word of mouth. The store is always packed—which is not surprising because it's only about seven hundred square feet, including our two ovens. Most of the space is given over to the bakers, so you can imagine how small it is up front. Considering how far off the beaten path we are— we're in the middle of the block in a residential area, below street level—it's really amazing how many of our customers are tourists. How do we know they're tourists? You can't miss them. They walk in with their guidebooks. Or wearing their Yankees baseball caps. I don't know. You can just tell. And they come here as a destination, having found us, I'm sure, through social media. *Yelp*, a blog that is user run, lists the best things to do in New York: First is Central Park; second is the Metropolitan Museum of Art; third is Levain Bakery, followed by the Brooklyn Bridge. Levain ahead of the Brooklyn Bridge? Come on, people! What's that all about?

And TripAdvisor is another one. For the past three years, in their listing of 11,583 top restaurants in the city, they cite us as either first, second, or third. So what happens when people coming to New York read that? They call us to make dinner reservations! Well, attention, TripAdvisor people: We are not a restaurant! We are a tiny little bakery with four metal stools and a stand-up counter. And we're just fine with that.

Pam Weekes

Connie and I started by knowing nothing about running a bakery. I remember asking my mother once, "How do you know you're ready to get married? How do you know you're ready to have a baby?" And she said, "You don't. You just do it and figure it out. If you wait until you know, you're never going to do it." Truth is, if we had known some of the things we'd have to deal with, we probably wouldn't have gone ahead. It's been a huge sacrifice; we both have given up a lot of things.

We've never really had assigned roles in the bakery. We've always just tried to do whatever worked best for the big picture. The good thing is, we have different strengths and weaknesses. Connie is more outgoing and feels more comfortable in the limelight. I'm quieter until I know people. I'm very detail oriented and organized for the most part. It's the Virgo in me. She's generally more laid back. She tends to be a lot more patient in some ways than I am. I'm much more direct. She'll say, "That's really nice but can you do it this way?" And I'll say, "Don't do it that way, do it *this* way."

We both interview and hire the new bakers, but as a rule, she trains them, because that takes an endless amount of patience. When we have to fire them, I try to make Connie do it. Everyone thinks I'm the tougher one. I might be tougher up front but if you push her to the wall, she can be really tough, too. You have to be when you have forty employees. We have very different personalities, but I think that the reason that our relationship works so well is that we have the same core values. You don't have to agree on everything. And we don't. But we do both believe in doing things as directly and simply as possible, especially having so many people involved. If you can keep it simple, then you can maintain quality, which is our singular goal. We will never sacrifice quality. Which is why we keep our products few in number.

We're now twenty years into working together. As we got more successful, we thought we should each get our own apartment, but then a friend in real estate told us we would get so much more for our money if we shared something. We found an amazing place with more space than I ever thought I would have in New York, and it's been our home ever since. Living and working together doesn't succeed for everyone, but it definitely works for us. We have three facilities now. One on 74th, one in Harlem, and one in the Hamptons. As a result, we're usually not in the same place during the day anymore, so we communicate by phone or text. If we're both back for dinner, we cook together at night, which is fun. But of course we end up talking about work, what happened where, with whom, what needs to be done. How to do things better. I think the biggest strain on our friendship is that we work too much. We used to do cool things together—biking, hiking, whatever. But it's really hard to plan ahead to do anything these days, because something at the bakery always seems to need attention from at least one of us. We've both missed family events, weddings, holidays, which has led to damaged relationships with certain people in our families. They don't understand that if you're in retail, holiday weekends are your busiest times and you simply can't leave.

I'm hoping that at some point I can slow down and start living a little bit more. I miss friends, family, having a relationship outside of the bakery. I have a stack of books this big that I want to read. We've both sacrificed close connections with others, but then I never had a burning desire to get married or have kids unless it was with the right person. Still, all of a sudden you turn around and you realize twenty years have gone by. Connie and I are both fifty-three. When we started, we were hiring people our own age to work with us. Now we're working with their children. That'll open your eyes. Do I have regrets? I don't think so. But sometimes I do wonder. I don't know if you can regret something, but you can wonder.

Bryce Shuman and
Eamon Rockey

BETONY

Talk about synergy . . . Here are two young men from the South, Bryce Shu-
man and Eamon Rockey, born a few years apart, both of humble backgrounds,
both schooled in culinary crafts. Both set out to find work in a fine New York
City restaurant. They meet in 2007 at Eleven Madison Park (EMP), one of
New York's most highly respected eating places. Shuman, a happy-go-lucky
guy with a boyish persona, goes into the kitchen, where he works his way up
to executive sous chef. Rockey, tall, angular, and the more serious of the two,
finds his place in the front of the house, eventually becoming, at twenty-three,
the youngest captain in EMP's history.

By 2013, Shuman is still at EMP, but Rockey has moved on to become
general manager and partner at several other restaurants. This is when
Andrey Dellos, a Russian expat and owner of a failing restaurant on 57th
Street, decides to shut it down and reopen with a whole new concept. A loyal
patron of EMP, he recruits Shuman by offering him his first solo effort as
executive chef. Shuman brings in Eamon Rockey as the GM. The name on the

*door changes to "Betony." The restaurant is a hit. It receives a string of acco-
lades from the critics, a three-star review in the* New York Times, *and suddenly these two are the culinary darlings of 57th Street. If Andrey Dellos isn't
patting himself on the back for this one, he should be.*

Bryce Shuman

Striking out on my own meant leaving South Carolina with a guitar
case and a bag of clothes; a twenty-five-year-old kid with cooking on
my mind. I worked in a few restaurants, bounced around a little bit,
visited the kitchens of Jean Georges, Joël Robuchon, and some other
really great places, but when I trailed at Eleven Madison Park, I knew
I was home. There was just something about it. A fire. An energy! The
chef, Daniel Humm, is crazy in the greatest sense of the word. He's so
passionate about cuisine that nothing else matters. Cooks walked off
the line because it was too hard. Chef fired people and threw them
out; always pushing, pushing those who remain. The kitchen atmosphere put me in mind of Bikram yoga or hardcore jungle music. And
it drew me in like a moth to a flame.

It's almost an unwritten rule that cooks stay for about a year at one
restaurant and then they're on their way to the next thing. But that
wasn't my plan. At my interview, I said to Chef Humm, "I want to start
at the bottom and work every station. I want to commit myself to you
indefinitely and to learn from you all I can." I'm guessing that's why he
agreed to take me on.

One day, not too long after I started, he said, "Okay, Bryce. You're
working fish roast." Not *garde-manger*, which is cold salads, the true

bottom, and which is where everyone generally starts. Not even hot apps, which is next in line. Fish roast was all the way up the hot line! I had been promoted even before I started. I worked as fish roast—you get your name from what you do—for a month, then I was meat roast for a month and then a few months after that, he promoted me to *sous chef*. *Sous chef* is an underboss. Like second in command. Did I deserve to become *sous* so early? I don't think so. I think he did it more out of necessity in the kitchen than anything else. People move on and spots open up. I remember someone telling me when I first started, "I've been here for eight months and I'm outta here!" I said, "Eight months and you're moving on?" "Yeah," he said, "eight months here is like ten years anywhere else."

Of all the lessons I learned from Chef Humm, the simplest and possibly the most important was this: Make it taste good. Easy? Not really. Can I whip something up with hydrocolloid and make the craziest foam in the world and freeze it with liquid nitrogen and smash it in the center of the table? Absolutely. But if doesn't taste like anything, then I've failed. So how do I know it tastes great? Because of the second Chef Humm dictum: Taste, taste, taste your food. Over and over again.

After spending six years at EMP, I felt I had literally done it all and I was ready to become an executive chef. I didn't want to be a *chef de cuisine* for another big chef who was opening another restaurant in his or her empire. That's very safe, and when you make mistakes, you won't fall that hard. In the end, though, nobody's ever going to hear about the *chef de cuisine* of a new restaurant that some other chef opened. If Chef Humm opened another Eleven Madison Park on Mars, and I ran that restaurant, even if I created all the dishes on the menu, trained the staff, and created inspiration, it would still be Chef

Humm's restaurant. So, no. That wasn't for me. At some point in time you have to stick your neck out a little, and probably more than a little. But I was willing to do whatever it took.

It wasn't long after making my decision to branch out that I got a call from Andrey Dellos, the man who owns Betony. He had opened it earlier under the name of Brasserie Pushkin to not much success and it eventually closed. But he had in mind to reopen it with a new chef and a new name. He said he was a big fan of EMP, and he asked me if I'd like to do a "tasting" for him. That's more or less a tryout. You prepare a menu and cook a number of courses to show what you can do.

There were three men at the table the day I did my tasting. Mr. Dellos, the head of his company, and his right-hand guy. I put together a menu of seven courses, and cooked and served them all. The first course was native persimmons with tarragon and watermelon radish snow, which is made with fresh watermelon radish juice. It's bright red and hotter than horseradish. I first froze it and then powdered it on top of this succulent persimmon. The tarragon gave it a nice balance. The second course was a venison carpaccio with wheat berries and pickled juniper. The third course focused on oysters. I roasted the oysters in pine branches until they opened. I added a *beurre blanc* with a bit of the pine, and whisked in butter. To go with it, I made a *sabayon* from matsutake—or pine—mushrooms. They're super aromatic and are just possibly my favorite fungus on the planet. Finally, I made a really great rib eye with potatoes. Dessert combined grapes and hazelnuts.

At the conclusion of dessert, I stood in front of these three men, waiting for a reaction. I knew every mistake that I made—like I might have forgotten to put this herb on, or this little shave wasn't exactly right, or there's a little line on the steak. Even one mistake to me is one too many and devastating. The only good thing was, I knew every-thing tasted great because I had tasted it. After a few minutes, they said, "Okay. Thank you." And that was it.

A few agonizing days later, the call I was waiting for came. I was to be the executive chef of a brand-new restaurant that was going to be called Betony, a name that refers to a medicinal herb in the mint fam-ily. The absolute best part of the deal was that it was then up to me to determine what kind of a place this 140-seat restaurant would be.

I knew precisely what I wanted. And what I didn't want. I didn't want to be the next high-end chef trying to teach the world about fine dining. I wanted to make sure that I was doing delicious food. I wanted it to be gracious, generous, welcoming, and friendly. People go out to dinner for many different reasons and I wanted to satisfy all of those reasons. I wanted my restaurant to be a place where diners have a bite before the theater or Carnegie Hall, which is just a block away. Maybe they come in and celebrate something special, like a birthday, anniver-sary, or some other special occasion. Or maybe they come in just because it's a Wednesday night and they want to have a great bottle of wine, eat a great piece of roasted chicken, and listen to some great music.

I started working on the project at the beginning of February. We installed a brand-new kitchen. I wrote and tested an entire new menu, which took me about a month or so. I kept it small: A good chicken, a great steak, a poached fish, a seared fish, a lobster, and a vegetarian pasta, a leafy salad, and some sort of charcuterie, like foie gras, hot and cold.

Next, I needed to find a general manager and beverage manager. For that job, I could think of no one better than Eamon Rockey. I knew him from the days when he was a captain at Eleven Madison Park. He was a partner in a restaurant downtown when I approached him, and

I was thrilled when he agreed to come aboard. When we discussed our vision for Betony, it was clear that we both saw things through a similar lens: I would handle the kitchen, and he would manage the dining room and the bar. No one can do both jobs well in a restaurant this size. But we realized right away that if we did things as a team, we would be better than the sum of our parts.

It was a race to the finish, to say the least. And we were full of metaphors. Because we decided that opening a restaurant is like jumping out of a plane, a week before we opened, Eamon and I went skydiving. We jumped—strapped to instructors—from fourteen thousand feet. It was awesome, and I think we just needed to let off some of the stress we were feeling. And then, the night before opening day, the whole staff got together and had champagne and a couple of beers and we put up a piñata—which represented that we were all breaking into something new. We took turns smashing it. When it broke, it spewed out all these little plastic rubber dinosaurs. Even now, sometimes you'll walk around the kitchen or in the restaurant and find one of these dinosaurs somewhere; people hide them around the kitchen as reminders.

Opening day was tremendous. Everyone was excited and charged up. We didn't do a lot of advance publicity, hoping to start slow and build as we became increasingly fine-tuned. The first night we did thirty covers, which doesn't sound like a lot but felt like madness at the time. Then we went up to sixty or seventy covers and that felt crazy again. When we went up to a hundred covers, I couldn't believe it! We were high-fiving each other all over the place, like little kids.

I'm a music lover, so once I felt we were on our way with the food and the space, I turned my attention to what our diners would hear as a background to their conversation. The choice of music in a restaurant is vitally important to me. I have thousands of records. I collect soul and jazz and funk. In fact, I often define myself as "the resident DJ of my living room"—much to the annoyance of the cats and my wife. Originally I had this idea that I would record all our music off of my vinyl collection so we could keep all the music along the same vein. At first I was recording just jazz. But something didn't feel right. In the décor of our restaurant, there's a lot of attention to detail—baroque flourishes here and there intermixed with hard, reclaimed barn-wood floors and intricate plaster. And I came to think that mixing all these elegant designs with this jazz music made it appear that we were taking ourselves too seriously. The songs that really felt great in the space, and fun, the ones that provided more of the effect we were aiming for were the couple of soul tracks I put on there. So I went back and recorded a ton more soul music.

I started out with four hours' worth so the diners wouldn't hear the same music twice, but after the first couple of weeks, my waiters were, like, "Bryce, I used to love this song, and right now, I hate it. You're ruining it for me." I realized immediately that I needed at least sixteen hours of music on my playlist so that my servers aren't hearing the same music over and over again and wanting to kill themselves. So back I went to my record collection and now, with a mixture of jazz and soul, I think we've got it right. At least I hope so.

We were open only a few months when Pete Wells, the restaurant reviewer from the *New York Times,* showed up. You never know in advance when he's coming—and you actually pray that he comes at all. He came in with three other people. Eamon recognized him immediately because he had served him at a few other restaurants prior to ours, but he needs to remain anonymous and we need to do our job to the best of our ability. And that's what everyone does.

The whole process of being reviewed is surreal. But every restaurant is in the same boat. It all goes down the same way. To keep his review fair and balanced, he usually comes into a restaurant four times over a brief period. He was here three times with three guests each time. I was expecting him to return a fourth time, which he never did. After he came in the first day, I told everybody that no one is getting a day off until the review comes out. All the *sous chefs* worked six days because I wanted to make sure we were at our best every single day.

A few days after his last visit, the *Times* called to say a photographer is coming, so we knew it would be soon. The restaurant reviews always come out in print on a Wednesday in the Dining section, but it shows up on the *New York Times* website the night before. That Monday night, before I expected it to come out, I stayed up all night long reading two-star reviews of really great restaurants to prepare myself. I told myself, "These are wonderful restaurants and they have two stars. Be prepared." The next day, Tuesday, I talked to the staff and cooks, and said, "Look, guys. We're a fabulous restaurant. We're really special. We have good stuff going on here. No matter how this review comes out, we have great things in store for us. Even to get reviewed, period, is a big deal. Thousands of restaurants open every year and they review only about forty-eight of them." Late that afternoon, Eamon went onto the *New York Times* website and there was nothing there. No website at all! We went crazy! We thought it was our computers so we kept hitting "Refresh" and waiting, and still nothing. Suddenly there's a notification on Twitter that the *Times* website is down and that Syrian hackers were taking responsibility. At six p.m., again he looked up the Betony listing under the *New York Times* restaurants. We still couldn't get the review but you could see the number of stars plain as day.

Three!

Three stars! Eamon came running into the kitchen. "Three stars, Bryce!" We started jumping up and down like little boys. When the full review finally came up on the screen, it was stellar. We were still in the middle of service, but I didn't care. I carried the paper around and read passages to my cooks: ". . . a big scoop of whipped chicken liver . . . is almost as smooth and luxurious as the foie gras. It came with toast that I kept forgetting to use; I got all the crunch I needed by dragging the liver mousse through a trail of fried chicken skin and caraway-rye crumbs, and all the sweetness from a bright purée of green apples and chervil."

As a chef, you devise a dish, and you work on it over and over until it's perfect and you hope your guests will love it the way you do. But to read someone else's take on it, particularly someone who commands words as effusively as Pete Wells, well, I can't even describe that feeling. I read them another passage: ". . . you know that the browned hunks of fat on the edge of dry-aged beef can be a treat. But do you know what happens if you melt that fat and stew a short rib in it for two days, then sear the rib over white-hot charcoal? Mr. Shuman knows, and I'll bet that a year from now other chefs will know, too. Accessorized with grilled romaine and one perfectly fried sweetbread, it's a dish worth stealing."

The entire staff was overjoyed. Around ten p.m., people started pouring in. Friends and friends of friends. After midnight, with only a few diners left, we gathered our staff, our friends, and the leftover diners; we got a slew of hot dogs and cases of beer, and with eighties and nineties hip-hop music blaring late into the night, we celebrated. It was an incredible night!

Eamon Rockey

I guess you could say I come by this profession naturally. My mother was a chef at the culinary program at the University of Southern Mississippi. My father was the chef of the Hattiesburg Country Club. My father was the first to recognize my passion. I still have this vivid memory of him coming into my room one evening when I was a senior in high school. I was sitting on my bedroom floor, fiddling around with something, when he dropped from his height a stack of pamphlets and brochures from the Culinary Institute onto the floor right next to me. I still remember the sound it made. And he said, "Eamon, if you're serious about cooking, you should think about going to Hyde Park."

Like many ambitious—and foolish—people leaving culinary school, I thought that I was destined early on for a management position in a fine restaurant. I started shopping myself around as though that were a possibility. I didn't realize how much I needed to learn. My first job was at Gilt, a restaurant in the New York Palace hotel. Chris Day, the GM, was kind enough to hire me and to humor me. I think he saw in me what I didn't know—namely, that I had a lot to learn. He was my mentor as I traveled through a variety of front-of-the-house positions. When I left Gilt and moved to Eleven Madison Park (EMP), I had to go through all the same positions again, starting at the bottom: runner, back waiter, front waiter. But the system makes sense. Each restaurant has its own culture, so even if you've been a runner at a million restaurants and progressed beyond that, you have to learn how it works all over again.

I was twenty-one years old when I became a captain at EMP. That's pretty unusual, but the restaurant was young and in a tremendous state of growth. While I was captain, I was also tending the bar. One day I would do one, the next day I would do the other. I loved doing both. Being a captain at a busy four-star restaurant and making it seem effortless can be a sport, but one that is all in your head. Tending bar is a sport too, but it's as much in your hands as your head. If you're going to excel, it's like shadowboxing. You have to know where everything is without seeing it, so you can turn around and grab something without giving it a thought.

My journey to Betony from EMP encompassed a number of years and a few different restaurants, but every one of the experiences I had was invaluable. My first landing was at Compose, a small cocktail bar and restaurant in TriBeCa. It was a little jewel. My role at Compose was general manager and my goal was to set the stage for tremendously talented bartenders to craft the best cocktails in the city. It turned out to be a bittersweet story for me, though. At first, Compose was everything I wanted it to be. But we ultimately decided to evolve the culinary component of the cocktail lounge and we started looking for a chef. That search led us to hire Matt Lightner, a tremendously popular chef at Castagna in Portland, Oregon. The problem was, with a talent like Matt's, to be secondary to cocktails was not going to be enough. So the name was changed to Atera, and the space evolved from cocktail-centric to food-centric. And that wasn't what I had signed on for.

I went from Compose to a restaurant called Aska, which I opened as a partner with a couple of the guys that I worked with at Atera. It was exciting and it was a challenge: How do I put together a world-class beverage program for a Scandinavian restaurant in a design studio in Williamsburg, Brooklyn, that legitimately becomes a crazy, 350-people-at-a-time club on the weekends? It was thrilling to watch it succeed the way it did. And so fast.

One day, Bryce Shuman came into Aska and sat down at the bar, without announcing himself. I originally met him when we were both working at EMP but we didn't know each other well. When I saw him, I was like, "Bryce, what's up, brother?" He said, "I'm just here getting food and drinks." I hadn't seen him over those few years, but we both lived in that neighborhood so it was certainly plausible to see him there. The next day, he e-mailed me, "Do you know anybody who might want to be the GM of the new project that I'm going to be the exec chef at?" I e-mailed back, "What exactly are you looking for? Are you looking for someone young and hungry? Do you want someone who has done a number of openings where you can do what you do and let them do what they do? Or do you want someone with a little bit of both, someone tenured but still learning? Young, with experience? A background in fine dining but not afraid to have some fun, too?"

I finished with, "Like me?"

The rest, as they say, is history. I kept my partnership at Aska, hired a GM to fill my role there, and signed on at Betony alongside Bryce in February 2013. I'm the general manager here, but I also run the cocktail program. Designing, devising, and serving unique and interesting drinks is fun for me. It allows me a creative outlet and I can get my hands dirty, so to speak. Some people think of a drink as just a drink. To me, every drink, particularly the ones I create, is a story. And more often, a personal moment. Looking back, I can connect many personal moments to drinks I have created. One in particular springs to mind. There was a drink on our menu until very recently which required the use of a seasonal beer, a cold Canard Noir from

Greenport Harbor. The first time I drank the beer, I thought to myself, "My granddad would love this." Out of that memory association, I devised a drink I called Old Dog Shandy. A classic shandy is a light beer mixed with lemon or lime soda. I've been making shandies for a long time, but this is not classic because it's based on a memory of my grandfather—hence the name, Old Dog Shandy.

Let me explain. When I was at the Culinary Institute, my grandfather would come visit and we drank dark beer together. Malty, rich, hoppy dark beer. So that's what I think of when I think of beer and my grandfather. I also think of a number of other things. When I would go visit him in Colorado, where he lives, we would go camping in the mountains. We always made a fire, and my grandfather smoked a lot of spicy Turkish tobacco. We cooked a lot at home too, and my grandma would make dishes with lots of vinegar. And for me, there was always honeycomb when I came to visit. You pull it out of the hive and you munch on the honeycomb.

Those memories became the genesis of the shandy. I started with beer that reminded me of him. And then I asked myself, "What do I put in it? What do we use as sweetener? Honey!" I associate honeycomb with my grandfather. What else will we do? Smoke? Perfect, because we made campfires all the time in the Colorado mountains. How do we get smoke in this? We smoke the honey. Now it's sweet and malty, but we need to balance it out. How do we do that? We can use citrus, like most will use, but the citrus won't integrate too well with dark beer and smoked honey, so let's use vinegar, that makes more sense. Grandma cooked with vinegar. What kind? Sherry vinegar, because it's dark. Dark beer, dark smoke, dark honey. It builds and builds.

Shandies express themselves really well in crushed ice because it eases off their round edges a little bit. Crushed ice in drinks is even better when you can smell some sort of aroma on the top. How do you get aroma in this? Okay, we have smoke but we don't have tobacco smoke, which is very different from other kinds of smoke. Are we going to do the Thomas Keller–Anthony Bourdain thing and steep cigarettes in something and make a dish? Or are we going to do something else? I pop in to see the tobacconist around the corner and pick up a small tin of Virginia pipe tobacco. And then I steep it in White Dog whiskey to get this thick, rich, powerful infusion that when you smell it, makes you feel like you are sitting in your grandfather's study. I mist that over the top of the drink and serve it.

When the drink comes to you, it's a glass of crushed ice, a homogenous dark liquid, and a straw. And that's it. When you look at it, it's pretty but certainly does not look special. You then taste it and you're assaulted with layer after layer of flavor and you're smelling tobacco, and tasting malt, and hops, and the vinegar is making you salivate but the sweetness of the honey is resting on your palate and satisfying you. The smoke, when you breathe out, is there on your breath and it's sweet and beautiful. At the end of it, you're looking at something monotone, on ice, in a glass with a straw. There's nothing unique about it. And yet there's not a person who has that cocktail that doesn't have some sort of memory like that. It's very cool. No one can escape the nostalgic impact of that flavor profile when smoke, honey, and tobacco combine. Everybody gets it.

Bryce and I spend a tremendous amount of time talking about how to motivate and inspire and push people to a place where both they and we are ultimately better for it. In the dining room, for example. If something is going wrong, if one of my team is falling aside from what is best for the restaurant, I have to address it. There are times when it's a struggle to strike the right chord between professional and personal, because I know that the people who work here take this personally. I also know that on a very busy night it can get very hard to keep the train on the tracks, to keep execution at the highest level of quality.

People make mistakes. It could be anything. The quantity of something ordered is mixed up, or food is served unevenly, or even something small like a piece of paper upon which a drink order was lost or forgotten about for too long a time. When that happens, I sometimes see tears in a staff member's eyes because they realize they have changed a guest's experience from what it should or could be, to what it now will be, which is in recovery mode. When I see the impact that even the smallest mistake can make on the leaders of my restaurant, I know I'm with a winning team and the passion that is in me is alive as well in them. It's a passion on both sides that I cherish.

Crowd Feeding

W e're spoiled. Generally when we eat, we exercise personal preference. We pick and choose; we eat what we want to eat, and mostly when we want to eat it. But in certain settings there are only two choices: Take it, or leave it.

In such settings, for one reason or another, people can't leave where they are or what they are doing to have a meal. So the food chosen by people other than themselves has to come to them—rendering them more or less a captive audience. The crowd feeders in this chapter include JoJo Esposito, a fireman who has been selected by popular acclaim as the designated cook for a group of firefighters in Rescue Company 5 on Staten Island; Stacy Adler, who specializes in catering to film crews working on location; and Department of Correction Commissioner Paulette Johnson, head of food services at Rikers Island, with twelve thousand prisoners and eight thousand staff to worry about.

Whereas the crowds Stacy and JoJo serve are only metaphorically confined—they get to go home at the end of the day—Paulette Johnson actually does serve a captive audience. Just a few of Rikers' more famous alumni—some of whom have even dined on Johnson's fare—include David Berkowitz, aka Son of Sam, a convicted serial killer who arrived on the premises in 1978; Guy Velella, Republican state senator found guilty of taking graft in 2004; former New York Giant Plaxico Burress, who checked in in 2009; and Mark David Chapman, who broke the heart of a nation when he shot down John Lennon in 1980.

The afternoon I went to Rikers Island to meet Commissioner Johnson, ominous storm clouds seemed to follow me on my cab ride out to Queens—adding an unwelcome touch of drama to my existing apprehensions about the day. My escort was waiting for me in his car on the prison's outer parking lot. Together, we drove across the Hazen Street bridge—the only way to get on or off the island—and through a gatehouse, where we were asked to identify ourselves. We made an immediate right into another lot—and pulled up behind AMKC, or Anna M. Kross Center, which was named for the department's second female commissioner and is the largest of the nine buildings that make up the prison complex.

You can't just walk into any of these buildings. You must first pass through a series of checkpoints. After providing my name and stating my purpose, I began the entry process by passing through a series of stations where I was vetted and revetted. There was a metal detector at one; I had my hand stamped at another, and entered and exited two steel-barred gates, each of which slammed behind me before the one in front of me opened. At the end of the line, I received a visitor's identification badge, along with a new escort. He was a massive uniformed guard who led me—single file and no talking, please—down a hallway so long I could barely make out the end of it. As I fell in behind him, I suddenly became aware that I was entering a world few people will ever see.

Two lines of yellow paint divide the cement floor into three traffic paths. We walked down the center lane, and I noticed in the distance a string of prisoners headed toward us on an outside lane. As we closed in on each other, the prisoners' guard motioned them to stop. As if choreographed, they slowly turned in unison and placed their foreheads against the wall, which took me by surprise. It turns out that this is standard procedure when visitors are in the vicinity. It ensures that they will neither see nor be seen by the inmates.

Finally, we arrived at the kitchen, where I met Commissioner Johnson. In my mind, I was picturing a Nurse Ratched or Queen Latifah (from the movie *Chicago*), but actually she was a diminutive sixty-year-old woman in a colorful suit, who welcomed me warmly. She and an assistant showed me around the vast space, which looked to me to be the size of half a football field. It was eerily stark and empty. And spotless, although the smell of chickens roasting filled the air. The equipment, an endless number of steel combi ovens and rotisseries—yes, filled with spiraling chickens—ringed the perimeter, while several rows of five-foot-high, one-hundred-gallon copper vats, each with a step attached so someone might peek inside, ran down the center. Prep counters filled in the open areas. And that was it. The reason the kitchen was so empty, Johnson explained, was because it was between meals. She assured me that soon enough the place would be turned over to the preparation of food for thousands. I did see one guard, however, who stood firmly against a wall watching as two inmates in white jumpsuits and paper caps polished an already clean-looking countertop. One of the inmates paused for a second, turned his head my way, and offered a hint of a smile before returning to his task at hand.

At the end of our interview, I reversed the earlier process, exiting through the same series of doors, receiving the articles I had earlier surrendered. I returned to the car with my host, and as we drove west over the bridge, revealing one of the most beautiful views of the city skyline I've ever seen, I took a final glance back at the facility from the car window. For some reason I thought about the young man in the white cap who had so diligently been washing down the kitchen counters. I hadn't yet decided where I would be having dinner that night, but I knew exactly where he would be dining.

Paulette Johnson

NEW YORK CITY DEPARTMENT OF

CORRECTION, RIKERS ISLAND

A calm, unpretentious woman, she speaks in the soft rhythmic cadences of the Jamaican native she is. As the chief overseer of the entire food service operations for the New York City Department of Correction, Assistant Commissioner Johnson directs the purchase, preparation, and service of 47,000 meals a day. Which is like serving a baseball stadium full of fans every day, seven days a week. Or approximately seventeen million meals a year.

I think it's safe to say the Department of Correction (DOC) has the largest kitchen in New York City. Which is not surprising, considering the number of people we serve. At any given time there are around twelve thousand inmates in the system. Rikers houses the majority of them in nine separate buildings. My department is responsible for feeding them each three meals a day. We also make daily meals for the inmates at three facilities located in the outer boroughs, and the prisoners in holding cells in several local courthouses. And we also prepare daily meals for a staff of around eight thousand.

Being in charge of a place of this magnitude is a once-in-a-lifetime experience. Not too many people can say they do what I do. Twenty years ago, when I applied for this job, I was working for a group of hospitals and nursing homes. It was a good position, but after a while I had pretty much accomplished all I had set out to do there and I was ready to move on. So when I heard the Department of Correction was scouting around for an executive director of the Nutritional Services division, I picked up the phone. There were three of us interviewed that day. When the guy who preceded me came out from his interview, I'm looking at a seven-foot-tall male. I'm only about five feet tall myself and I'm thinking, "Oh, man. They'll never select me! A five-foot female? In a prison facility of this size? Not a chance."

Still, I walked into that interview full of confidence because I knew I had a very impressive résumé. Five or six men, including the chief general counsel and the deputy commissioners, started throwing questions at me. They asked me about budgets and how I felt about working multisite facilities. I explained to them that I already had a pattern of doing that; I currently had a system in place for three facilities. Then they asked, "How do you feel about managing so many people?" To which I answered, "It's really not the size of the gun, sir, it's the effect of the bullet."

When I told my friends I was moving into the world of corrections, they thought I was crazy. But for me, life is all about challenges. I tend to seek them out. Besides, I'm a very positive person. I believe that if something needs to be done and if someone has to do it, why shouldn't that someone be me?

Each of our twelve facilities has a kitchen but only five are fully equipped and used for actual cooking. One of them, the AMKC facility, houses what is likely the largest kitchen in New York. It's around forty thousand square feet, almost the size of an acre of land. And yet, we use only three types of cooking equipment: vats, combi ovens, and rotisserie ovens. When we designed the place, we looked for equipment that could handle our huge numbers. The hundred-gallon vats were perfect for that. Each vat is an institutional-sized copper pot about five feet high that has a step-up attached to the side so you can see what's cooking inside. AMKC has twelve of them. Our requirements for the three rotisserie ovens were that they could each turn out four hundred servings of roast chicken in about the time it takes to watch half a segment of *Law & Order*. Our combi ovens can accommodate five times that. When everything is in full swing, it's quite an operation. But once you get used to the magnitude of it all, it's not at all hard to keep things running smoothly. "Organization" is the operative word here.

Some of the inmates help us out in the kitchen, but mostly they do the cleaning. They clean the floors, the tables, and all the work surfaces. They scour the baking pans or other implements as needed. They transport food inside the kitchen from one station to the next, and assist the cooks and bakers in preparation, working alongside them but never actually cooking. I've often wondered if these men and women volunteer to work in the kitchen or get assigned to it. I know, given the choice, I'd volunteer to be here. I think it's a fun place to be!

Even though there are guards assigned to watch the prisoners who are working in and around the kitchen, preparation knives are obviously of great concern to us. Our knives are kept in locked boxes that are secured in a specified area. These locked boxes are called "shadow boxes." They hang on the wall, and when they're opened, there's a picture at the back of the box that looks like a shadow of a specific piece of equipment. For example, if there are twelve French knives, they will be lined up on hooks in front of the shadows of twelve French knives in that box. If one is removed, that leaves an empty shadow, which tells us that something is missing. When a knife is needed, a civilian staff member signs it out, and signs it back in. If I'm using a knife to cut up a chicken, I sign it out. I cannot leave the kitchen without turning it in. As a result, in this kitchen, you'll never see a knife lying around.

The inmates eat three times a day. Breakfast is at five a.m., lunch at eleven, and dinner at four p.m. These are the state commission standards. I didn't plan them. I'm not sure what time they get up in the morning, but this is when we provide the meal. We have approximately one hundred and seventy inmate dining areas here on Rikers. They're called either "pantries" or "congregate." Fifty prisoners eat in each of the pantries, and three hundred and up in the congregate feeding areas. Those who are served from the pantries line up in their housing area—always under the watch of guards—and walk single file into a dayroom, which is actually a multipurpose room, equipped with television, tables, and chairs. It's adjacent to their cells. The food is brought in from the kitchen, plated by inmates under the supervision of staff in the pantry, and passed through "blind feeding windows" to the inmates in the dayroom.

If they're eating in the congregate room, they come out of their housing areas, line up, and walk into huge dining rooms with tables and chairs that are designed specifically for prisoners. They walk in a line, show their meal cards, and a tray is handed to them with their meal. They take their tray, get a drink from the beverage dispenser, and sit at one of the tables. The officers direct them for the most part to where they can sit.

Those prisoners who are on therapeutic or special diets eat in the same dining room as their fellow inmates, but they're not eating the same thing. Kosher and halal prisoners get precooked, prepackaged meals, which we just heat and serve. These come from approved vendors and are stored in a separate freezer for religious meal items only. And we color-code their trays so they don't get mixed up and they are maintained separately.

A lot of people, when they think of prison food, they think of slop. They think of putting everything in a pot, stirring it around, and dumping it on a tray. They think of inferior food being prepared and served in an inferior manner. This is the total opposite of what's happening here. The staff eats the same meal as the inmates, just not at the same time. What the staff eats today at noon is what the inmates will eat for supper. For lunch today, the staff is having chicken, rice, and vegetables, and the inmates are having a pasta casserole. For supper, the inmates will get the chicken and rice.

Here's something people don't generally know. Every prisoner on Rikers Island is currently eating a heart-healthy diet. That, to me, was a dream come true. The prisoners don't get anything fried. Nothing. And it's whole grains only, as well. We started this process twenty years ago when the DOC undertook a kitchen renovation project. First thing we did was get rid of the fryers. No fryers? No fried foods! Easy enough.

Then in 2006, the Department of Health eliminated all trans fats, which was a big plus. Around the same time, Mayor Bloomberg created a food policy task force, which included all twelve city agencies, to make changes in the food we bought and served, changes geared at eliminating heart disease. In 2008, Executive Order No. 122 mandated that we meet those guidelines. Which was exactly what I wanted.

We started out by reducing portion sizes. But how to do that without complaints? I knew if we put a smaller quantity of food on the same plate that once contained a larger quantity, it would be very noticeable. So we came up with a slightly smaller-sized plate that made the quantity of food look more or less like the same amount. It was no secret. We explained this to the inmates before we did anything, and surprisingly, I didn't get any protests that there wasn't enough food or that they left the dining room hungry.

And believe me, I would have heard from the dietitians in the clinics. We also have a grievance box where inmates can drop comments, and scheduled inmate council meetings where they meet with the dietitians. If I serve something for lunch and for some reason they don't like it, you know I'm going to hear about it—if not during the meal, then directly afterward. They'll tell the officers and the officers will tell the captains, and we're flooded with phone calls. When that happens, I investigate immediately. But I'm pretty careful to see that it doesn't happen often. A special menu committee tests everything I serve in the prison before I serve it. Everything we do here is planned, tested, and retested before it's rolled out.

For breakfast, the prisoners eat pretty much what you might expect: Hot or cold cereal, bread, fruit, and coffee or tea. It's a "continental-style" breakfast except for once a month they get a hard-boiled egg. Lunch and dinner include a protein, starch, vegetable, fresh fruit, and salad. Over the course of the day, the Rikers Island inmates probably eat much healthier than most people.

We release around sixty-one thousand inmates back into society every year. Most of them return to their homes. Hopefully, they'll take with them some of the good eating habits they've learned from our kitchens. The highlight for me is to be able to get some of those households to change the way they eat, particularly the lower-income families that really need to know about healthy eating.

Apropos to this, I heard about an interview between a member of the media and an inmate that took place when we changed from white to whole wheat bread, from regular food to low-sodium meals, and from whole milk to 1 percent. The interviewer asked the prisoner what he thought about the changes, and the prisoner said he felt much better and had more energy. The announcer asked, "When you are discharged from Rikers, what are you going to take away from your experience here in terms of the food?" The inmate said, and I'm paraphrasing, "Well, I haven't had fried food, or salty food, or junk food for so long that the first thing I'm going to do when I leave here is go to the closest KFC and get me some greasy fried chicken. I'm going to eat that with some French fries just to satisfy my taste for the bad foods. Then, I'll go home and say to my girl, 'Listen, we've got to cut this bad stuff out.'"

The one food item we're most famous for here is our carrot cake, which is little known outside the prison's walls, but renowned within them. The prisoners help the bakers make it for Thanksgiving, Christmas, and Ramadan. Everyone in this facility—inmates, staff, and visitors if they're lucky—is crazy about this cake. Actually, anyone who tastes it loves it. The way we make it, each loaf, which is chock-full of carrots, raisins, and walnuts, weighs nine and a half pounds and serves twenty-five people. We put out roughly twenty-five hundred loaves a year. The recipe is below.

Rikers Island Carrot Cake

Recipe for 25 loaves of carrot cake

25 pounds sugar	8 ounces baking soda
25 pounds flour	8 ounces salt
8 ounces cinnamon	20 pounds raisins
6 ounces nutmeg	25 pounds carrots
4 ounces ginger	8 pounds walnuts
4 ounces clove powder	25 pounds eggs
6 ounces allspice	3 gallons vegetable oil
1 pound baking powder	8 ounces vanilla extract

1. Place in a mixing bowl: sugar, flour, cinnamon, nutmeg, ginger, clove powder, allspice, baking powder, baking soda, and salt. Use a paddle mix on slow for 5 minutes.

2. Add raisins, carrots, walnuts, eggs, vegetable oil, and vanilla extract, mixing on slow speed for an additional 5 minutes.

3. Increase speed to medium for 10 minutes.

4. Pour into loaf pans. Pans should be three-quarters full.

5. Bake at 350°F for 40 minutes.

JoJo Esposito

RESCUE COMPANY 5, STATEN ISLAND

Growing up on Staten Island, he remembers himself as being the only kid in the neighborhood who never even thought about being a fireman. But when he turned twenty-one, his brother, a fireman himself, encouraged him to take the test. He passed it, signed up, and never looked back. Now he's a part of Staten Island's elite unit known as Rescue Company 5. There are only five such units in New York City, one for each borough. If a fireman goes down or a technically complex rescue is required, the rescue unit handles it. "We've had people trapped in cars, trapped underwater, trapped in construction site cave-ins, sewers, elevators. You name it, we've pulled someone out of it."

JoJo's brother died on the job on 9/11. So did eleven members of Rescue Company 5.

Staten Island has twenty-four firehouses. Most are double houses—an engine company and a ladder company. The engine company has the hose and pump, and handles the fires. The ladder carries out the rescues. Our firehouse is different. We have both an engine (six guys on each shift) and a rescue unit (six guys on each shift).

I've always been with the rescue company. From the day I started, I felt like this was where I belonged. It's the whole atmosphere of the fire department. The way of life. Everything we do. We're always helping someone. Every time we come on the scene, people are glad to see us. I'm sure being a cop is great, too, but they're law and order. People aren't always happy to see the cops. We, on the other hand, we're life and death. We're always the good guys.

Contrary to popular opinion, we don't just hang around all day waiting for a fire. We do practice drills, check our tools, clean the place, and of course we cook. And we eat. If the company's on a twelve-hour shift, we're eating three meals a day on-site. Unless, of course, an alarm comes in and throws everything off for the day. Breakfast and lunch are up for grabs. There's always food around for those meals, but you make them for yourself. Six nights a week we have a real meal. On Sundays, we'll either order in pizza or Chinese food.

The engine and rescue companies always eat together. Every other month we switch off: One month the engine company is in charge of meals, and the next month the rescue company is. When Engine has the meals, we're all on diets because they don't buy enough and the refrigerator is empty all the time. The mice even leave for vacation because there is no food around. You know when Rescue is cooking because guys are eating leftovers for three days after. It's always good to have extra food around when the guys come in hungry from a job. And it doesn't cost you much more. Maybe a dollar more per person. When it's Rescue's month on, I'm usually the designated cook. Notice, I didn't say "chef." I'm a cook. Plain and simple. Why me? Take a look. I'm the heaviest guy in the room. So okay. So I swallowed a lot of aggression when I was young. And a lot of pizzas. But you know what? I'm also a pretty good cook.

And don't get me wrong. I love to do it. For me, cooking is the best job in the firehouse. My favorite meal is rigatoni with sausage, a recipe I learned from my mother. It's really easy. You fry the sausage, add two large cans of tomato sauce, throw in some onions, olives, and sundried tomatoes, and mix it all together. Pour it over some just-cooked pasta and it tastes great. I can make that for fifty people if I had to. Add a loaf or two of Italian bread. Done. And the guys love it. You can't get too carried away with this stuff, of course. I mean, we *are* here to put out fires. When we get a call while cooking, we're literally out of here in under a minute. I just shut the fryer down, cover the stuff I've done, and go. If, when we come back it's a little cold, we just heat it up and it's good to go. There's not a meal that I make that you can't heat up and it's just as good later.

Whoever's cooking the meal that night decides the menu and then, right after roll call, we all get together, we put on our gear, and we go food shopping. The whole company has to go together, because if we get a run, that's where we're leaving from. For the same reason, we take the truck to the grocery store. We try to find a spot to park it, but sometimes we end up double-parking and everyone thinks the grocery store is on fire. Usually the officer on duty stays in the truck to listen to the radio.

When we walk into a store, people stop and stare at us because we're all dressed in our gear and also because we're loud and funny. We know it. But we're so serious on the job and it's so tense that it's fun to goof off where we can. So we'll stand in the aisle: "We getting this?" "No, put that back." "This?" "No, ain't getting that, either." We walk around helping people who can't reach things. Just stupid stuff. We're a bunch of kids, sometimes. Just a bunch of sixth-graders having a good time. Sometimes in the store we're picking out food, and a woman will ask us, "What are my taxes buying you tonight?" I'm the first to tell her, "Lady, you're not buying us anything! The City of New York does not pay for our meals. *We* pay for our meals." These people have no idea how many of those meals—that we pay for—get abandoned in the middle of cooking or eating.

The only thing about cooking that I don't appreciate is the criticism. Every so often someone will break my balls and right away I tell 'em, "Yeah? You try it! Go on, make something for everyone." They run away like a headless chicken. But some of them will take me up on it. Like the one guy—no names—who thinks he's a chef and every time he cooks it's horrible. He's made stuff like chicken with cream cheese. Combinations you can't even imagine. The other guys wanted to throw up. The young guys in the company watch these cooking shows, so they try all this new stuff. One time one of my buddies got so crazy with this kid's food, he said, "Look. Do me a favor. Cook like a man, okay? Make a meatloaf. Make a potato. Toss on a few string beans and we're good. None of this hoity-toity shit."

In just about every firehouse in the world, the kitchen is the center of the universe. That's where it all happens. It could be a shrink's office for a lot of what goes on there. You got a problem at home, you got a counselor in there. Got a problem with the kids, problem with your wife, someone in the kitchen can advise. Sometimes more than a few are there to help. Got legal troubles, you got a lawyer in the kitchen. Something wrong with you? There's a doctor at the end of the table. There's nothing we don't talk about or that we can't solve. And if we can't solve it, someone will give you a number of a guy who can, because it's a world of information in that kitchen. Of course, don't say anything you don't want published because it's not like Las Vegas. Where what happens in Vegas, stays in Vegas. There's nothing sacred in the fire-house. So you'd better remember that. If you say, "Listen, I'm telling you this but don't say nothin'." "Yeah, sure. I won't say nothin'." Next minute, boom! Everyone knows.

Stacy Adler

Y-CATS CRAFT SERVICE

Her commissary is in a large warehouse in a sleepy neighborhood called Green-
point, the last subway stop in Brooklyn before Queens. Many of the old ware-
houses in the area have been converted to film studios. And one serves as Y-Cats
headquarters. This is where she and her staff prepare most of the food before
shipping it out to clients throughout the city, and where she runs the show from
her office. She's worked hard to make her business the success it is, and even
after all these years, she still can't believe her luck.

After ten years doing mostly the business end of restaurant work, I'd had it up to here. A friend of mine is a production manager in the film industry, and when I told her I was at a crossroads, she suggested I consider something called "craft service," which essentially is catering for film crews on location shooting a film. She took me down to her film set, I saw what the caterers were doing, and I thought, "I can do that! You cook stuff, you set it up, you serve it. What's the big deal?"

Two weeks later, I had quit my job and was on my own. That first day, I sat down with a phone book for twelve hours and cold-called people. My selling point was service. A lot of people in the catering industry are known for providing tasty food, but I knew how to take it from just food on a table to that feeling of being at a banquet or a wedding. I explained how my presentation would be a little different from everyone else's, and I guess my feigned confidence didn't hurt, because by Friday I had my first call to do a job on Monday.

It was for a German film production company that wanted me to feed fifty people. Outside. In January. In the middle of Central Park. I cooked the food—snacks, sandwiches, sweets, pick-up stuff—in the kitchen of my apartment and I loaded as much as I could into my little two-door hatchback. I arrived in the middle of the park to ten degrees and eight inches of snow on the ground. It was still snowing and blustery as I set up my table outside. I knew in advance that there would be a truck with a generator and I used it to plug in my coffee urns and whatever other heating elements I had. But anxiety? Don't even go there. And freezing! I'm not sure what I expected, but I certainly didn't expect to be standing outside for fourteen hours. I hadn't worn enough layers and I shivered my way through the day. But there was no option for failure because I had quit my job. For me it was do-or-die time.

After that German shoot, I kept cold-calling and slowly got more and more business. Then, after six months, I landed the big one. I was hired by the reality show *Queer Eye for the Straight Guy*, and that provided me with my first steady eight months of working. It's great when you have a TV show, because you know that you'll pay the bills that month. You work Monday through Friday and feed fifty people a day lunch, snacks, drinks, and coffee. After a while it becomes routine. So I made sure I did a special signature something every day. Like my homemade soups. I make Tuscan white bean, Manhattan chowder, vegan soups, vegetarian soups, beef stew, chili. I learned fast that when you're feeding people for thirty days at a clip, it doesn't matter how great the chicken soup is, you don't want them to say, "Chicken soup? Again?" They love you the first couple of days, but you have to focus on the last day because for sure that's the only day they'll remember.

Eventually, I started getting calls from the producers of music videos—mostly from the big rappers with the million-dollar budgets, and by default, I suddenly became the music video caterer. As my business increased, I moved out of my home kitchen and into a bigger space. I hired part-time workers, and the part-time workers eventually became full-time workers. There were days where I had five jobs going out at once. I bought a small, used minivan, and then a brand-new van, and then another brand-new van a month later. Then we went to a small truck, and then a bigger truck. And now, fifteen years later, I own seven vehicles, including two huge trucks we can turn into kitchens if we need to.

It took me a long time to feel successful. Being raised by a single mother, I always felt like I was in survival mode. My mantra throughout the early days was: Failure is not an option. If it meant staying up for three days straight to make sure my client was happy, so be it. If I had to travel miles and miles, that's what I did.

An average film shoot in New York is a twelve-hour day. Right now it's Super Bowl season. When I'm called to do a commercial, I know in my head it's going to be a sixteen-hour day. This means my team and I have to come to the shop a couple of hours beforehand, load the truck, give an hour or two to drive to location, work the twelve-hour shoot day or, if the day goes longer, fifteen hours, wrap out, come back to the shop, unload the truck, and hopefully you'll have four hours before you have to come back to work the next day.

I just worked on a monster commercial for Bud Light for the 2014 Super Bowl. The crew filmed for four days straight. Our call time was to be at the location of the old World Trade Center site—it's now called the Freedom Tower—at seven in the morning. Six of my staff came to the shop at four a.m. to load the trucks. We left Greenpoint at five thirty a.m., giving ourselves enough time to get to the location. There's never any parking anywhere in New York, but for this particular commercial, parking people held spaces for us. The Tower was not completed yet, so it was a perfect place to shoot. And because it's wide open and we were on the fiftieth floor, we saw some of the most beautiful views of Manhattan I've ever witnessed.

We pulled in with our big trucks about six thirty a.m. It took the parking troops about thirty minutes to pull us into the right spot, and then we had to schlep and unload trucks full of food and equipment up to the fiftieth floor of the building. Trying to move things from a truck that's parked in the middle of the street in Manhattan is crazy! People scream and curse at you. The whole nine yards. We slowly progressed into an elevator where twenty other departments were loading all their equipment, and had to wait again. We're the food people, but as important as we think we are, we're at the bottom of the barrel. The camera guy, director, producers, and art department take precedence. It sometimes took us two hours just to get upstairs.

We served everything from crudité to cheese platters, to dried fruit, nuts, organic fruit, different soups, chili, chicken wings, grilled cheese, baked cookies, heroes. Anything you can imagine. The first day, we fed a hundred people; by the last day, that number escalated to five hundred. When you watch the commercial, you see the stadium with hundreds of people in the bleachers. Or people walking the street. All those people have to be fed. It was a huge deal. There were all kinds of A-list celebrities in the shoot. The budget on the commercial could have been five million dollars. Who knows?

The crew was supposed to walk away for lunch. That means the production company gives them money to go out to eat. But this week, it was zero degrees and we were on the fiftieth floor, so nobody wanted to go out and bear the cold or wait forty-five minutes for the elevator. That left us rolling with the punches, trying to feed whoever asked us. In the building, we weren't allowed to have any open flame so we had to use whatever equipment I had that's electric. I used portable convection ovens and soup crocks. It was like glorified camping. The first day, by the time we got back to the shop, it was eleven p.m. Technically, the first day started at four thirty a.m. and by the time we punched out it was like ten thirty p.m. That's a sixteen-hour day, and that's a ballpark average shoot day.

Everything in the entertainment industry is "gotta have it yesterday!" Particularly commercials. They'll book at the last minute because, for example, they'll find out that Michael Jordan is available Friday, and so Nike will shoot on Friday. They'll call me this afternoon and say, "Plan on fifty people for breakfast and lunch. Tomorrow." And then they'll call me tonight and say, "It's actually going to be one hundred people." Now, if you're entertaining at home and suddenly you find six people instead of four are coming for dinner, you go crazy. At the very least, you have anxiety. But for me, feeding fifty extra people, I don't even stop to think about it. I guess I've mastered it.

Things are a little different when you're doing food service for a movie or a TV show that's using the streets of Manhattan as backdrop for their film, The film company needs a permit from the mayor's office. They go to the mayor's office and say, "We would like to shoot on Sixteenth Street," and they pay a fee to the city. As soon as they get a permit, the "No Parking" signs go up along several blocks in a row. That's followed by a parade of enormous trailer-sized trucks carrying all the components for the shoot that pull in right along the block. Residents in those neighborhoods hate these shoots, not only because they eat up all the parking spots and snarl traffic around them, but also because sometimes they can't even walk down their block. And because we are the ones who are standing outside at the tables with all the great-looking food—which, by the way, is not for them—they hate us, too.

If I'm working on a movie that stars someone very cool, my buddies always want to know the lowdown: "What's he like?" "Did she talk to you?" That kind of stuff. Actually, the bigger the celebrity, the nicer they are. It's all the ass-kissing people around them that are the ones that drive you insane. Like Kanye West. When he walked past us, his people asked us to turn our heads and not look at him. That was bizarre. Mariah Carey routinely shows up hours late—but that doesn't affect me because I get paid overtime to be there. We fed Justin Timberlake before he was anybody, and Martha Stewart before she went to jail. George Clooney? A sweetheart, cutie pie, delicious, regular guy.

Of course, most of the day these guys are working. Or they're in their trailer. It's not like they're just hanging out with us, bullshitting all day. But one time George walked over to grab a hot dog, and people on the street watching started screaming his name bloody murder. He's such a superstar. When he's on the street, you feel his energy all over the place. I've seen them all. Jennifer Lopez is a sweet, regular girl.

Madonna? Couldn't get near her. Twenty people surround Madonna every time she steps to the left or the right. Jay Z, Beyoncé? A beautiful couple. I did Beyoncé's music video this summer. It was a two-day shoot, sixteen hours each day. It could take thirty-two hours on set for a three-minute video. And that doesn't include all the prepping and editing off location.

I've been at this for fifteen years now. The only real break I took was when Hurricane Sandy hit. Sandy was devastating for so many people. I live in Long Beach and my newly purchased dream house—the one that I watched for years before it came on the market and I finally could afford to own it—that house, and everyone else's, was destroyed by the hurricane. A couple of clients in the industry called me to say they wanted to help. They knew I had food trucks, and they told me to go where people didn't have food. Places like Staten Island, the Rockaways, and Queens. They called all the production companies and told them to hire me to take my trucks to feed people who had no power or food or water in their homes. Some for more than a month! The production companies were so generous. I was able to feed my town of Long Beach twice. The day before Thanksgiving, I provided a huge Thanksgiving meal for the first responders and the homeless. One day I went to City Hall and fed all the politicians and the cops. We were all over the place for two months. We literally fed thousands of people. I called our purveyors and ordered what I could. Then I would make fifty pans of mashed potatoes and pasta and grilled chicken, fried chicken. We just wanted to get them hot meals. We did egg sandwiches and gave them hot coffee in the morning. It was amazing because it didn't give me a chance to think about my personal life, or my dream home that was gone with the wind.

My mother still thinks what I do is insane. All the hours and everything. But when I couldn't think of a name for my company, she was the one to come up with it. She said, "Why don't you call it 'Y-Cats'?" "Y-Cats?" I said. "What's Y-Cats?" And she said, "That's Stacy backwards!" She said it worked for Oprah, whose production company is called Harpo. So I figured, Hey! Why not? If it works for Oprah . . .

PART IX

Counter Culture

New York is a town full of food-savvy eaters, people who can and do argue knowledgeably about the merits of six- versus eighteen-month manchego, or whether the Guérande's *fleur-de-sel* beats L'Île de Ré's. But that doesn't necessarily mean they cook, whether because they can't be bothered or they've never learned how. Fortunately, they don't have to. In this city, the twin pillars of "eating at home" are take-out and delivery. And we're not just talking pizza or Chinese. How about paper-thin slices of Serrano ham and New Zealand cockles to start, followed by freshly killed and steamed lobsters and a fennel gratin, with a Meyer-lemon-and-fig galette for dessert? Of course if it's a business dinner for twenty international guests, you might want to do a teeny bit of upscaling—like get the "courses" out of their telltale cartons and onto nonpaper plates before anyone is around to witness their provenance. But that's easy. It's all easy if you know which take-out counters to hit. There are many, many subcultures in New York, but the culture of the counter is too major to be counted among the mere subs.

Personally, I plan to hit up said counters later today when a group of friends comes for dinner. They all claim they'll eat anything, but I have in mind at least one healthy course and I want to cook it myself.

The main course will be some kind of fish. I live on the Upper West Side of Manhattan so I generally shop along Broadway, from 74th Street to 80th. Within that range, and on the west side of the street alone, there are nine food establishments that are either markets or restaurants where you can buy "take-out." Of the markets, I seem to always favor three.

My first stop is Fairway, a 24,000-square-foot institution that started during the Depression era as a fruit cart and still sells fruit and vegetables from stands that line the sidewalk in front of the store. There's just no place that feels like this one. Fairway has it all. Want some artisan truffle ravioli for your dinner party? Check! Need some fruit-and-dark-chocolate Kashi granola bars because that's all your kid will eat? Check! There's nothing you can dream up that Fairway doesn't carry. So why don't I go there all the time? Because the place is a zoo, with no rhyme or reason to its layout. The pre-cut watermelon butts up against the balsamic vinegar, which is across the aisle from the chocolate-covered almonds (although they *are* amazing chocolate-covered almonds), and there are at least fifty different types of vinegar. (See what I mean?) And if that's not confusing enough, there are no rules to navigating the already too-tight aisles, so you can almost count on getting your heels run into by a crusty Upper West Side granny if you're blocking her access to the ready-made banana pudding. So why go at all? Because it has more help than you could possibly ask for, fresh meat like a local butcher, and a prepared-food department with choices you didn't even know you wanted. For my hors d'oeuvres tonight, I'm going to do a *crema di carciofi e tonno* dip to go with the *haricots verts*. Now, where is it again . . . ?

Since I want fish for my main course, there's no way I'm going anywhere but Citarella. Directly next door to Fairway, it is one of the last bastions of civility in Upper West Side marketdom. If you want a shopping cart, Citarella doesn't want you. So be prepared to purchase only what you can fit in the little orange basket you sling over your wrist. Whatever you decide to put in there—exquisitely manicured celery strips, Campari tomatoes so perfectly shined you want to cry—you can count on receiving it over the counter by a faultlessly groomed man or woman, head covered, hands gloved. The fish are so fresh here, you can almost smell the salt water. Tonight I'm making red snapper, which I hesitate to ask the monger to butcher for fear he'll bloody his fresh apron, but I do. Everything about Citarella says "clean, fancy, expensive." Most days, the market is a bit pricey for my blood, but for special occasions like this, why not?

Saving the best for last . . . Zabar's. Okay, I admit it. I'm a Zabar's groupie. On oh-so-many levels. Let's start with the smell of the place that assaults me full blast as I enter. That mixture of pickles, cheese, smoked fish, fresh bagels, and coffee transports me back to Miami Beach, circa 1964, when my father took me to Arnie & Richie's deli for "two slices of roast beef—and slice them thin." Seriously? If I could bottle that smell, I would open up a little stand outside of the store and be set for life. There's nothing not to like about Zabar's. Sure, it's packed. If I had a nickel for every time I hear or say "sorry" to someone I'm gridlocked with in one of the aisles, I could buy a lifetime supply of the store-brand chocolate babka. But for food this good I am willing to overlook the crowds. And speaking of that babka, I throw a loaf into my basket. Okay, make it two. And then I move to the smoked fish counter for tonight's appetizer—a pound of Nova sliced thin enough to read the *New York Times* through. But I won't have just anyone do the slicing. It's Lenny Berk or no one. And that means I'll have to wait in line.

Lenny Berk

At eighty-four, he's the last Jew to be slicing lox here. After forty years as a CPA, he sold his practice and "bounced around" looking for something new to do that didn't involve numbers. One day he heard from a friend who'd seen a New York Times *ad from Zabar's for a lox slicer. Having been a Zabar's customer for years, he thought that sounded interesting. "I figured, why shouldn't I apply? Whenever I bought smoked salmon, I'd buy a big chunk and go home and slice it myself. I could do this." That was about two decades ago.*

I sent a fax to Saul Zabar, the owner, listing my credentials one through ten. I'm dependable, etc., etc. He called me and he said he didn't believe that a CPA would want to slice salmon. He said, "I don't know. Maybe you should come down here. I want to take a look at you and we'll see." As a CPA, I was making two hundred dollars an hour. I don't think he believed that I really wanted the job, but he couldn't not let me try.

So I came down, and right away he gave me a white jacket and put me behind the counter. At that time there was a guy named David

Yang, a Chinese lox slicer, working here. In fact, at that time, most of the lox slicers were Chinese. So he put me behind the counter and he said to David Yang, "Show Len what to do." David Yang was a man of very few words. And when Saul left the counter, David Yang turned to me and said, "Watch!" That was it. One word.

So I watched. And maybe about an hour later, after I stood back there watching and watching, the store got a little busy and some lady came to the counter. "Are you available?" So I jumped in and started working. Saul came down at the end of the first day and he had a little conversation with David Yang. Then he said to me, "You want to come back tomorrow and the next day and we'll try you out?" I said, "Sure!" I remember being behind the counter those few days. One guy is talking to me in Spanish in one ear and the other guy in Chinese in the other ear. I didn't know what any of them were talking about but I just kept nodding because I didn't want to offend anyone.

After a few days, Saul came downstairs, and he said, "I'm willing to try you out, but since you never did this before, you're going to have to do it on a pro bono basis." You tell a guy that's coming into a job slicing lox that he's going to do it on a pro bono basis? Most people don't even know what "pro bono" means! But I agreed and I came back and worked two hours a day for two weeks. Finally, he called me up to his office and he said, "Okay. Forget about the pro bono. I'll pay you for whatever time you put in."

Personally? I think he just wanted to say "pro bono."

Eighteen years later, I'm still here. What keeps me coming back are the customers. Very interesting people come into this store. This is New York. And it's Zabar's. They all come. One time, a lady walked into the store, she must have been eighty, maybe older. She was with a companion and she came over to the counter and she said to me in a distinct Jewish accent: "I don't want salty!" This was maybe five years into my time here and I was determined to use the most challenging customer as a learning tool. "Okay," I said. "No salty." And she'd come back every week and over a period of a year, and she always waited until I was free. I could see she began to trust me. So when she came to the counter, she no longer had to say anything. We developed a kind of very interesting smoked-salmon relationship. We smiled at each other. We talked about fish. And then one day, the companion came in without her. I asked after the lady and the companion said she wasn't coming that day. "Is she okay?" "She's okay." So I thought, "Well, if she's ordering lox, she still has an appetite and that's a good thing." Also, lox costs thirty-five dollars a pound, so she must be able to afford it. Another good thing. Then the companion said, "You know who she is, don't you?" I said I didn't. "She's Woody Allen's mother."

It's amazing how you can like someone without that person having said a word. And dislike someone without that person having said a word. Visceral connections travel between people—even across the lox counter. There are those I don't like but I don't think they would know that I don't like them because I try to treat everybody with respect. The first ten years, I didn't care who they were; I was going to treat them like they were queens. After ten years of that, I kind of lost a little of that feeling that I have to take someone who is disrespectful and nasty and treat them nicely. So I have a sharp tongue at times and I guess sometimes I let go a little bit. Not too much. When the time comes that I can't control that, I'll move on and see what I want to do next.

Some people come in—we call them "tasters." "Can I taste the Nova?" they ask. "Sure." They don't want to buy it. After that they say, "Is your whitefish good?" "It's excellent." "May I taste it?" "Sure." After that, "What about your sturgeon?" Finally, I'll say, "You know, you're only allowed two tastes." Years ago, I would have given them as many tastes as they want, but I'm not serving lunch. There are people who specialize in that and we can spot them a mile away.

This job keeps me in the mainstream. I'm active, I'm alert, and working to me is a very, very important thing. Always has been. I don't think I could come up with a job better than this. I slice, I talk, I engage with the customers. It's funny. Some of my colleagues say, "Oh, I only have an hour to go and I'm off." I say, "I only have one hour to go, but thank God I'm coming back tomorrow."

Chris Borgatti

BORGATTI'S RAVIOLI & EGG NOODLES

New York's real Little Italy is not in Manhattan. It's in the Bronx, along Arthur Avenue, a venerated street of sausage, pastries, pasta, and all things Italian. His shop is just off the avenue. It's small, brightly lit, two connecting rooms lined with photographs depicting generations of Borgattis. The pasta here is rolled out and cut to order, as it has been done for over eighty years. This particular afternoon, a customer stands watching the clerk behind the counter turn sheets of fresh-made noodles through a hand cutter, where they emerge in one-eighth-inch strips of linguini. The clerk weighs it, wraps it in butcher paper, and the customer is on her way.

Chris Borgatti and I head for the back room, where we sit at a small metal table that's been in use since the days of his grandfather. He points out a patch worn of its paint and muses about the table's history: How many meals must have been eaten on this very surface? How many bills paid? How many recipes devised? He's in his fifties, but looks far younger, which he credits to the fact that "life is good . . ."

Arthur Avenue is not just a street, it's a community. I've been here since 1976, and I've seen businesses come and go. Nobody leaves because they want to. It's more like circumstances force them out. There are third-, fourth-, fifth-, and maybe sixth-generation businesses in this neighborhood. The Teitel Brothers, a Jewish family that imports Italian specialty foods, has been here almost a hundred years now. Mario's Restaurant is in its fifth or sixth generation. Artuso Pastry has been here over sixty years. Egidio Pastry Shop since 1912. Biancardi Meats, maybe four generations. The fish markets, Randazzo's, Consenza's. Too many to count.

I myself am third generation. My grandparents, Lindo and Maria Borgatti, immigrated from just outside Bologna, bringing with them their six sons, one of whom was my father. My grandmother was a great cook and so they settled on this little store where they would sell food from her recipes, always made from scratch. Mostly her ravioli and egg noodles. They started this place on a shoestring. It got them, along with their six sons plus a few foster children, through the Depression. I don't think we'll see a generation like that again.

As my grandfather got older, my father's brothers eventually went on to other things, and my father took over the business. Then, in 1976, when I graduated high school, it was my turn to decide if I'd go on to college or come here. To me, it wasn't even an option. It was all about working with my dad. Generally, as we're growing up, our fathers are so busy at their jobs that the kids see them only on occasion. Working here would let me spend time with my father 24/7. So at the age of eighteen, I became the third-generation Borgatti to enter the business. And here I am, almost forty years later, still working with him. He's ninety-six years old now, so he doesn't come in every day like he used to. But he comes in enough. Believe me.

There are two kinds of father-son teams in business. One, where the son is just waiting to change everything. Can't update it fast enough. And then there's *my* type. I've always been the kind of son who goes along with the principles that came before him. My father's philosophy has never changed. He says, "Keep it simple, Chris. Keep it simple." What he means is: Make the ravioli exactly the way your grandmother made it. And for the most part, I do. But sometimes the future calls, you know? Every businessman will tell you, you can't hold back progress, because if you try to, things will move ahead without you.

The Internet has definitely changed how people shop. So if customers don't come into a store as often as they used to, you have to take your product out to them. That's always been part of my larger plan anyway—to have Borgatti ravioli distributed in other specialty stores. The problem is, our name has always been synonymous with quality. Am I prepared to risk losing control by expanding? Not really. Not yet, anyway. I am starting to change things here, though. If slowly.

In the past year or two, my father took a few steps back, which unleashed me a little bit. Whereas he's still touting your basic cheese, meat, and spinach ravioli, calling everything else "just a fad," I have very quietly ventured out on my own with a few new things. For example, this year we made a pumpkin-filled ravioli for the fall, and ricotta, spinach, and mushroom. I also came up with a recipe I like that incorporates dried imported porcini mushrooms and a Chilean mushroom combination in that filling. And every time we make fresh dough for noodles, I include some exotic batches. Like today, when he's not here, we made squid-ink pasta.

I mean, can you *believe* this? I'm fifty-five years old and I'm still sneaking things in, away from my father.

I'll always think of this as my grandparents' store. It's amazing what they did with so little, and what this place has become. Lately, because we're such an Arthur Avenue staple for so long, we've gotten a lot of TV and newspaper coverage. As a result, tour busses stop here and tourists check out our store. They take group pictures inside, next to the old-fashioned noodle cutter that stands in the front of the store. But in fact the majority of people who come through our doors are not here to take pictures. They're here to buy our fresh pasta. In that respect, my father is right. In the end, Borgatti's is only about the ravioli.

Alan Tony Schatz

SCHATZIE THE BUTCHER

We are seated on wooden stools at the back of a small butcher shop on the Upper West Side. Directly behind us, a giant steel door leads to the refrigerated room, which is where he ages and stores his inventory. To our left is a gleaming case loaded with every kind of meat imaginable. Except chopped. A sign in its place tells customers: "If You Want Chopped Meat, We Will Grind It for You Fresh."

Hanging on the wall opposite the meat case is the original cooler door from the 1930s. As his grandfather moved his shop from one location to another, he took that door and placed it on each new refrigerator. He still has and continues to use his father's fifty-year-old Biro saw. An affable man with a deep, melodic voice, he's dressed in a white butcher's coat that pulls across his belly, and looks as if he's had a busy day. As we talk, a flirty woman of about fifty stops at the door with her dog. By law, she cannot bring her dog into the shop, so she calls her order from the threshold and leaves. "I love the women," he says. "They're the best part of this job. Always have been." He's sixty-eight.

I've been a butcher for fifty-five years. My father, grandfather, and great-grandfather were butchers. Four generations. But it was my father's assistant who taught me how to butcher when I was a kid. Eleven, twelve. My father couldn't do it himself because it's difficult to teach your son. You end up always fighting with him. Ask me. My son works here with me now and I fight with him all day long. He doesn't want to work as much as I do. Kids. You know? First I got upset because I can see that he's not going to work seven days a week, eighteen hours a day like I did. But the more I thought about it, the more I realized, he really doesn't have to. He doesn't have to get here as early as I do because people don't come in that early anymore. I still have the work ethic that makes me do this, but not him. I spoiled him. He went to private schools. He went to camps. He went to Europe. He did whatever he wanted. Ah, but now he has to figure out how to make a living. So here he is.

What I really wanted to do was to be a singer. I finally got the courage to follow my dream and I was on my way to California to try my luck when I learned my father had died. So I had to come back to the Bronx to run his butcher shop and that was it.

Things have really changed over the years. When I was younger, I got up every morning at about four. I had my own truck and I'd go to the market in the Bronx and pick up my meat and come back to the store and stay there until seven when it closed. Six days a week. We were closed on Sunday, but we'd spend Sunday in the store checking the machines, making sure everything was working right. That's what my father did. So that's what I did. In 1969, after fifteen years, I moved from the Bronx to the Upper East Side of Manhattan. To Madison Avenue. It was summer, and what I noticed immediately was that all the other butcher shops were closed on Saturday. The first thing I did, I said to my wife, "Let's open on Saturdays. We'll be the only store open. We'll be busy." Some busy! The first Saturday I took in twenty dollars. Second Saturday, she came over with the baby in the carriage. It was one o'clock in the afternoon and I had taken in fifteen dollars. I said, "That's it. We're not opening on Saturday anymore." No one on the Upper East Side shops on Saturday because they're all in the Hamptons in their second homes. I came here to the Upper West Side two years ago because my rent on the East Side went up unbelievably. So now I'm open seven days a week again.

Things are so different today. When I was younger, women would be coming in the store at ten in the morning and buying all day long. Today those women are lawyers. They're not home taking care of babies. So it's pretty quiet all day until four o'clock, when we start getting really busy. And on Saturday, it gets really busy. Thirty baby carriages come in the store with men pushing twenty-eight of them. They're like old women, these guys. I think they've changed more than the wives.

I remember when the women's movement started. I can tell you stories, you'll think I'm making them up. I'm laughing just thinking about it. One Saturday, a guy comes in the store and he's with his wife. She comes walking in ahead of him. And she's looking at everything. "Hey, Schatzie," she says. "How you doing?" He comes in behind her pushing a toddler in a stroller. On his back he's wearing a backpack, and on his front he's carrying a baby in one of those baby carriers. Now the wife is talking to me and the baby in the stroller is fussing because he wants milk. So the guy is trying to get the bottle out of the backpack, but he can't reach all the way around because the other baby is in the front. God forbid he should say anything to her. He leaves her alone. I'm watching this, see? So he puts the baby down. Then he takes the backpack off and everything falls on the floor. And he's trying to get the milk. Then the kid starts to cry and he doesn't know what to do. And she's busy inspecting the mozzarella cheese.

He's scrambling for the milk and he doesn't know what to do. He looks at me. I look at her. And she's still looking at the cheese, oblivious. Give the guy a little help, you know? I'll tell you one thing. Maybe I'm old-fashioned, but I would never put up with that.

The reason there are so few butchers left is that they're all dead. Nobody wants to be a butcher anymore. They want to be movie stars. I'm looking around. You know anyone who wants to be a butcher? No. People don't think that it's a classy job. And it's not. But personally? I'm much more geared to money than I am to "classy."

People look down on this profession. That doesn't bother me anymore, but it sure did when I was younger. I don't think I've ever asked anybody what he or she does for a living. Ever. First of all, I don't care. And second, what difference does it make? Still, in New York City, nine times out of ten, I meet you, you're going to tell me what you do three minutes into the conversation. You're going to have to because you're going to have to find out whose is bigger.

And I'm willing to bet if I was at a party and somebody said to me, "What do you do?" and I said, "I have a butcher shop" and then they said to my brother, "What do you do?" and he said, "I'm a brain surgeon," I think the perception of who we both are would be that he's in a much loftier place than I am.

That sets up a whole thing that I never liked. When I was working in the Bronx, after my father died, I ran that store for twelve years. It was in a black and Puerto Rican neighborhood. Those people would come to my store at night and walk me to my car. You were almost revered. You were the owner of a business. The guy in the cigar store, the same way. The guy in the furniture store, too. Then I came to Madison Avenue and they all thought I was a delivery boy.

I think the only thing that kept me who I am is that I made a lot of money. So even though I don't think that's a way to view yourself, if you need it and it helps you, go for it. When I was twenty-seven years old, I bought an apartment on Park Avenue. And I bought a Cadillac every three years. And that made me feel as good as the guy who's working on Wall Street or maybe working in the garment district who thought that he was so much better. It made me feel better.

The vegetarian movement that's been floating around for years hasn't affected me in the least. That's because people who are real veggies don't come in here. Honestly? I don't care what people do as far as what they eat. You want to be a vegetarian? Fine. Just don't lecture me about selling animals.

People these days are so hung up about what they put in their mouths. They want to know exactly what the meat they eat eats. Imagine this. They'll ask, "Is this meat grass-fed?" And I say, "Yes." Then they ask, "Is it grass-finished?" "Grass what?" What does that mean? I say, "It's grass-fed." They say, "That doesn't mean it's grass-*finished*." So I think this, but I hold my tongue, "Then don't buy it! What do you want me to tell you?" I don't know what grass-finished is supposed to mean. But they probably don't either. I'm sure they read it somewhere.

I sell chickens. Regular chickens. For $2.98, $3.29 a pound. These are free-range chickens. I also sell organic chicken for $6.98 a pound. I don't make as much money on the organic chickens, but people want it. It's such bullshit. What makes an organic chicken is it's raised on organic water and organic food. The government certifies it. Organic water and organic pastures and you're paying twenty-one dollars for a three-pound organic chicken—which I'm happy to sell them if they insist—although my regular chickens are just as good. There are no preservatives and no additives in my regular chickens. But no. They insist it be organic. Pure, pure, pure. Okay, so just imagine an organic chicken is out in the backyard and the chicken is grazing on pure organic grass, and a bird flies over the yard and poops on the grass. Is that grass still organic? It's so obscene. In order to get a truly 100 percent organic bird, you have to keep this bird in a coop. They can't go outside and exercise and have a ball game and then come back. They don't do that. That's the real organic. They look like shit. They don't taste like anything special, and you're happy that the animal was treated humanely.

When Richard, my son, was about ten years old, a lady came into the store and he wanted to help but he was too little, so he'd watch. I said, "Can I help you?" And she started to talk to me about this baby cow and how cruel it was that it was killed so young. She likes the idea that they're humanely treated. So this little ten-year-old says to her, "Yeah, after they're humanely treated, then they kill them. Is that humane?" The lady looked at him. She wanted to be assured that her veal cutlet was treated nicely while it was walking around.

You can buy fresh meat, you can buy free-range meat, and you can buy meat that's certified that's different from organic. Organic meat is fed organic feed and organic water and it can't touch anything else, but you know that that's not going to happen.

Meat comes in four categories. From best to worst they are: prime, choice, select, and canners—that's dog food. Most supermarkets sell choice and select. I sell prime. Prime is only 2 percent of the kill. It's prime that goes to the Waldorf Astoria, the Palm, and all the fancy restaurants. And by the way, you can't buy prime organic meat. Why? Because prime meat feeds on grain. The more grain you feed it, the fatter the animal. If it eats grain, it's a lighter, paler red with fat running through it. Fat running through it is marble. That's what you want. Fat is what makes meat prime. The way I'm built, I would be considered "prime." I got a lot of fat. So with meat, the more fat the animal, the more prime it is.

Organic beef feeds on grass. It doesn't feed on fat. If a piece of meat eats grass and nothing but grass, it's going to be red when you kill it, no marbleizing. What I think is, when you're going to buy steak, I don't think you should be worrying about health. I think you should be saying to yourself, "I want the best prime meat I can buy and I'll eat a steak every week or every two weeks, rather than eat this sub-prime stuff every other day."

The West Side is a state by itself. The Upper West Side of the United States of America. East Side and West Side of New York are like night and day. The people over here think they're much smarter than the people over there and the people over there think they're much richer than the ones over here. I do believe they're smarter over here. But they think that they're really smart. In a neighborhood like this, we sell chickens for $9.98 with two sides. With tax it comes to $10.87. Do you know how many people come in here and say, "It's supposed to be $10.85"? There was a mistake on that sign and I never fixed it. Two cents!

East Side customers ask, "How much?" You tell them and they say, "Fine." Over here on the West Side? "Put it back. I don't want it. It's too much." It's a different neighborhood. But you have a lot more people here. A guy and his wife come in here and they look around and they look around, and they're here for twenty minutes. "Can I have one sausage?" I want to tell them, "This is a butcher shop, not a clothing store." East Side? They don't buy sausage, too fattening. West Side, they buy it. But they complain. The whole experience is so different. So interesting.

A butcher shop like mine is over, dead, not coming back. The kids today don't care about a shop like mine. They go to the supermarket. They call FreshDirect [an online grocery]. They don't have any idea what they're eating. They don't care. You have a certain amount of people who, if they make a chicken themselves, they think of themselves as "foodies." So it's so nice when someone comes in and says, "Wow! An old-fashioned butcher shop. Give me a steak." I love that. I pick a steak. I put it on the scale. I weigh it. I wrap it in butcher's paper. They buy it, and that's it. Just like the old days.

Rob Kaufelt

MURRAY'S CHEESE

His grandfather, Isaac Kaufelt, a Polish immigrant, owned a grocery store in New Jersey. After World War II, Isaac and his son opened a small supermarket, the first in that area. That grew into a string of upscale supermarkets under the name Mayfair, which was where Rob landed after graduating college in 1972. Eight years after working every department in the chain, he became the company president.

Maybe this isn't true for everyone, but for me, working with family, no matter what your title is, can be very difficult. Particularly when you have your own strong ideas. Which I did. So at thirty-eight, I decided the time had come to leave Mayfair and strike out on my own. To say my father was not happy with my decision would be an understatement. But there it was.

My first solo venture was a small specialty-food shop in Summit, New Jersey, which I followed by another one like it in Princeton. The store in Summit was very successful, but I opened the second store right around the time of the '87 stock market crash. The Princeton store was an expensive proposition that didn't end as successfully as I would have liked. In fact, it collapsed completely. Once that one went out of business, I decided I'd had enough of New Jersey. I sold the Summit store and, now unemployed, came to New York to decide what I was going to do next.

I moved into my brother's old apartment in the Village and started searching for jobs in the food industry, but I couldn't find anything I liked. Then one day, while I was standing in line to get a sandwich at Murray's Cheese Shop—a little store near my apartment—I overheard the owner, Louis Tudda, say he was closing up shop and moving back to Italy. Louis was an Italian immigrant from Calabria, who had been a clerk for Murray Greenberg, the store's founder. Murray sold Louis the store in 1970, and now Louis was ready to retire. One thing led to another, we struck a deal, and I became the third owner of Murray's, New York's oldest cheese shop.

At the time, I was still feeling pretty bad about my earlier failures, and all I wanted to do was lead what I considered a quiet Village life— which I thought owning this small shop would let me do. I didn't feel like I had to make a killing. I figured, if I could make fifty grand a year, I could pay my rent and take a couple of weeks' vacation. I had no expectations that any of it would work. None. Meanwhile, my father and I still were not on good terms, but I called him anyway to tell him what I had just done. He said buying a small cheese shop at a time when everyone in the world is worrying about cholesterol was—well, actually? He told me I was out of my fucking *mind!* In hindsight, maybe those words gave me the impetus to prove him wrong, but at the time, I figured that he was probably right.

We opened Memorial Day of 1991. And I admit it, I was a little nervous. As I had learned with my earlier ventures, owning your own business is never easy. But as the new kid on the block, I was fortunate enough to get some help when I needed it from my next-door neighbors, the Zito brothers. Zito & Sons bakery was even older than Murray's. The brothers were the sons of the original owners, both immigrants. I sold some of their bread in my store and every so often I would go over there and they would give me business tips.

I'll never forget, one morning, I was in their store when a lady comes in. There's Zito, this grouchy sixty-year-old Italian guy behind the counter, and she walks up and she says to him, "Is this bread fresh?" Now, I grew up in a small town in New Jersey where our store's clientele was predominantly Jewish, and every single day people would call up my mother or my father to complain about something in our store. So I was used to customers saying all kinds of things. And I was raised to be very polite. The customer is always right. All those good things. But now I'm hearing Zito say to the woman, "What did you say?" The woman: "I said, is this bread fresh?" Zito: "Get out!" The woman: "What do you mean?" Zito: "Get out! Nobody asks if my bread is fresh!" So she apologizes for hurting his feelings. And he says, "No. Too late." And he threw her out of the store. I said, "Wow. Zito. I can't believe you did that! This lady's going to go home and she'll tell twenty of her friends, and they'll tell twenty more and that's four hundred, and pretty soon no one in New York will come to buy your bread." And he said, "Naw, I'm not worried. She'll want it more than ever. She'll be back." And she was. I'm sure there was a lesson to be learned in that interaction, but I'm not sure what it was.

Entrepreneurs and small businessmen the world over live in a constant state of fear. What you fear, of course, is failing. You do feel a little more secure over time, and if you're successful, you get more confidence, but that fear never completely goes away. Failure is not the end of the world, though. I don't think in hindsight that you can be a successful entrepreneur without some failures. And fear is not your enemy, either. Whether it's at the higher levels, like Steve Jobs and Apple, or a more local level like Murray's Cheese Shop, you have to have that fear in there because when you make a mistake, it forces you to think about what you did wrong. And if you think about it, you may be able to figure it out and not repeat those mistakes.

Aiming in that direction, some of the things I learned right up front were to not be highly leveraged in debt and not to spend an inordinate amount of capital, which, of course, is easier said than done. Food retailing can be very expensive because it requires so much refrigerated equipment. Rents are very high in the city and cheese is very labor- and inventory-intensive. If you think about it, everything that a modern Internet company, say, or financial company might not be, the food business is. Very old-fashioned in terms of labor and equipment, for example. I remember once I was in Naples and went to Pompeii, where they restored an ancient marketplace for tourists. They had the wine merchants and the oil merchants and the olive merchants, and I thought, "That's the same business I'm in. It hasn't changed in two thousand years." Somebody was producing or buying the oil or the wine, and bringing it to the marketplace and selling it for a little more than it cost. Capitalism at its finest.

To be successful in the cheese business, a thousand variables have to be taken into account. For example, your inventory is perishable, so you have to control it. Also, you're at the mercy of unexpected disasters, like a power outage, which is rare, but can happen. And there are a ton of agencies in New York City—people who come around inspecting things or charge you for things or perhaps have the ability to fine you or even close you down. So there's that element. Plus, the margins are small and the competition is fierce. The food business by its very nature is highly competitive. The good news is that it doesn't lend itself to a virtual reality. You have to have the food in your house or in your stomach, and you can't outsource it to a foreign land. You can outsource your accounting to India, but you can't buy your groceries there. And because food is consumed on a regular basis, it needs constant replenishing. In the end, it's a matter of having the right product at the right prices, convenience, and good service. That's it.

Right now, I find myself in three food worlds. First, there's the specialty or retail world—we currently have two gourmet stores and we have Murray's cheese shops in supermarkets all over the country. Second, we are wholesalers to countless high-end restaurants that include cheese courses on their menu. Finally, we're in the restaurant business. We've just opened our first restaurant next door, and we plan to expand to more of them in time. The fact that so much has happened in the space of twenty-some-odd years since is nothing short of a miracle. I have to give a lot of the credit to our terrific staff of about a hundred very sharp young people with the average age of thirty. Putting all those people to work makes me very happy. It also makes me feel like a Republican, sometimes, which oddly enough is not as bad a feeling as you might think. And I've long since reconciled with my dad who, believe it or not, has become my greatest supporter.

Charlie Sahadi

SAHADI'S

I read somewhere that a customer asked Charlie Sahadi, "What's the best olive?" To which Sahadi replied, "If there was a best olive, why would I need thirty-two?" That pretty much sums up the tone and the personality of both the store and its owner.

Walk into Sahadi's on any Saturday and you'll find the place packed with customers jockeying for position at the deli counter, piling containers of dried figs and olives into their baskets, greeting neighbors, chasing down their children, and shooting questions at the blue-smocked staffers. He loves the chaos. Thrives on it, in fact. He's a tall, warm, friendly man with graying hair and a twinkle in his eye when he tells a visitor, "If you want to work here, the first question you'll find on the application is: 'Are you crazy?' If your answer is yes, the job is yours."

I never really had dreams about being anything else. What I was trained in was this market. As a kid, weekends I was here. Would I rather have been playing basketball? Sure. But the family business called, and I actually liked being part of it. Even back in the early days, we sold all kinds of specialty foods, plus mountains and mountains of sweets and nuts. So, yeah, I was your veritable kid in a candy store. What could be bad?

Back in the fifties and sixties, when I joined the business, our store was different from most. You went into a deli, they sliced your meats and cheeses, you got a couple of prepared salads, maybe, but the rest of the store was all packaged goods. Not here. We were, and still are, more of an ingredients store. Meaning we sold whatever you wanted by the pound. Bins and sacks of ingredients were located all over the store. So if you had a recipe that called for, say, "three tablespoons of pine nuts," you could come to Sahadi's and we could sell you a few ounces.

Also, we were strictly a Middle Eastern food store. That's where you went if you were Syrian, Lebanese, or Egyptian, because when you asked for bulgur wheat, they knew what you wanted. When you asked for tahini, they knew. Don't forget, health food stores were not yet around, so you couldn't find these things. And regular supermarkets were not yet into ethnic.

Today, everybody is health conscious. Look around this market, everyone is reading packaging labels. Not just women. Men, too. And teens. They say the second most reading done in the United States after libraries is in grocery stores. I believe it. You watch people pick up a jar, or a can, or a box of cereal. "Oh," they say, "three hundred and eighteen milligrams of salt! Eleven grams of fat, thirteen grams of sugar." They drop the package like a hot potato, pick up the box next to it, and start checking out the facts on that one. And people say nobody reads anymore. That's a laugh!

You can't say we're not doing our part for good health. Remember how, in a store like this, you used to stick your hand into an open jar or bin and you pulled out a handful of figs or nuts or candy? Today, a customer standing next to you sees you do that, he'll smack your hand so fast you won't even see it coming. Every customer thinks he's the "health police." And they're right. It's not the most sanitary thing. Our store is geared to the Mediterranean diet—supposed to be the healthiest way to eat. Olive oils, fish, nuts, chocolate. We have thirty-two kinds of olives, every dried fruit you can think of, including kiwis and pears. Twelve kinds of almonds, from blanched to cinnamon roasted. Pistachios from half a dozen countries. Dates sourced from nine regions of the world. Almond flour, quinoa, goji berries. We even have chia seeds. This is nothing new for us. In the Middle East, yogurts and all these things have been in vogue forever.

We're still one of the only stores around that sell in bulk. But with the times, we've had to modify that policy a bit because of the time it takes to personally service a customer. You come in and you want two pounds of chickpeas, I weigh the chickpeas, stick the price on it, get ready to hand it to you, and you change your mind. "That doesn't look like enough. Could you make that three pounds?" So I gotta open the bag and make it three pounds. Ring it up, put a new sticker. "Oops, just a bit too much. Do you mind, Charlie?" On a Saturday or during the holiday season, something like that can kill you.

People always think of Turks and Lebanese sitting around, a demitasse cup of coffee balanced on their knee. That's not me, though. I've never had a cup of coffee in my life. It's true. I don't touch the stuff. Customers are always asking me, "What's the best flavor?" "What's the strongest?" Even though I don't drink it myself, I can safely describe the characteristics of half the coffee we sell. How? Because if you listen to your customers, you learn things without tasting. But if someone wants to know which is my favorite, I tell them the truth. I say, "I'm a Pepsi guy." That's all.

I don't need to lie to sell stuff. That's my feeling. First of all, you have to be very smart to lie, because you tell every person a different story and who can remember what you said? "What the heck did I tell this lady the last time she was here?" If you tell the truth, your story may deviate a little bit—just by human nature, you can't remember every detail. But it's within a caliber that you can live with. I tell that to my staff, too. "Don't tell people it's coming tomorrow if you don't know for sure it's coming tomorrow, 'cause they'll come back tomorrow, and they'll be very unhappy if the goods aren't here."

I love to comparison shop. To compare, I go to Zabar's, which to me personifies the term "specialty foods" or "gourmet foods." We should all thank Saul Zabar for starting an industry that wasn't here. Just like we should thank Colavita, the olive oil people who created the term "extra virgin" in the United States. There was no "extra virgin" oil in New York before 1982. We had pure, and we had something else—I don't remember—blended oil, which was something else with olive oil. The categories changed in 1982 when Colavita came on the market. And now, you go to the shelves, and every olive oil on the shelf is extra virgin. "Extra virgin" means first pressing. It has to have a certain acidity level. Other oils, which are chemically processed, go under the term "pure." And then, you get to the bottom of the barrel, which is called "pomace." Pomace is oil that's derived from the pits of the olives, after you've taken the oil, now you want to suck up the last little bit. A chemical extractor takes it from there, and you get a very, very bland oil, basically tasteless. Now, to make it taste decent and have color, you add 5 or 10 percent extra virgin oil to give it a little color and a little taste, but it's deceptive. Again, I'm all about being honest. Olive oil has a lot of medical benefits, but when you get to this chemically extracted stuff— you may as well just wash all the health benefits down the drain. I always say, you wanna save money, buy a cheap shirt and when you're finished with it, throw it out. You wanna put something in your body, buy something good, because your body is nourished from this, and if you put crap in, you get crap out.

This body is built by chocolate and ice cream, my dear. And I don't mean dark chocolate, because no one told me at the time that dark chocolate was good for you. Chocolate and ice cream keep me going, and I have nothing to apologize for. I've had a good run. When the subject of retirement comes up—and it comes up more often these days than I'd like—I just flick it off like an unwelcome gnat. I still love what I do, the customers that come in. They've known me for years. Some of them are actually older than I am. It's hard to believe there are people out there older than me, but there are.

I try not to let too many things get under my skin, but every once in a while, I get really ticked off. A guy once bought a five-pound bag of pistachios. They were probably five dollars a pound at the time. A week or ten days later, he came back with a pound and a quarter in the bag, and said, "I want to return these pistachios." I said, "What's the matter?" He said, "We didn't like them." I said, "Okay." I put it on the scale and it weighed a pound and a quarter. So I gave him back five dollars. He said, "I paid twenty-five dollars for those nuts!" I said, very calmly, "You bought five pounds. You returned a pound and a quarter. You're telling me you had to eat three and three-quarter pounds before you decided you didn't like them? Did you think they were going to get better as you got down to the bottom of the bag?" He glared at me and then he said, "I'm never coming back to this store." To which I replied, "Could you put that in writing?"

Afterword

N ew York is a city that lives in the moment—perhaps even ahead of the moment. In the three years since I began this project, I've watched the food scene change at a pace that would send a marathon runner sprinting just to keep up. These changes are everywhere: in restaurants, in the professionals who provide our food, and in the patrons whose attitudes toward what and where and how they eat drive this ever-fluctuating metric.

For starters, an astonishing number of restaurants around town have closed. And yes, closing restaurants are a natural part of the life-and-death cycle of the food service industry. But why so many? And why now? One unmistakable factor is the city's skyrocketing real estate. Sammy Anastasiou and Luísa Fernandes spoke of how shattered they were upon learning that their beloved workplaces—Manhattan Diner and Park Blue, respectively—would fall victim to the wrecking ball, making way for yet another high-rise condominium. The Union Square Cafe—a perennial New York favorite that has stood just off Union Square for nearly thirty years—must now relocate, a casualty of hungry landlords. All around town, windows that once proudly displayed an inviting menu are papered over with signs declaring "Lost Our Lease."

Another contributing component is, quite simply, out with the old. This past summer we learned that as of July 2016, the Four Seasons, often considered the country's first modern American restaurant, will no longer be housed in the Seagram Building, the sleek architectural landmark it has called home since 1959. Despite the fact that the restaurant's Grill Room still hosts power lunches of steadfast clientele, and the Pool Room remains one of New York's most notable and beautiful venues, the building's current owner decided it was time to bring in downtown darlings Rich Torrisi and Mario Carbone (read: *younger*) to run the new (read: *buzzier*) space. What that will mean for veteran cooks Guyo Ketavanan and Albie Chauca is anyone's guess.

But new restaurants have opened, too. Jelena Pasic is set to debut her second edition of Harlem Shake in the spring of 2016. Wilson Tang has added Fung Tu, a Chinese restaurant on Orchard Street, to his long-established Nom Wah Tea Parlor. Shatzie moved uptown and has appended a burger joint to his new butcher shop. Dominique Ansel has opened Dominique Ansel Kitchen, where burrata ice cream and rosemary brownies (but *not* Cronuts) are on the menu, and Ed Schoenfeld's chef Joe Ng is wowing them downtown with Decoy, a duck-specialty restaurant that in its prior iteration was a laundromat.

Street food, not new by any means, has become more interesting, diverse, and accessible. As waves of new immigrants arrive in the city, the imported offerings they bring with them are changing the way city dwellers experience food. Once borough-centric, New Yorkers now move seamlessly throughout the five boroughs sampling dishes and flavors that earlier required international travel. And the pace seems to be escalating daily. For just a few dollars and a subway pass, anyone can travel to Jackson Heights, Queens, to enjoy the endless lineup of food trucks and stalls offering Columbian, Tibetan, and Thai fare. Hop on the Bronx-bound D train to sample Ghanaian, Jamaican, Puerto Rican, and Nigerian cuisine. And at Brooklyn's famed Red Hook Ball Fields, an abundance of Latin American food vendors will happily offer you a choice of *papusas*, ceviche, goat meat tacos, and *elotes* (corn on a stick, dipped in mayo and chili powder).

And here come the food halls. In 2010, Mario Batali and Joe Bastianich blazed a trail when they opened their wildly popular high-end Italian food hall Eataly, a 58,000-square-foot space that combines under one roof a multitude of restaurants, food, cooking products, and communal dining spaces. Not surprisingly, the concept has fast been emulated by a surge of new—and successful—venues: City Kitchen in Times Square, Le District in Battery Park, the Gansevoort Market in Chelsea, and Gotham West Market in Hell's Kitchen. In fact, so many entrepreneurs have jumped on this fashionable culinary bandwagon, it's a wonder there's any room left on Manhattan Island for Anthony Bourdain's forthcoming eponymous food hall. But you know there is. And it's coming soon to a pier near you.

New Yorkers have a passionate interest in anything new—which includes seeing and being seen at the place of the moment. So how do we know where the "it" place is? No need to wait until Wednesday for the sage words of the *New York Times* restaurant reviewer. Instant gratification seekers have only to flip open their laptops or switch on their phones. Yelp has turned us into star-dispensing critics; Instagram into food photographers; Facebook into neighborhood guides. And it all happens in real time. Sharing segments of our lives with friends and strangers is fun. And it's even helpful, if—and this is a big if—you go into it with your eyes open. If you don't believe me, I suggest you reread what the women from Levain Bakery have to say about TripAdvisor.

Of course, some things never change. Because New York is a city that never stops eating, there can be no demarcation between night and day for those indefatigable food pros who feed us. At eight-thirty *p.m.* in the South Bronx, Sam Solasz parks his car, grabs his white coat, and heads out for his eighteen-hour day at Master Purveyors. At three-thirty a.m., Sandy Ingber can be found wandering around the Fulton Fish Market selecting the day's seafood supply for the Grand Central Oyster Bar. At three a.m., Carmen Melendez ties on her apron at Tom Cat Wholesale Bakery and gets ready to flour the boards. And at eight a.m., just as Paulette Johnson is crossing the Haven Street bridge to Rikers Island, Jonathan Parilla is leaving Cafeteria and heading home to sleep.

I have unwavering respect for these people. For their resilience, their determination, their passion. And even though I turned off my tape recorder at the close of each interview, I never really left them behind. Often, as I sat at my computer, I thought about them, about where they might be in the future. I wondered, for example, whether Michael Burke's daughter would one day make it four generations at Denino's Pizza, or whether eighty-five-year-old Sylvia Weinstock would finally retire. Will John Greeley open that skateboard shop on a beach? Will David McQueen ever be able to justify calling himself a sculptor/waiter?

I'm guessing that many of these people will be precisely where they are now. But new people and new trends lie ahead as well. Maybe meat and potatoes will become the new kale; Israeli-Arab food the new fusion. Perhaps fancy French restaurants will make a comeback and tipping will become a thing of the past. Hopefully, with a little luck, Lenny Berk will still be slicing lox at Zabars.

Hopefully.

Stay tuned.

The Kitchen Brigade

In 1903, in an effort to streamline kitchen duties and bring order to the kitchens of fine restaurants, the French chef Auguste Escoffier devised what he called *La Brigade de Cuisine*—the Kitchen Brigade. It was modeled on a military hierarchy, employing a strict chain of command whereby each kitchen position had a station and a set of well-defined responsibilities. And each was directly responsible to the position above. This chain of command and the specific responsibilities of the kitchen personnel are below. In an effort to streamline these definitions, I have on occasion used the pronoun "he" but it is well known that an increasing number of women are occupying these positions at every level, in just about every kitchen in the city.

The Brigade

Executive chef or sometimes called simply "chef." In larger restaurants or restaurant chains, rather than cooking, the executive chef runs the business end of the kitchen, sets the menu, hires and fires staff, creates recipes, and purchases food. He may also expedite the service.

Chef de cuisine, also known as the "cooking" or "hands-on" chef. In situations where a single person or group owns a number of restaurants, the *chef de cuisine* is responsible for the day-to-day cooking in one of those restaurants. However, if there is only one restaurant, the *chef de cuisine*'s responsibilities will be interchangeable with those of an executive chef. And he often cooks as well.

Sous chef. Second in command to the executive chef or to the chef de cuisine. His general duties include scheduling, overseeing the daily food production by the line cooks, and helping with food ordering and inventory. When necessary, he may fill in for the chef or any of the line cooks.

Chef de partie or station chef. Runs a particular station if there is more than one cook at that station.

Pâtissier or pastry chef. Responsible for all baked items, pastries, and desserts, and may work alone or have a staff of cooks working under him.

The Stations/Line Cooks

Each line cook is responsible for the preparation of food served from one of many stations along the pass. Depending on the size of the restaurant, some stations may be combined or not exist at all. In the brigade system, stations along the line have their own hierarchy, which from the top down, is as follows:

Saucier or sauté cook. Sautés dishes and prepares sauces and stocks to complete the protein dishes. This is one of the most demanding positions on the line because *sauciers* often have to juggle ten pans at a time—throughout the service—which is why it carries so much prestige.

Grillardin or grill chef. Second in command to the sauté cook. He is responsible for all grilled and broiled foods.

Rôtisseur or roast cook. On an equal level to the *grillardin*. The two positions may be combined in smaller restaurants.

Friturier. Responsible for all fried foods. The position may be combined with the duties of the *rôtisseur*.

Poissonier or fish cook. In charge of all fish and seafood preparation, from sautéing to poaching.

"Hot Apps." Responsible for all hot appetizers on the menu.

Entremetier or vegetable cook. Responsible for hot vegetables, soups, pastas, and other starches and garnishes, which make up most of the accompaniments on a diner's plate.

Garde-manger or pantry chef. Responsible for the preparation of all cold foods, including cold appetizers and salads, dressings, and pâtés. This is usually the entry-level job for most cooks, independent of how much prior cooking experience they may have.

Tournant. Swing cook who is experienced enough to fill in as needed at any station.

Commis. An apprentice or junior cook who works a specific station and reports directly to the *chef de partie*.

Communard. Prepares the family meal, which is served daily to the kitchen staff.

Glossary

Aging. The process of hanging beef in a climate-controlled environment for a period of up to thirty days, during which time the natural enzymes break down, improving texture and deepening the flavor of the meat.

Amuse-bouche. French for "amuse the mouth." A bite-sized appetizer of the chef's choosing—a tiny cup of soup, for example, or a single canapé—that is presented as a gift to the diner before the meal is served.

Back waiter. The liaison between the dining room and kitchen; places orders from the captain, monitors the progress of orders in the kitchen, informs the chef when a table is ready for the next courses to be prepared.

Bain-marie. A pan filled with hot water into which smaller receptacles are placed during cooking to control the heating of delicate foods, such as custard.

Bastads. Swedish-made clogs often worn by kitchen staff.

BOH. Back of the house: (1) areas in and around a restaurant kitchen where food is produced; (2) staff that work in the kitchen, including chefs, line cooks, and dishwashers.

Busboy. Front-of-the-house staff member whose duties include delivering trays to the station, refilling water glasses, offering bread, clearing and crumbing the table, and resetting it between diners.

Captain. Responsible for a group of tables in the dining room. The captain interacts with the guests, explains the menu, takes orders, and makes sure each of his tables is served and maintained by the front and back waiters.

Chef de cuisine. See Kitchen Brigade.

Chef de partie. See Kitchen Brigade.

Combi. A versatile oven that can produce a combination of steam heat and dry heat, allowing users to control the humidity of the air inside the cooking chamber.

Commis. See Kitchen Brigade.

Comp. To give something away for free or to take an item off the final bill.

Cover. Denotes an individual guest in the dining room.

Drop the check. Present the bill to the customer.

Dupe. Ticket that gets submitted by the waiter to the kitchen so the cooks can prepare the ordered dishes.

Eighty-six, 86. Remove an item from the menu because the kitchen has run out of it. An "86 list" tells the purchasing agent what the kitchen is out of.

Expediter. Kitchen traffic controller, sometimes also the chef. Generally stands at the spot on the line where the kitchen meets the dining room (the end of the pass), receives incoming orders, dispatches them to the cooks, and examines finished plates before they are served to the diners.

Extern. Also known as an intern, this refers to a cook who works in but is not an official employee of a given restaurant, who may or may not get paid.

Family meal. Also known as "staff meal," usually served family-style. All staff eat together, either before or following service, at the family meal.

Fire! Command by the expediter to the line cooks, telling them to start cooking a dish that has been previously "ordered." In this way, all dishes for a single table are ready at the same time.

FOH. Front of the house, or dining room. Also refers to the staff that holds those positions.

Front waiter. Responsibilities vary by size of restaurant, but may include setting the table, taking the order, serving the food, refilling wine and water glasses, and clearing the table after each course.

Garde-manger. See Kitchen Brigade.

Grillardin. See Kitchen Brigade.

Gueridon. A silver rolling trolley used in upscale restaurants to present roasts or fish to a table for tableside preparation.

Halal. Meat prepared as prescribed by Muslim law.

Hood. Rests above a high-heat cooking apparatus and is designed to pull hot air, steam, and smoke out of the kitchen.

"In the shit." Seriously in the weeds (see below). Expression used to denote when a line cook is overwhelmed by orders and frantically trying to cook and plate his dishes.

"In the weeds." Expression used by line cooks to denote running behind and helplessly watching things back up in the kitchen almost to the point of no return.

Kashering the kitchen. Turning a nonkosher kitchen into a kosher one by means of a rabbinically sanctioned cleaning process.

Kosher. Food that meets kashrut, the Jewish dietary laws set forth in the Torah.

Line. The area in a professional kitchen where food is prepared during service.

Line cook. See Kitchen Brigade.

Lowboy. An under-the-counter refrigerator.

Maître d'. Individual who, during service, oversees and supervises the dining room staff, works with the reservationist, greets and seats guests.

Michelin Guide. French hotel and restaurant guidebook that reviews and rates restaurants around the world on a zero-to-three-star scale. Michelin stars are the most coveted honor a restaurant can receive.

Mise en place. Translated in French as "everything in its place." All of the prepared items and ingredients a cook will need for his specific station, for one night of service. Always gathered in advance of the beginning of service.

Molecular cuisine. A modern style of cooking using natural processes like flash freezing to reduce certain ingredients in order to form edible creations such as transparent pasta, powdered caviar, or deconstructed desserts like mango foam and salted caramel dots.

Omakase. Translated in Japanese to "I trust the chef." A style of service—usually in a Japanese restaurant—where the chef decides that day what dishes he will be serving. Usually based on that day's freshest available ingredients.

"Ordering!" Command called out by the expediter to the line cook to tell him it is now time to begin preparation of a dish that has earlier been ordered.

Pass. In the kitchen, a long, flat, metal surface where cooks pass their food to the chef for plating, and where the chef examines it before turning it over to the wait staff for delivery to the dining room.

Pâtissier. See Kitchen Brigade.

Plate. To assemble a finished dish on its serving plate.

Poissonier. See Kitchen Brigade.

Prep. Work that is done in advance of actually cooking a dish.

Proofing. Allowing yeast to activate and dough to rise. This process takes place after the dough has been shaped and before it is baked.

Protein. Generic term given to the protein component of a dish, e.g., meat, fish, or poultry; an entrée.

PS ticket. Letters jotted on an order in some restaurants to signify a regular patron or a VIP.

Rôtisseur. See Kitchen Brigade.

Runner. Picks up food in the kitchen and brings it to the dining room. Often his duties are interchangeable with those of the back waiter.

Salamander. A broiler-style cooking apparatus.

Saucier. Sauté cook. See Kitchen Brigade.

Sauté. Fry quickly in a pan on top of the stove.

Server. Preferred term for waiter or waitress.

Service. Actively preparing food for diners and serving it to them.

Shokunin. A person who makes sushi; a master craftsman.

Slammed. Overly busy, sometimes to a point of no return—meaning almost impossible to catch up on what has fallen behind. See also "In the weeds."

Sommelier. Wine steward or wine waiter.

Sous chef. See Kitchen Brigade.

Stage. French term, pronounced *staah-je*. An extended "trail." After completing a "trail" (see below), if the chef likes a line cook applicant, he will be granted a *stage*, which can last for a few days to a month or two. It's considered a learning experience for the potential cook, and free labor for the kitchen.

Stagiere. A person who is working a *stage*.

Station. A group of tables waited on by a particular server, or, in the kitchen, the area where a cook stands when preparing food.

Tasting. A tryout for a position of chef where a job applicant prepares a menu and cooks a number of courses to show what he can do. "Tasting" can also refer to a tryout by the executive chef and staff members of new recipes before putting them on the menu.

Top. Number of people at one table in a dining party or the size of the table. For example, an eight-top refers to a dining party of eight or a table that seats eight people.

Tournant. See Kitchen Brigade.

Trail. After interviewing with the chef, an applicant for the job of cook will be invited to "trail" or work for a day in the kitchen, so the chef and other staff can see how the applicant works and how much he knows.

Turn a table. To replace a party of diners who have completed their meal with a new party.

Two-second rule. Maximum amount of time that can pass from when an item of food, say a roast half duck, hits the floor to when it's picked up and returned to the pan or the plate. (If the culprit is lucky, no one will see him. But in a busy kitchen, forget that ever happening.)

Walk-in. A refrigerated room used to store perishable items and to temporarily conceal overheated, overworked, and/or overwrought kitchen staff.

Working. Food that is actively being cooked.

Acknowledgments

No one writes a book alone. I knew that from past experience. But when I started this book, I could not have imagined how *many* people would play a part, and how very grateful I would become to each and every one of them.

Specific thanks begin with my sagacious, sharp, and eternally upbeat editor, Kerri Kolen, who loved this project from the start and whose enthusiasm has only grown with time. Kerri guided me with objectivity, excellence, and her signature attention to detail (translation: pages and pages of notes). I feel so lucky that my book landed in her hands. And I am, as always, deeply indebted to my agent, Kim Witherspoon, who, with a calmness and wisdom I've come to count on, has been with me every step of the way. Thanks, too, to her assistant, Monika Woods, and to Allison Hunter, an early supporter.

Every book is an expedition into unfamiliar terrain and this one is no different. Susan Squire, writer and editor extraordinaire, was my food guru, who with great fortitude (and a requisite sense of humor) shone a light on many of the insider culinary happenings in town. My gratitude to her knows no bounds. Marcel Sislowitz is Woody Allenesque in his devotion to New York City. As such, he assumed the roles of both historian and tour guide, cheerfully offering an endless wave of facts I never knew I needed to know. His resolute support and encouragement through the research and writing of this book merit a special note of thanks.

High fives to Putnam/Penguin Random House for the most energetic and dedicated production group an author could ever hope for. For the book's beautiful aesthetics, I extend my gratitude to the greatly talented design team, including Design Director Claire Vaccaro and Gretchen Achilles, and to Rita Carroll, who provided the perfect visuals for each of the chapters. Kudos as well to Art Director Monica Benalcazar, and to illustrator Josh Cochran, who together created the book's fantastically imaginative jacket.

For a great job serving up *Food and the City* to the public, a deep bow to Publicity Director Alexis Welby, Katie Grinch, and Ashley Hewlett and to Ashley McClay, Director of Marketing, who graciously taught me the importance of "platform" and how best to showcase a book on social media. A big thank-you to publishing attorney Karen Mayer, who kept me on the straight and narrow, and an extra helping of gratitude to editorial assistant Alise Hofacre, who was always there when I needed her. You don't appreciate the value of a good copyeditor until you realize the glaring mistakes you might have made. I was blessed with *two* such editors. Dorian Hastings and Marie Finamore saved me from potential embarrassment when they gently pointed out—to give just one example—that I had John Wallace playing center for the New York Knicks when absolutely *everyone* in New York knows he played forward.

Sheldon Czapnick, Richard Drubel, Roz Siegel, Suze Yalof Schwartz, and Leslie Tenzer were early readers of this book. Their invaluable comments are greatly appreciated. Debby Aqua was meticulous in her transcription of hours and hours of tapes. I was touched by the generosity of the following people—avid food lovers all—who gave so freely of their valuable time and expertise assisting me in my understanding of the dynamics of New York's food culture: Louis Balducci, James Bynum, Miguel Castillo, Keith Cohen, Eric Friedman, Raymond Guadalupe, Nick Kapelonis, Wayne Lammers, Maribel Lieberman, Mark Maynard-Parisi, Mike Morgenstern, Collette Peters, Alexander Petrossian, Sarah Powers, James Rath, Herb Rose, Ahmed Sherif, Robert Shields, Mark Strausman, Lauren Tyrell, Barbara Uriarte, Alex von Bidder, Saul Zabar, and Lora Zarubin.

Finally, a gigantic thank-you to my "cast of characters" for opening your doors and your hearts to a stranger. It is only through your vivid narratives that outsiders can observe and truly understand the exciting, demanding world of food in this, the world's greatest city. I am eternally grateful to each of you and I hope you realize how much the sharing of your lives has brought this book to life. None of this would have been possible without you.

Index